EX LIBRIS

MAY BLESSINGS BE UPON THE HEAD OF CADMUS, THE PHOENICIANS

OR WHOEVER IT WAS THAT INVENTED BOOKS — CARLYLE

M. O

By George Santayana

PERSONS AND PLACES: THE BACKGROUND OF MY LIFE
REALMS OF BEING
THE REALM OF SPIRIT
THE REALM OF TRUTH
THE PHILOSOPHY OF SANTAYANA: SELECTIONS FROM THE WORKS
    OF GEORGE SANTAYANA
OBITER SCRIPTA: LECTURES, ESSAYS AND REVIEWS
THE LAST PURITAN: A MEMOIR IN THE FORM OF A NOVEL
SOME TURNS OF THOUGHT IN MODERN PHILOSOPHY
THE GENTEEL TRADITION AT BAY
THE REALM OF ESSENCE
THE REALM OF MATTER
PLATONISM AND THE SPIRITUAL LIFE
DIALOGUES IN LIMBO
POEMS
SCEPTICISM AND ANIMAL FAITH
SOLILOQUIES IN ENGLAND AND LATER SOLILOQUIES
CHARACTER AND OPINION IN THE UNITED STATES
THE SENSE OF BEAUTY
INTERPRETATIONS OF POETRY AND RELIGION
THE HERMIT OF CARMEL AND OTHER POEMS
WINDS OF DOCTRINE
THE LIFE OF REASON: OR THE PHASES OF HUMAN PROGRESS

    I.   Introduction and Reason in Common Sense
    II.   Reason in Society
    III.   Reason in Religion
    IV.   Reason in Art
    V.   Reason in Science

LITTLE ESSAYS DRAWN FROM THE WORKS OF GEORGE SANTAYANA
By Logan Pearsall Smith, *with the collaboration of the author.*

Charles Scribner's Sons

PERSONS AND PLACES

GEORGE SANTAYANA

From a Harvard University class photograph, 1886

PERSONS
and
PLACES

The Background of My Life

BY

GEORGE SANTAYANA

NEW YORK
CHARLES SCRIBNER'S SONS
1944

THIS BOOK IS
MANUFACTURED UNDER WARTIME
CONDITIONS IN CONFORMITY WITH
ALL GOVERNMENT REGULATIONS
CONTROLLING THE USE OF PAPER
AND OTHER MATERIALS

PRINTED AND BOUND IN THE U. S. A. BY
KINGSPORT PRESS, INC., KINGSPORT, TENN.

CONTENTS

PERSONS AND PLACES

CHAPTER I

TIME, PLACE AND ANCESTRY

A DOCUMENT in my possession testifies that in the parish church of San Marcos in Madrid, on the 1st of January, 1864, a male child, born on the 16th of the previous December, at nine o'clock in the evening, at No 69 Calle Ancha de San Bernardo, was solemnly christened; being the legitimate son of Don Agustín Ruiz de Santayana, native of Zamora, and of Doña Josefina Borrás, native of Glasgow; his paternal grandparents being Don Nicolás, native of Badumés, in the province of Santander, and Doña Maria Antonia Reboiro, native of Zamora, and his maternal grandparents being Don José, native of Reus, Catalonia, and Doña Teresa Carbonell, native of Barcelona. The names given him were Jorge Agustín Nicolás, his godparents being Don Nicolás Ruiz de Santayana and Doña Susana Sturgis; "whom I admonished," writes Don Joaquín Cabrasco, who signs the certificate with his legal *rúbrica* or flourish, "of their spiritual relationship and duties."

A shrewd fortune-teller would have spotted at once, in this densely Spanish document, the two English names, Glasgow and Sturgis. Where did they come from, what did they forebode? Might not seeds of my whole future lie buried there? And if the diviner had had preternatural powers, he might even have sniffed something important in those last, apparently so effete and per-functory words, that Doña Susana Sturgis, who was my mother's daughter by a former marriage and then twelve years of age, had been forewarned of her spiritual relationship and duties: not that she should forbear marrying my godfather, my uncle Nicolás, who was a major in the Spanish army, with a wife and child, and

1

forty-five years old; that was canonical red-tape nothing to the purpose; but that she was called by Providence to be really my spiritual mother and to catechize my young mind. It was she that initiated me into theology, architecture and polite society.

With parents evidently Catalans of the Catalonians how did my mother come to be born in Glasgow, and how did she ever marry a Bostonian named Sturgis? These facts, taken separately, were accidents of travel, or rather of exile and of Colonial life; but accidents are accidents only to ignorance; in reality all physical events flow out of one another by a continuous intertwined derivation; and those odd foreign names, Sturgis and Glasgow, were in fact secretly allied and their presence here had a common source in my grandfather's character and circumstances and in the general thaw, so to speak, of that age: incongruous wreckage of a great inundation.

Not that I would nail the flag of fatalism to the mast at the beginning of this retrospective voyage. What we call the laws of nature are hasty generalizations; and even if some of them actually prevailed without exception or alloy, the fact that these laws and not others (or none) were found to be dominant would itself be groundless; so that nothing could be at bottom more arbitrary than what always happens, or more fatal than what happens but once or by absolute chance. Yet in the turbid stream of nature there are clear stretches, and traceable currents; and it is interesting to follow the beginnings and the developments of a run here and a whirlpool there, and to watch the silent glassy volume of water slip faster and faster towards the edge of some precipice. Now my little cockle-shell and the cockle-shells of the rest of my family, and of the whole middle and upper class (except the unsinkable politicians) were being borne along more or less merrily on the surface-currents of a treacherous social revolution; and the things that happened to us, and the things we did, with their pleasant and their hopeless sides, all belong to that general moral migration.

My grandfather, José Borrás y Bufurull, belonged to a well-established family of Reus, of the sort that possess a house in the town and a farm in the country. In this as in other ways many old towns near the Mediterranean preserve the character of ancient cities or *civitates,* and Reus in particular is a place of great dignity in the eyes of its inhabitants, who are reputed to speak habitually of "Reus, Paris and London." But José was a younger son, and the law of entail or *mayorazgo* still prevailed at that time in Catalonia, so that the house and land and an almost Roman authority as head of the family fell to his eldest brother. Yet dignity to the classic mind does not involve great wealth or much territory, and younger sons, even in Reus, had to seek their fortunes away from home. They might indeed expect hospitality or a little aid from their families in time of stress, but were well aware that in the ancestral estate and community there was no place or occupation for more than one household at a time. There was the Church always tempting them, if it tempted them; there were the other professions, and there was the New World, or at least Cuba and the Philippines. One of my grandfather's brothers had actually combined these opportunities, become a monk, and later been established as a parish priest in Montevideo or in Buenos Aires.* The ultimate resource, among all my Spanish acquaintance and relations, was some post under the government; and my grandfather might very well have sought his fortunes no further afield than Barcelona, or at most Madrid; but he went much further. Economic considerations were probably not uppermost in his mind; if they were, his career must have disheartened him. Those were unsettled and unsettling times, the repercussions of the French Revolution had not spent themselves, and emancipation of mind was sure to follow, if it had not preceded, being cast

---

* A history of the Borrás family of Reus has been published, but it contains hardly any information about my grandfather and none about my mother. In some respects the traditions recorded there diverge from those that my mother handed down; they may be more accurate, as my mother had no great interest or respect for the past. The exact facts in any case are not important, and I report the impressions that I have gathered.

loose upon the world. In any case we know that my grandfather, far from becoming a monk, like his brother, became a Deist, an ardent disciple of Rousseau, and I suspect a Freemason; and when a French army entered Spain, in 1823, to restore the shaken authority of Ferdinand VII and the absolute monarchy, José Borrás was compelled or thought it advisable to leave the country. The story goes that he fled first to Las Palmas, in the Balearic Islands, where he saw and wooed Teresa Carbonell, a stout blonde with very blue eyes (my mother's eyes were also blue and large); and that after a romantic marriage he persuaded her to follow him in his wanderings. In my certificate of baptism, however, Teresa Carbonell is set down as a native of Barcelona, which is not strictly incompatible with her living later at Las Palmas, or her family belonging there; but she and her whole history are wrapped in some obscurity, and suggest various problems that I have no means of solving.

One of these problems is why my grandfather should have chosen Glasgow for a place of refuge, and what he did there. Mahon, in the neighboring Minorca, had long been in British occupation, and occasions may have presented themselves to sail from there to Scotland, or perhaps to Lancashire; and he seems to have remained in those parts for some years, probably giving Spanish lessons and in any case learning English. This exile in poverty and obscurity, in so remote, cheerless, and industrial a scene, may not have been altogether unwelcome to him. Catalans are industrially and economically minded; novelty and distance allure them; and who knows how many utopias and ideologies, and what reflections on the missed opportunities of human government may not have kept his brain and heart warm in that chilly climate. All I can say is that his thirst for exploration or his longing for a simpler and more ideal society carried him eventually across the Atlantic, to rural, republican, distinguished, Jeffersonian Virginia. Here, if anywhere, mankind had turned over a new leaf, and in a clean new world, free from all absurd traditions and tyrant mortgages, was beginning to lead a pure life of reason and virtue. With slavery? Perhaps that was only a temporary necessity, a kindly apprenticeship to instill into the simple negro a love of labor and of civilized arts; and as the protection of industries might be justified provisionally, until they could become well-rooted, so domestic servitude might be justified provisionally, until the slaves were ripe for freedom.

Be that as it may, José Borrás either came well recommended or ingratiated himself easily into the democracy of Winchester, Virginia, becoming (as a florid testimonial averred) one of its most honored and beloved citizens; so much so that as the years revolved, and a change of government in the liberal direction had occurred in Spain, his Winchester friends induced Andrew Jackson, then President of the United States, to appoint him American Consul at Barcelona. Thus his cordial attachments in exile enabled him eventually to return home, not only safely but gloriously, and with some prospect of bread and butter.*

* THE PRESIDENT OF THE UNITED STATES OF AMERICA·
to all who shall see these presents, greeting.

No ye, that reposing special trust and confidence in the abilities and the integrity of Joseph Borras of Spain, I have nominated and by and with the advice and consent of the Senate do appoint him consul of the United States of America for the Port of Barcelona, in Spain, and for such other parts as shall be nearer thereto than the residence of any other consul or vice-consul of the United States within the same allegiance,—and do authorize and empower him to have and to hold the said office and to exercise and enjoy all the rights, preeminences, privileges, and authorities to the same of right appertaining, during the pleasure of the President of the United States for the time being; HE demanding and receiving no fees or perquisites of office whatever, which shall not be expressly established by some law of the United States. And I do hereby enjoin all captains, masters, and commanders of ships and other vessels, armed or un-armed, sailing under the flag of the United States as well as all others of their citizens, to acknowledge and consider him the said Joseph Borras accordingly. And I do hereby pray and request Her Majesty, the Queen of Spain, Her governors and officers to permit the said Joseph Borras fully and peaceably to enjoy and exercise the said office without giving or suffering to be given unto him any molestation or trouble, but on the contrary to afford him all proper

An element of mystery or mystification hangs about this home-coming. The date of my mother's birth, according to her official papers, was 1828, but there is reason to believe that in reality it was 1826. When she was brought to Spain in 1835 the shocking fact appeared that she had never been christened. Was there no Catholic priest in Glasgow in those days, and none in Winchester, Virginia? Had no travelling ecclesiastic been met with in all those wanderings? No doubt her father's enlightened principles made him regard all religious practices, morally and philosophically, as indifferent, while socially it was advisable that everyone should be affiliated to the religious customs prevalent in his country. But what was to be my mother's country? If it were to be Scotland or Virginia, she ought to be christened and brought up a Protestant: if it were to be Spain, it was imperative that she should be a Catholic. The matter therefore had to be suspended until the question of final residence was settled: although it may seem singular that my grandmother should have wholly acquiesced in this view and allowed her daughter to grow up, as they say in Spain, a Moor. Now, however, the matter had to be patched up as expeditiously and quietly as possible. Friends and relations, even clerical advisers, are very accommodating in Spain and very in-genious. The age of seven, the canonical age of reason, when one begins to sin of one's own accord, was the right age for confirma-tion; young Josefina was small for her age; let her official age be reduced to seven years, let a private christening, to supply the

---

countenance and assistance; I offering to do the same for all those who shall in like manner be recommended to me by Her said Majesty.

IN TESTIMONY WHEREOF I have caused these letters to be made patent, and the seal of the United States be hereunto affixed.

GIVEN under my hand at the City of Washington, the third day of March in the year of our Lord one thousand eight hundred and thirty-five, and of the Independence of the United States of America the fifty-ninth.

(Signed)   ANDREW JACKSON
          By the President

(SEAL)   John Forsyth, *Secretary of State.*

place of the missing documents, be smuggled in before the confirmation, and then the child would be launched quite legally and
becomingly in her religious career, with confession and communion to follow immediately. This wealth of sacraments, raining
down on her unprepared and extraordinary self-reliant little soul,
seems not to have left much hunger for further means of grace.
My mother always spoke of such things as of troublesome and
empty social requirements; and even ordinary social requirements,
like visiting, rather annoyed her, as if they interfered with her
liberty and interrupted her peace.

On the whole, however, her ten years or more of girlhood in
Barcelona seem to have been gay and happy—the only frankly
happy period of her life. Without being robust, her health was
perfect, her needlework exquisite, her temper equable and calm;
she loved and was loved by her girl-friends; she read romantic
verses and select novels; above all, she danced. That was the
greatest pleasure in life for her: not for the sake of her partners—
those were surely only round dances, and the partners didn't
count; what counted was the joy of motion, the sense of treading
lightly, in perfect time, a sylph in spotless muslin, enriched with
a ribbon or a flower, playing discreetly with her fan, and sailing
through the air with feet that seemed scarcely to touch the ground.
Even in her old age my mother never walked, she stepped. And
she would say in her quaint, perhaps Virginian English: "Will
you step in?" She was not beautiful, and prematurely regarded
herself as an old woman, and put on a white lace cap; but she had
good points and made a favorable ideal impression, even if she
did not positively attract. I can imagine her in her young days,
agile of foot and hand, silent and enigmatic behind her large
sunken blue eyes, thin lips, and brown corkscrew curls, three on
a side, setting off her white complexion. If men did not often
make love to her, especially not the men who care specifically for
women, she amply took her revenge. Her real attachments, apart
from her devotion to her father, were to her women friends, not
to crowds of them, but to two or three and for life. To men as

men, even to her two husbands, she seems to have been cold, critical and sad, as if conscious of yielding to some inevitable but disappointing fatality.

I will translate a letter written to her by my father, dated Jan. 28, 1888, when I was in my second year at the University of Berlin, and it began to seem clear that I should drift into an academic life in America.

"My dear Josefina; I have had much pleasure in taking note of your kind letter and of the verses which, while thinking of me, you wrote twenty-five years ago. A volume would be requisite for me to recount the memories I have of our relations during now little less than a half a century. When we were married I felt as if it were written that I should be united with you, yielding to the force of destiny, although I saw plainly the difficulties that then surrounded such a union, apart from those that would not fail to arise later. Strange marriage, this of ours! So you say, and so it is in fact. I love you very much, and you too have cared for me, yet we do not live together. But it is necessary to keep in mind the circumstances peculiar to our case. I have always believed that the place in which it would be natural for you to live was Boston, in consequence of your first marriage which determined the course of your whole life. My position has offered and now offers no inducement, none, to balance the propriety or necessity of that arrangement. On my side, I could not then or later leave my own country for good, in order to live in Boston, when in view of my age and impediments it was impossible for me to learn to speak English well and to mix in that society. Here I have been a help to my family, and there I should only have been an encumbrance.

"I should have wished that Jorge should not have been separated from me, but I found myself compelled to take him in person and leave him in your charge and in that of his brother and sisters. Unhappy compulsion! Yet it was much better for him to be with you than with me, and I prefer his good to my pleasure."

How much in this was clearness of vision, how much was modesty, how much was love of quietness and independence? It is not a question for me to decide, but there was certainly something of all those motives. Education such as I received in Boston was steadier and my associations more regular and calmer than they would have been in Spain; but there was a terrible moral disinheritance involved, an emotional and intellectual chill, a pettiness and practicality of outlook and ambition, which I should not have encountered amid the complex passions and intrigues of a Spanish environment. From the point of view of learning, my education at the Boston Latin School and at Harvard College was not solid or thorough; it would not have been solid or thorough in Spain; yet what scraps of learning or ideas I might have gathered there would have been vital, the wind of politics and of poetry would have swelled them, and allied them with notions of honor. But then I should have become a different man; so that my father's decision was all for my good, if I was to be the person that I am now.

CHAPTER II

MY FATHER

THE name Santayana is derived by phonetic corruption from that of a small town in the Cantabrian hills, not far from the sea and from Santander. This name was originally Santa Juliana, doubtless that of some shrine or hermitage; but in Latin, as in Italian, *J* is only a double *i*, or *y*, the consonant, and the consonant *y* in Spanish is often confused with the stronger sound of *ll*, or the Italian *gl*; so that Santa Juliana could obviously yield in the vernacular to Santa Lliana, Santallana, Santayana, and Santillana. This last is the present name of that village; and on the other side of Santander, towards the Southeast, lies the village of Espinosa; so that my witty friend and translator, Don Antonio Marichalar, Marqués de Montesa (from whom I borrow the above etymology), half in banter and half in compliment finds in those seaside mountains, opposite one another, the native soil of Spinoza and of myself. But if I cannot be mentioned without a smile in the same breath with Spinoza for greatness of intellect, he cannot be compared with me for Spanish blood. He was a Jew: his ancestors could have found their way to Espinosa only as they did later to Amsterdam, or he himself to The Hague, or I to America; whereas if the reader will look back to the first page of this narrative, he will see that my grandfather was born in the province of Santander though not at Santillana, and that his wife and my father were born at Zamora, in Leon, my grandmother having the distinctly Portuguese or Galician surname of Reboiro: so that my ancestry on my father's side points distinctly to northwestern Spain, and Celt-Iberian blood; while my mother's origins were as unmistakably Catalonian and Balearic; rooted, that is, in those northeastern shores that look towards Provence and towards Italy and have linked Spain for many ages with the whole Mediterranean world.

The name Santayana is tolerably well known in Spain. My father had a book of the eighteenth century written by one of the family on the subject of international trade, advocating the Spartan policy of isolation and autarchy. My father didn't call it Spartan, but monkish; and it was based perhaps more on fear of heresy than on love of political independence; but the author was not an ecclesiastic, but a man of affairs. My two forlorn unmarried aunts, older than my father, used to tell me that our family was noble and allied to the house of a Marqués de Santayana then existing in Madrid; but they had no means of tracing the relationship, nor did my father give the least attention to questions of this kind; so that I know nothing of my ancestry beyond his own time. Moreover our family name is really Ruiz, a very common one; and perhaps the addition of de Santayana was as accidental in our family as the addition of de Espinosa must have been in a family of Amsterdam Jews. Dropping Ruiz and retaining only Santayana was my father's doing, and caused him some trouble in legalizing his abbreviated signature in formal documents. He loved simplicity, and thought plain Agustín Santayana as pompous a name as his modest position could carry. I sympathize with the motive; but why not drop the Santayana and keep the Ruiz, which was the true patronymic? Legally I still possess both; and the question has no further importance, since with me our branch of the family becomes extinct.

If I were looking for ancestors there is only one known to fame to whom I might attempt to attach myself, and he is Gil Blas, whose blood I should rather like imagining I had in my veins. I feel a natural sympathy with unprejudiced minds, or if you like with rogues. The picaresque world is the real world; and if lying and thievery and trickery are contemptible, it is because the game is not worth the candle, not because the method is unworthy of the prize. If you despise the world, and cheat it only to laugh at it, as the Spanish rascals seem to do, at least in fiction, the sin is already half forgiven. When the rogue tires of the game or is ruined by it, he may unfeignedly turn his free spirit towards higher things, or at least, like the good thief in Calvary, may recognize their existence. Those who lack the impudence and nimbleness of the rascal cannot help admiring his knowledge of things, and his quick eye; and the very meanness and triviality of his arts will keep him from thinking, as sinners do on a larger scale, that they are altogether heroes. Gil Blas doesn't become a saint— his biographer is a Frenchman—but becomes a good bourgeois, rich and happily married. It is a sort of redemption, though the Spanish spirit in him demanded another sort. The worthy solution would be found not in prosperity (too nearly what the unregen- erate Gil Blas was pursuing) but rather in devotion, religious in its quality, even if not in its object: the solution that the poet Zorilla, a friend of my father's in their youth, puts into the mouth of the reformed Don Juan, reformed, that is, by love.

> ¿Nos es verdad, ángel de amor,
> que en esta apartada orilla
> la luna mas clara brilla
> y se respira mejor?

> Angel love, is it not true
> that on this sequestered shore
> the moon shines as ne'er before
> and to breathe is something new?

Gil Blas represents also the sort of spiritual democracy that is characteristically Spanish, Christian, or Oriental. An unprejudiced man will be ready and happy to live in any class of society; he will find there occasions enough for merriment, pleasure, and kindness. Only snobs are troubled by inequality, or by exclusion from some- thing accidental, as all particular stations are. Why should I think it unjust that I am not an applauded singer nor a field-marshal nor a puppet king? I am rather sorry for them; I mean, for the spirit in them. Success and failure in the world are sprinkled over it like dew: it does not depend on the species of plant that receives it, save that the plant must exist and must spread its living texture to the elements. That is a great privilege, and a great danger. I would not multiply or inflate myself of my own accord. Even the punctilious honor of the Spanish gentleman is only an eloquent vanity, disdaining many advantages for the sake of a pose. Why assume so much dignity, if you have it not? And if you have it, what need have you of parading it? The base and sordid side of life must be confessed and endured humbly; the confession and the endurance will raise you enough above it.

The Spanish dignity in humility was most marked in my father. He lived when necessary and almost by preference like the poor, without the least comfort, variety, or entertainment. He was bred in poverty, not the standard poverty, so to speak, of the hereditary working classes, but in the cramped genteel poverty of those who find themselves poorer than they were, or than they have to seem. He was one of twelve children, imposing the strictest economy in the household of a minor official, with insecure tenure of office, such as his father was. For supper they had each a small bowl of garlic soup—something that my father loved in his old age, and that I also liked, especially if I might break a raw egg into it, as those twelve children were certainly never allowed to do. You fry some garlic in a pan with some olive oil; when crisp you remove the larger pieces of garlic, add hot water according to the size of the family, with thin little slices of bread, no matter how dry, *ad libitum*, and a little salt; and that is your supper. Or perhaps with a further piece of bread, you might receive a slice of cheese, cut so thin that the children would hold it up to the light, to admire its transparency, and to wink at one another through the frequent round holes.

That oil and water will not mix is disproved by this excellent garlic soup but also by a salad, *gazpacho*, that somewhat corresponded to it in the South. Bread, tomatoes and cucumbers, with oil and vinegar, and some slivers of raw onion, if you were not too refined, composed its substance, all floating in an abundance of water; so that if hunger was partly mocked, thirst at least was satisfied, and this is the more urgent need in a warm climate.

If supper at my grandfather's was only bread and water, with condiments, breakfast probably included a tiny cup of thick chocolate into which you might dip your bread, before you drank your water; for a glass of water after chocolate was *de rigueur* in all classes in old Spain. The difference between simplicity and luxury was only this: that the luxurious had an *azucarillo*, a large oblong piece of frosted sugar blown into a light spongy texture, and flavored with lemon, to be dissolved in a glass of water. At midday the daily food of all Spaniards was the *puchero* or *cocido,* as the dish is really called which foreigners know as the pot-pourri or *olla podrida.* This contains principally yellow chick-peas, with a little bacon, some potatoes or other vegetables and normally also small pieces of beef and sausage, all boiled in one pot at a very slow fire; the liquid of the same makes the substantial broth that is served first.

My father was educated at Valladolid, I don't know first under what schoolmaster, but eventually at the university there, where he studied law; and he at least learned Latin well enough to take pleasure in translating the tragedies of Seneca into Castilian blank verse; a pure work of love, since he could expect no advancement, perhaps rather the opposite, from such an exhibition of capricious industry. Nor was that his only taste; he also studied painting, and quite professionally, although he made no great progress in it. His feeling for the arts and sciences was extraordinarily different from that which prevailed in the 1880's in English-speaking circles. As to painting all in England was a matter of culture, of the pathos of distance, of sentimental religiosity, pre-Raphaelitism, and supercilious pose. Even the learned and gifted that I saw in Oxford were saturated with affectations. My friend Lionel Johnson was typical: although thirty years later, during the war, I had other distinguished friends in Oxford, Robert Bridges and Father Waggett, who were not in the least affected. But my father could not understand the English mind, greatly as he admired and respected the practical lordliness of Britain. Speaking once of Newman, he said he wondered why Newman broke with the Anglican establishment. Was it so as to wear a trailing red silk gown? I had some difficulty in making him admit that Newman could have been sincere; perhaps it was possible, if, as I said, Newman had never doubted the supernatural authority of the Church. But of inner unrest or faith suddenly born out of despair my father had absolutely no notion. Could he ever have read the Confessions of his patron saint, Saint Augustine? Was that not a natural sequel to the tragedies of Seneca?

As to painting, my father's ideas were absolutely those of the craftsman, the artisan, following his trade conscientiously with no thought or respect for the profane crowd of rich people who might be babbling about art in their ignorance. This jealous professionalism did not exclude speculation and criticism; but they were the speculation and criticism of the specialist, scientific and materialistic. He viewed the arts in the manner of Leonardo, whom probably he had never read. In talking about the pictures in the Prado, which I had seen for the first time, he approved of an observation I made about *El Pasmo de Sicilia*, that all the figures were brick-colored except that of Christ, which was whitish—a contrast that seemed artificial. He said I had been looking at the picture to some purpose. But he was disappointed when he questioned me about the Goyas, because I said nothing about the manner of painting, and only thought of the subjects, the ladies' fashions, and the sensuality of the eighteenth-century notion of happiness, coarser in Goya than in Watteau.

His methods were not less workmanlike than his thoughts. His easel, his colors, ground by himself with a glass pestle and carefully mixed with the oil, his palette and his brushes were objects of wonder to my childish heart. I was too young to catch the contagion and try to imitate him; but afterwards, when drawing became a pastime for me (as it still is) I wondered sometimes if my father's example and lessons would have helped me to make the progress in draughtsmanship which I have never made. And I doubt that they would have helped me. Because composition and ideal charm which are everything to me in all the arts seemed to be nothing to my father. I might have acquired a little more manual skill, and corrected a few bad mannerisms; but I should soon have broken away and turned to courses that he could not approve. Yet I think that he himself suffered in his painting, as in his life, from the absence of any ideal inspiration. He was arrested by the sheer mechanics of the art, as I was arrested by ignorance of them; and he remained an amateur all his life in his professionalism, because after measuring his drawing, and catching the likeness (since his paintings were all portraits) and laying on his first strata of color, he would become uncertain and discouraged, without a clear vision of what might render his picture living, distinctive, harmonious, and in a word *beautiful*.

When I once asked him, apropos of his liberal politics, the hollowness of which I already began to feel, what ideal of society he would approve, he said he had no *ideal*. "I don't know what I want, but I know what I don't want." We laughed, and the matter ended there, since discussion with him was rendered difficult by his extreme deafness; and few things seem worth saying when one has to reduce them first to a few words, and to make and impose an express effort in order to communicate them. But in my reflections afterwards it has often occurred to me that this position, knowing what you don't like but not knowing what you like, may be sincere enough emotionally, but not intellectually. Rejection is a form of self-assertion. You have only to look back upon yourself as a person who hates this or that to discover what it is that you secretly love. Hatred and love are imposed on the spirit by the psyche; and though the spirit may have no image of the end pursued, but only of jolts and obstacles on the way, there could be no jolts or obstacles if the life of the psyche had not a specific direction, a specific good demanded, which when discovered to the spirit will become an ideal. Not to know what one wants is simple absence of self-knowledge. It is abdication—my father was inclined to abdicate—and the insistence on *not* wanting this, or *not* wanting that, becomes an unamiable exhibition of the seamy side of your nature, the fair face of which you have turned downwards. Now my father hated shams, among which he placed religion, and hated complicated purposes or ambitions, with all the havoc they make; from which expressed dislikes it would be easy to infer that he loved the garden of Epicurus, with simple natural pleasures, quietness, and a bitter-sweet understanding of everything. This garden of Epicurus, though my father would have denied it, was really a vegetable garden, a convent garden; and it seemed strange to me that a man who had been so much at sea, and seen many remote countries, should take such a narrow and stifled view of human nature. He was tolerant and kindly towards the minor vices and the physical ills of mankind; he was tightly and ferociously closed against all higher follies. But is it not an initial folly to exclude all happy possibilities and condemn oneself to limp through life on one leg? If it be legitimate to live physically, why isn't it legitimate to live morally? I am afraid that my father, unlike my mother, was not brave.

In some directions, however, my father was docile and conservative. He had a great respect for authority in science or letters, and would quote Quintilian in support of his own preference for limited views: *Ad cognoscendum genus humanum sufficit una domus: For exploring human nature one household is large enough.* Yet when authority made for boldness of thought or for ambitious aims, he mocked it. In the region of Avila, which is some 4000 feet above the sea level, the heath is strewn with many boulders, large and small, often fantastically piled one over another; and one day when we noticed a particularly capricious heap of them, I said what a pity it was that we hadn't a geologist at hand to tell us about the origin of this odd formation. "What would be the use of that?" said my father. "He would tell us his theory, but he wasn't there to see the fact." Hobbes had said the same thing: "No discourse whatsoever can end in absolute knowledge of fact"; and I have made the *authority of things*, as against the presumption of words or ideas, a principle of my philosophy. Yet we materialists cannot consistently reject the evidence of analogy between one thing and another, since materialism itself is an interpretation of appearance by certain analogies running through things, and helping us to trace their derivation. There are glaciers in movement today in other mountainous regions the effects of which on the rocks they carry with them may be observed, as also the effect of running streams and beating waves in rounding and smoothing pebbles: so that those boulders on the skirts of the Castilian mountains may be plausibly explained by analogy. But my father feared to be cheated: and whenever he suggested anything a bit paradoxical, he would hasten to disown any personal responsibility for it. "I haven't invented that myself," he would say; "I have read it in a printed book, *en letras de molde.*" There seemed to be a curious mixture in his mind of the primitive man's awe for any scripture, with the skeptic's distrust of every theory and every report. And yet this very distrust tempted him to odd hypotheses at times to explain the motives behind what people said or imagined. If a visiting lady told us something interesting, which in my relative innocence I supposed might be true, it would startle me to hear my father say, as soon as she had turned her back: "I wonder *why* she said that."

Respect for authorities is fatal when the doctors disagree and the pupil is not self-confident enough to give direction to this freedom. My father's style in painting, for instance, inclined to clear shadows, pure outlines, and fidelity to the model, with little thought of picturesque backgrounds or decorative patterns. Had he had greater decision and dared to follow the ideal that he denied he possessed; had he simplified his surfaces boldly and emphasized characteristic features and attitudes without exaggerating them, he would have painted like Manet. But perhaps when he was at work on a canvas that promised well, he would visit the Prado, and some lurid figures by Ribera would catch his eye, or the magic lights in darkness of Rembrandt, and he would come home and spoil his picture by incongruously deepening the shadows. Stronger imaginations than his have been distracted and defeated by rival contagions; he at least was conscious of his defeat, and finished very few of his portraits; and he deputed even these to be finished when in reality they were scarcely begun.

He stopped halfway also in the law, which was his chosen profession, but for different reasons. Here he had not the blessed independence of the painter, consulting only his own inspiration. He had to think of tradition, of clients, of magistrates, of personal and political influences and intrigues; and his natural diffidence and dislike of rigmarole stood in his way. His family had no influential connections, and when still a very young man he accepted a post in the government service in the Philippine Islands. In this career, save for the effect of a tropical climate on his health, he did very well. Modesty combined with intelligence are prized in subordinates; and I had myself an opportunity, without any supernatural privilege of watching my father with his superiors in Manila before I was born, to see how he had behaved. My father's last post had been that of financial secretary to the "Captain General" or Governor General of the Philippines, who at that time had been General Pavía, Marqués de Novaliches. Now at the time of the revolution that dethroned Queen Isabella II, this general, then in Spain again, had been the only one to remain faithful to his sovereign, and actually to oppose Prim and Serrano in a battle at Alcolea, in which he was wounded and easily defeated. In 1871, when my father and I were living alone in Avila, my mother and sisters having gone to America, Novaliches and his lady came to live in Avila, in the palace that was later the Military Academy; and in their solitude and provincial retirement they seemed to relish the society of my father, with whom they had so many old memories in common. They had a carriage—the only one then in Avila—in which they took a daily drive along one *carretera* or another, or perhaps to the green hermitage of Sonsoles at the foot of the mountains opposite: a favorite walk of ours also. Sometimes they would send word, asking my father to accompany them; and as he

and I were then the whole family, it was inevitable that I should
go too.

Conversation on those occasions was naturally above my head,
as I was seven years old; and after the first day I was promoted to
a seat on the box beside the coachman, where I could watch the
horses and the front wheels in motion to my heart's content. The
landscape of that region has character, but no charming features
such as a child might notice; indeed it is striking how entirely children and common people fail to see anything purely pictorial.
Women and babies seem to them lovely, and animals attract their
attention, as being human bodies curiously gone wrong or curiously over-endowed with odd organs or strength or agility; but the
fact escapes them that light and shade or outlines in themselves
are something. It was unusually mature of me, in ripe years, to
re-discover *essences*—the only things people ever see and the last
they notice. From that coachman's box my young mind saw nothing but the aesthetics of mechanism; yet my unconscious psyche
kept a better watch, and I can now evoke images of impressions
that meant nothing to me then but that had subtler significance.
Now I can see how deferentially my father sat on the front seat of
that carriage, listening to the General's thick voice: for he had
been wounded in the jaw and tongue, so that he had an impediment in his speech and wore a black beard—of the sort I don't like
—to conceal the scar. Every now and then he made a one-sided
grimace that I still recall, as well as the serene silent figure of the
Marquesa at his side, dressed in black, passive and amiable, but
observant, and when she spoke saying something always kind and
never silly. She had the air, so common in Spanish ladies, of having suffered, being resigned, and being surprised at nothing.

My father couldn't particularly have relished the General's talk
which must have turned upon the politics of the hour, the intrigues
of his rivals and his own wrongs; but my father had heard such
talk all his life, and was not impatient. He liked to know and to
read the opinions most opposed to his own. He actually preferred
El Siglo Futuro, the Carlist and clerical newspaper, to the liberal

sheets. I daresay it was written in purer Castilian, but that was not his chief reason for reading it: he wished to understand, he said, why Spain made so little progress. "Progress" of course meant material development and assimilation to England and France. I think that intellectually my father had no other political criterion; yet emotionally he remained a patriot, or at least, without considering what virtues were proper and possible for Spain, he suffered at the thought that his country should be inferior in anything.

We soon left for America, and Novaliches and his lady also left Avila on the return of the Bourbons, and resumed a place in the great world: not a leading place any longer, but a sort of grandfatherly place in the background of affairs. Once, some twelve years later, when I was to pass through Madrid, my father gave me a letter of reintroduction to the old General. I was then, 1883, in that appealing phase of youth when one's heart and intelligence are keenly active, but unpledged; and if Novaliches or the Marquesa should take a fancy to me, might they not still have enough influence to secure a place for me in the army, or at court, or in some government service, where my knowledge of foreign languages might be useful? English, my strong point, was as yet little studied in Spain, and even my elementary German might have seemed an accomplishment: unfortunately it was my Spanish that limped, although that defect would soon have been remedied had I remained in Spain. These illusions floated, I know, in my father's mind, and they tempted me also imaginatively; but practically, had it ever come to a choice, I should have dismissed them. They would have led me into a slippery and insecure path, full of commitments, personal obligations, and false promises, very different from the homely plank walk across the snow that was to open to me in America. I have never been adventurous; I need to be quiet in order to be free. I took my letter to the General's house, but he was out of town; and this little accident, which we might have foreseen, as it was midsummer, sufficed to discourage us. We took it instinctively for an omen, symbolizing the insurmountable difficulties in the way of our hopes. We had no money. We had no friends. My mother not only would not have helped, but would have regarded my action as an ungrateful rebellion against her and a desertion of my duty. The desertion, though excusable, was really hers, because nothing would have been more natural and proper than for her to return to Spain, being a Spanish subject, especially a few years later when for her daughters it then would have been a most welcome change. Only her son Robert, then thoroughly Americanized and planning marriage, would have been separated from her, not my father or my sisters or me. But her will was adamant, once it had taken shape: and without her aid—apart from the unpleasantness and responsibility of the quarrel—I could not have weathered the storms and the prolonged calms of such a voyage in Spanish waters. How her passionate will found expression in words may be seen in a letter, unusually rhetorical for her, that I will translate literally: it deals with this very point of a possible military career for me in Spain, although the essential question—sticking to her or sticking to my father and my country—is not mentioned.

No date (about 1880).

"I am glad that our son has no inclination to be a soldier. No career displeases me more, and if I were a man it would repel me less to be a hangman than a soldier, because the one is obliged to put to death only criminals sentenced by the law, but the other kills honest men who like himself bathe in innocent blood at the bidding of some superior. Barbarous customs that I hope will disappear when there are no Kings and no desire for conquest and when man has the world for his country and all his fellow-beings for brothers. You will say that I am dreaming. It may be so. Adieu."

In repeating the part of this letter about the hangman and the soldier, my father once observed, "I wonder in what novel your mother had read that." Perhaps it had been in a novel; but I suspect that the words may have come from her father's lips, or out of the book of maxims drawn from all sages, from Confucius to Benjamin Franklin, that my grandfather had collected and published, breathing the spirit of Locke, Rousseau, and *Nathan der Weise.* My father was as strong a liberal as my mother; but he had studied Roman law and looked upon government as an indispensable instrument for securing peace and prosperity. Arcadia and the state of nature were among the ideals that he refused to have. He had lived among the Malays in the Philippines, the most blameless of primitive peoples, and he spoke kindly of them; but the only Malays he respected were those that had become Mohammedan and warlike—pirates if you like—and had kept their independence. He was modest enough not to hate superiors, as my mother did; he admired them.

When I ask myself what it was that he admired, say in the English or in the Romans, and what he respected them for, I think it was not that he had any inner sympathy with their spirit. The English I know he didn't understand: their whole poetic, sporting, frank, gentle side was unknown to him. He thought them only stiff, determined, competent and formidable. They were all captains of frigates pacing the quarter deck. And they were all rich, oppressively rich; because in his respect and admiration for the English there was an undercurrent of contempt—as towards people who are too well dressed. If you wish to be thought a gentleman among the English, he would say, you must shave and change your linen every morning, and never eat with your knife. The only time I remember him to have been annoyed with me was during my first visit to him in 1883, when we had made an excursion to the Escurial, going third class at night from Avila, because in the morning, before we had breakfast, I wanted to wash my face and hands, and asked the waitress for some soap. "*¡Cuantos requisitos!*" he exclaimed. How many requirements!

As to the Romans, I am uncertain of his feelings. He often quoted them as great authorities, especially the line of Lucretius about *Tantum religio potuit suadere malorum.* But it was the thought, the political wisdom in them, that he cared for. He took their Greek refinements, as the true Romans took them, for mere accessories and matters of fashion. When I once wrote out for him (he had few books) the well-known little ode to Pyrrha in the first book of Horace, he was arrested at the word *uvida*, and remarked on the interweaving of the concordance between adjectives and nouns. Of the poetry, of the Epicurean *blasé* sentiment, he said nothing. If I had written out the first ode of the fourth book, through which so much pierces that is disquieting, what would he have said? He might have shrugged his shoulders at pagan corruption: societies are like human bodies, they all rot in the end, unless you burn them up in time. But he was no soldier, not merely no soldier temperamentally in that personally he shrank from conflicts, but no soldier morally or religiously in that he saw nothing worth fighting for. Of course, you fought for your life, if attacked: that was a mechanical reaction of the organism. But he could have felt no sympathy with the martial regimen and martial patriotism of an ancient city. There was something sporting about it, a club of big boys, only hereditary, sanctified, made eloquent and mysterious by religion. The Spaniard is an individualist; he can be devout mystically, because that is his own devotion to his own deity; but socially, externally, he distrusts everything and everybody, even his priests and his kings; and he would have distrusted the *Numina* of Romulus and Remus.

In his old age my father's eyes became so weak that it was almost impossible for him to read or write. Painting he had long since abandoned; and in order to while away the time he took to carpentering and to framing and polishing steel clothes-horses of which there was soon one in every room of the house. I think he was happier in these rude occupations than when he had been more occupied with politics and ideas. He felt better, and his mind could choose its own themes, rather than the unpleasant events of the moment. Nature is far kindlier than opinion. When one faculty perishes, the others inherit a modicum of energy, or at least forget gladly, now that they are free, that formerly they were subordinate. Anything suffices, if nothing else is demanded; and mankind, let us hope, will dwindle and die more contented than it ever was when it waxed and struggled. I at least have found that old age is the time for happiness, even for enjoying in retrospect the years of youth that were so distracted in their day; and I seem to detect a certain sardonic defiance, a sort of pride, in the whining old beggars that look so wretched as they stretch out a trembling hand for a penny. They are not dead yet; they can hold together in spite of everything; and they are not deceived about *you*, you well-dressed young person. Your new shoes pinch you, and you are secretly racked by hopeless desires.

The house in which my father spent his last years, and which afterwards fell to me and was the only property I ever had in Spain, was built by an Englishman named John Smith, who had come to Avila as a railway foreman or contractor when the main line from the French frontier to Madrid was constructed. He had settled in Avila and established the hotel—*la fonda del inglés*—opposite the cathedral, to which all foreigners stopping in Avila were compelled to go. I must have seen him, but have no clear memory of him; only of the stories told about his outrageous Spanish, and of his long friendly relations with my father. They were once in England together; it must have been in 1867 when my father took Robert to London, or in 1873, on his way back from Boston to Spain. Anyhow Smith conducted him to Grantham, his native town, and regaled him with an oxtail soup that in my father's estimation, was "fit to resurrect the dead." The relish of it I am sure confirmed him in his rooted admiration for England. The fundamentals are fundamental and in England they were solid. Who, on such oxtail soup, would not conquer the world? It seems that on some occasion—perhaps at that convivial moment—my father had lent Smith a considerable sum of money; which Smith naturally never found it quite convenient to pay back; on the other hand a little more ready cash, especially if you are establishing a hotel or moving out altogether from one country to another, is eminently useful; so that it was agreed that my father should buy Smith's house, who would thus cancel his debt and get a little ready money in addition.

This house, one of the first in the town as you come from the

Station, was opposite the Church and convent of Santa Ana, where above a stone cross and a modest row of trees, the rocky soil rises a little above the road and forms a sort of terrace or little square. It was a working-man's dwelling, what in England is called a cottage, but commodious; there was ample room for my father and aunt, and for me and Susana, and eventually for my other old aunt and my cousin Elvira. In the first place it was a whole house, not divided into apartments; and it possessed a walled space, called a garden, in the rear, with a low wing on one side, which with its kitchen formed a complete dwelling by itself. This "garden" contained an apricot tree and some bushes, and one accidentally picturesque feature, which perhaps I was alone in noticing. The back wall, of uncut stones and mortar, coincided with a private aqueduct belonging to another convent in the neighborhood, called popularly *Las Gordillas*; and between the top of our wall and a broad arch of this aqueduct, there remained a semicircular space, exactly like those filled by Raphael's frescoes in the *Stanze* at the Vatican; only that instead of the *School of Athens* or the *Dispute of the Sacrament*, nature here had painted a picture of the *Valle de Amblés*, to which Avila owes its existence, with the purple Sierra beyond: a picture everywhere visible to the pedestrian round about Avila, yet here concentrated and framed in by its stone setting into a perfect and striking composition.

The ground before this little house was neither town nor country: virgin earth with rock emerging in places, and preserving its irregular surface; but stone paths had been laid across it roughly, in the directions that people were likely to take, and served as stepping-stones in case of mud or pools of water; for there was no drainage. We had a well with an iron pump, in the house, so that only the water for cooking and drinking needed to be fetched from the public fountains. Sometimes in summer, when the purest water was desired, a donkey with four large jars in the pockets of a wicker saddle brought it from some reputed spring in the country. This primitiveness was rather pleasant and on the whole salubrious; we lived nearer to mother earth; nor was it exclusively

Spanish. At Harvard I used to bring up my coal and water daily from the cellar of Hollis Hall, or water in summer from the college pump opposite.

Going to the fountain (as it was called) was a chief occupation for servants in Avila, whether girls or men, and also a chief amusement as were the innumerable errands they were sent on; it gave them a breath of air, a little freedom from the mistress's eye, and a lovely occasion for gossip and for lovemaking. Without going to the fountain and without errands (since all messages were sent by word of mouth, never by written notes) the life of domestic servants would have been prison-labor. As it was they knew everybody, heard everything, and saw wonderful things.

John Smith had built his house in the style of the country, but on a plan more regular and symmetrical than usual. A passage paved in stone like the paths outside, and on the same level, led from the front door to the garden; and on each side were square sitting rooms with alcoves: every sitting room in Spain having such a whitewashed sleeping cubicle attached to it. I always occupied the room immediately to the left of the entrance; while my father had the back room upstairs (the other being the kitchen) because it was the only sunny room in the house. There had been an open veranda running outside this room, through the whole width of the house; but my father turned it into a glazed gallery, himself making and fitting all the woodwork necessary. This, with my father's room behind it, was the pleasantest place in the house, and we habitually sat there, and made it the dining room. There was little furniture of any sort: a table and a few chairs could be easily moved anywhere: only the bookcases and a *chaise longue* remained always in my room, which had been meant for the study: while the room over it, possessing a sofa, two armchairs with oval backs, and an oval mirror, suggested the ladies' parlor. Susana occupied it whenever she came to Avila, and on other occasions my cousin Elvira.

All this formed a meager, old-fashioned, almost indifferent stage-setting to my father's life: the real drama was his health. He was a wiry and (for a Spaniard) a tall man, and lived to the age of seventy-nine; and long walks and long sea-voyages in comfortless old sailing vessels were nothing to him. Yet he was a hypochondriac, always watching his symptoms, and fearing that death was at hand. Whether this was congenital or the effect of insidious ailments proper to tropical climates, I do not know: but the sense of impediment, of insecurity, was constant in him. It defeated any clear pleasure in any project, and mixed a certain bitterness with such real pleasures as he enjoyed. They were snatched, as it were, from the fire with a curious uneasiness, as if they were forbidden and likely to be punished. And this when theoretically he was absolutely rationalistic, materialistic, and free from moral or physical superstition. Perhaps, if a man's bowels are treacherous, he cannot trust anything else. Dysentery removes all the confidence that the will has in itself: the alien, the irresistibly dissolving, force is too much within you. Moreover, my father had other obvious discouragements to face: poverty, deafness, semi-blindness: yet these, if his digestion had been good and strong, I don't think would have cowed him. He had plenty of Castilian indifference to circumstances and to externals, plenty of independence and capacity to live content with little and quite alone. But the firmness of the inner man must not be undermined by a sour stomach: that, at least, seems to have been my father's experience. Intelligence and brave philosophy were mixed strangely with this discouragement. On one of the many occasions when he thought, or dreaded, that he might be on his deathbed, he felt a sudden desire for some boiled chicken, without in the least giving up his asseveration that he was dying; and as his deafness prevented him from properly modulating his voice, he cried out with a shout that resounded through the whole house: ¡La Unción y la gallina! "Extreme Unction and a chicken!" Extreme Unction only, be it observed. That is the last Sacrament, to be received passively, without saying a word. It would put him to no inconvenience. To have asked for confession and communion would have implied much talking; he was too far gone for that. Extreme Unction would do

perfectly to avoid all unpleasantness regarding his funeral and
burial in holy ground. Nobody would need to be distressed about
his soul. And meantime, since these were his last moments, and
the consequences of any imprudence would make no difference,
why not boldly indulge himself one last time, and have some
boiled chicken? That, I am confident, was his thought. And he
had the chicken. The last Sacrament, this time, was not required.

CHAPTER III

MY MOTHER

I HAVE already recorded my mother's parentage with what little I have gathered about her childhood; and in the sequel there will be occasions to mention many other events in which she was concerned. Yet the crucial turn in her life, her migration to Manila, and her first marriage, remain to be pictured: I say pictured, because the bare facts are nothing unless we see them in a dramatic perspective, and feel the effect they had on her character and the effect that her strong character had on them. Between her father's return to Barcelona, to act as American Consul there, and the time, thirty years later, when my own observations begin, I must interpolate a little historical romance: because my mother's history during those years, her sentiments, and even her second marriage were intensely romantic. Romantic in a stoical key, when the heroine is conscious of her virtue, her solitude, and her duty.

Those dancing years of girlhood, with their intense girl-friendships, their endless whisperings and confidences and discussion of toilets and tiffs and other people's love affairs, with their practice at the piano, their singing-lessons, and their lessons in the languages—for my mother could read and half-understand French, although she never spoke it—would have had a natural end in being courted and married; especially in Spain, where young people easily become *novios*, or acknowledged sweethearts without any formal engagement to be married. To go to the papa and make an express demand for the young lady's hand, and to obtain leave to visit the family daily, would be an ulterior step, on which the wedding would follow presently; but to have *relaciones* or to be *novios* is a free and indefinite courtship, permitting no liberties, and involving no blame, should the courtship be broken off by either party. It might be described in Anglo-Saxon terms as a trial engagement. Now this normal development seems not to have occurred in my mother's case; I never heard the least hint that she had ever had a *novio* either in Barcelona or in Manila. In her the first flower of youth did not bring its natural fruit; it was cut short by the pruning hook.

Whether my grandfather's appointment lapsed with the change of Presidents in the United States, or whether those strictly legal fees to be received by him were disappointing, or whether other difficulties arose, I do not know: but he was still a Spanish subject, and after a change of government in the liberal direction had occurred both in France and in Spain, his friends were able to obtain for him what promised to be a lucrative post in the Philippine Islands. This was further geographically than Virginia, but politically and socially much nearer home; and perhaps the oceanic distance and the idyllic state of nature of the natives in those unspoiled latitudes tempted his imagination, as much as the easy life and future pension tempted his advancing years. At any rate, he decided to go; and it was obvious that his daughter, who was devoted to him and was the apple of his eye, must accompany him. Distant lands were not unknown to her, nor colored people. Her first memories were about a "Grandmother Locke" in whose house they had lived in Virginia, and the darky children that ran half-naked about it. The sea had no terrors for her; perhaps she positively preferred the excitement of a real danger, with the sense of her own courage in facing it, to the fading trifles that had entertained her until now. The problem was her mother, who seems to have been less willing to leave her friends and country for the second time. They were really her friends and country, something that was not true in her daughter's case nor, in a moral sense, even in her husband's, because with his opinions a certain irritation at all things Spanish was hardly to be avoided. It is easy to acknowledge the backwardness or poverty of one's country, and to be happy there, when one thinks those things relative and unimportant, and the contrary advantages treacherous and vain. The Arab is not ashamed of his desert, where he is alone with Allah; but the pupil of the French Revolution, dreaming of multitudes all possessing a multitude of things, and of the same material things, cannot rest in a few old customs and a few simple goods. He has a bee in his bonnet; or rather his head is a veritable beehive, and the only question for him is in which direction to fly. My grandfather, though perhaps a little weary, was determined to launch forth again in pursuit of fortune: but my grandmother wouldn't go. She was very fat; she was not young; perhaps she felt that she had not much longer to live; perhaps she had a premonition that this adventurous project might go wrong, and that her husband and daughter might come back to her before they expected. If so, she would have been half right, as are the best premonitions. She died soon; her husband never returned; and new dawns opened before her daughter in which she counted for nothing.

The voyage from Cadiz to Manila, round the Cape of Good Hope, lasted six months, included the inevitable worst storm the Captain had ever encountered, with death yawning before the passengers in every hollow between the black waves; and it included also the corresponding invention of something to do in good weather. My mother then made the first of her bosom-friendships with a young lady I believe of Danish or Dutch extraction but Spanish breeding named Adelaida Keroll; she learned to play chess; and her father gave her lessons in English to brush up her Virginian baby-talk, which must have been rather forgotten during her ten years in Barcelona.

And what language, I may ask incidentally, would she have habitually heard or spoken in Barcelona between 1835 and 1845? Castilian, no doubt, officially and in good society; but surely Catalonian with the servants and in the streets; and was not Catalonian also the language that her parents spoke when alone together? Perhaps not. That was not yet an age when disaffected people were nationalists; they were humanitarian and cosmopolite: they were purists in politics and morals, theoretical Brutuses and Catos, inspired by universal ideals and categorical imperatives of pure reason. In any case I have only heard a very few words of Catalonian, bits of proverbs or old songs, from my mother's lips. Yet she may have spoken it fluently at one time. Had we not lived in America later, I might never have heard her say a word in English, which had been one of her first languages; even in America she never spoke it easily or if she could help it. Her Spanish, however, was far from perfect; and perhaps a certain confusion and insecurity in her language contributed to render her so prevailingly silent. The things she was likely to hear or able easily to express were of little interest to her; and it annoyed her to be troubled about them.

In the 1880's, when we lived in Roxbury (a decayed old suburb of Boston) a rich widow who lingered in a large house round the corner, and had intellectual pretensions, came to call and to invite my mother to join the Plato Club—all the very nicest ladies of the place—which met at her house once a fortnight in winter. My mother thanked her, and excused herself. The president and host of the Roxbury Plato Club would not take no for an answer. Might not my mother *develop* an interest in Plato? Would she not be interested in *meeting* all those superior ladies? In what then *was* she interested? What did she *do?* To this my mother, driven back to her fundamental Philippine habits, replied without smiling: "In winter I try to keep warm, and in summer I try to keep cool." Diogenes could not have sent the President of the Plato Club more curtly about her business.

I am convinced that this contempt of the world, this indifference and pride had a double root in my mother. Partly it was native independence, like that of the wild bird that refuses to be tamed; but partly also it was a second mind, a post-rational morality, induced in her by the one great sorrow and disappointment in her life, of which I shall speak presently. She put on a resigned despair, a profound indifference like widow's weeds or like a nun's veil and mantle, to mark herself off as a stricken soul, for whom the world had lost its savor. The sentiment was sincere enough and rendered easy to adopt by that native wildness and indolence of the bird soul in her which it seemed to justify rationally; yet her change of heart could not be complete. It was romantic, not religious. She kept intact her respect for the world in certain directions, and even a kind of negative snobbery. She could not forgive the shabby side of things for being shabby, or the weak side of people for being weak; while she sternly abdicated all ambition in herself to cultivate the brilliant side, or to hope for it in her children; and this renunciation was bitter, not liberating, because she still craved and needed that which she knew she had missed.

Was it only English that her father taught her during those six months out of sight of land? What better occasion for instilling true wisdom into a virgin mind, so ready to receive it? Just at the crisis, too, when frivolous amusements were being abandoned together with all familiar faces and ways, and a violently different climate, frequent earthquakes, torrential rains, a new race of human beings and a simpler more primitive order of society were to be encountered. I like to believe that during some of those starlight nights or lazy afternoons under an awning in the slow swell of a tropical sea, my mother must have imbibed those maxims of virtue and philosophy to which she always appealed: commonplace maxims of "the enlightenment" but taken by her, as by her father, for eternal truths. Pope's *Essay on Man* contains them all in crisp epigrams; and it was in this oracular form that my mother conceived them, as if self-evident and recommended by their luminous simplicity to every virtuous mind. All else was unnecessary in religion or morality. Nor was there any need of harping on these principles or of preaching them. Hold them, appeal to them in a crisis, and they would silently guide you in all your actions and judgments.

I never accepted these maxims in my own conscience, but I knew perfectly what they were, without being expressly taught them, as I was taught the catechism. They were implied in every one of my mother's few words and terrible glances. And she was almost right in thinking that, without much express admonition or direction from her, they would suffice to guide us safely in all circumstances; because they were not really confined to being "virtuous." We knew that it was equally obligatory to be "refined." To be a *persona fina* was to be all right: refinement, to her mind, excluded any real vices. Her notion of what was right, like the Greek notion, did not divide the good from the beautiful. And this had a curious reverse effect on the education of her children. We were expected to be refined, but that did not mean that we were to have any advantages or accomplishments. It was quite sufficient to be virtuous. Of course we were to be educated: enlightenment and virtue (again a Greek notion) were closely allied. It was not religion that made people safely good, it was reason. If she had not felt so poor, no doubt we should have been sent to the best schools or had the best private tutors, according to prevailing fashions. But the object, in her mind, would still have been to make us personally more virtuous and enlightened; it would not have been to widen our interests or our pleasures and to open the way for us to important actions or interesting friendships. Nor, in the case of the girls, would the reprehensible object have been that they should find distinguished rich husbands, or any husbands. They could be virtuous at home, where they belonged; and if they were virtuous, they ought to be happy. The result of this was that two of her children had little education and led narrow dull lives; while the other two, Susana and I, had to make our friends and pick our way through the world by our native wits, without adequate means or preparation, and without any sympathy on her side—quite the reverse. Our new interests —religion, for instance—separated us from her and from the things she trusted. We were not virtuous.

Whether or not the seeds of this stern philosophy were sown in my mother's mind during those six months at sea, the end of the voyage put that philosophy to a severe test. Not all vessels took so long, even going round the Cape of Good Hope; and there was also the overland route by Alexandria, and camelback to Suez. Despatches from Spain, sent after my grandfather's departure, had reached Manila before him; and he learned to his dismay that in Madrid there had been a change of ministers, and that the post promised to him had been given to somebody else. Yet as justice does not exclude mercy in God, so injustice does not always exclude it in men. The Captain General of the Philippines enjoyed some of the prerogatives of a viceroy, since distance from superiors always leaves some room for initiative in subordinates; and another post was found for my unfortunate grandfather, an absurdly modest one, yet sufficient to keep body and soul together. He was sent as Governor to a small island—I think it was Batang— where there were only natives, even the village priest being an Indian. Terrible disappointment, do you say? But was not this the very ideal realized? What a pity that Rousseau himself, so much more eloquent than poor José Borrás, could not have been sent instead to that perfect island, to learn the true nature of virtue and happiness!

I am not sure that Rousseau or my grandfather need have been disappointed with the moral condition of Batang: perhaps it was just what they would have desired. Or if there were any unnatural chains binding those blameless children of nature, the chief gaoler and tyrant in this case was happily the philosopher himself, who might devote his energies and his precepts to relaxing those bonds and might win the supreme reward of making himself superfluous. No: the real obstacle was not moral: perhaps the real obstacle never is moral. If it were, the surrender of some needless prejudice, a slight readjustment of some idle demand, might immediately solve it. Are those blameless children of nature, for instance, promiscuous in their loves? Instead of crying, How shocking! the moralist has only to familiarize himself with their view, sanctioned by the experience of ages, in order to recognize that promiscuity may be virtuous no less than a fidelity imposed by oaths and fertile in jealousy and discord. But here the physician and the historian may intervene, and explain the origin of exogamy, monogamy, and the cult of virginity. Perhaps, as a matter of fact, promiscuous tribes are weaker, more idiotic, easier to exterminate than those that take it into their heads, no doubt superstitiously, to observe all sorts of sexual taboos. Perhaps it was the ferociously patriarchal family that made the strength of the Jews and of the Romans. The force as well as the obstacle in nature is always physical. So it was with my unlucky grandfather, and so it would have been with Rousseau, had he ever found himself safe and sovereign in his ideal society. The state of nature presupposes a tropical climate. A tropical climate is fatal to the white race. The white race must live in the temperate zone, it must invent arts and governments, it must be warlike and industrious, or it cannot survive. This fatality of course is not absolute or immediate; white men may live in the tropics, protecting themselves by a special regimen, and returning home occasionally to recover their tone; but if they leave children in those torrid regions, the children will die out or be assimilated, in aspect and temperament, and probably also in blood, to the natives.

Now when my grandfather found himself relegated to Batang, he was not a young man; he was a battered and disappointed official, a man of sedentary habits, studious, visionary, and probably careless about his health. It was noticeable in Spain and Italy, until very recent times, how little most people seemed to sleep, how much they smoked, how they never bathed or took exercise, how yellow was their complexion, how haggard their eyes. I don't know that my grandfather carried this neglect of the body and abuse of its powers further than other people did; probably he was more continent and abstemious than the average. He was an enthusiastic moralist and idealist, and it is only fair to suppose that his life corresponded with his principles. But now, in the decline of his life, he was suddenly transferred to a tropical climate entirely new to him, without advice or such resources, medical or other, as even a tropical colony would have afforded in its capital city; and he succumbed. His wife also had meantime died in Barcelona; and my mother was left an orphan, without property or friends, alone at the age of twenty in a remote island peopled only by Indians.

It was at this crisis that she first gave proof of her remarkable courage and strength of character. With what ready money she could scrape together, and with her jewels for security, she bought or hired a small sailing vessel, engaged a native skipper and super-cargo, and began to send hemp for sale in Manila. If she was without friends in a social sense, the people round her were friendly. Two of her servants, her man cook and her maid, offered to remain with her without wages; and her skipper and agent proved faithful; so much so that in a short time a small fund was gathered, and she began to feel secure and independent in her singular position. She adopted the native dress: doubtless felt herself the lady-shepherdess as well as the romantic orphan. And she was not without friendly acquaintances and friends of her father's in Manila who were concerned at her misfortunes and invited her to come and live with them. In time, offers of protection came from even greater distances. Her uncle, the monk, then in charge of a parish in Montevideo, wrote asking her to join him, and be his housekeeper. Although I have heard nothing, I cannot help thinking that her other uncle or cousins in Reus, and her mother's relations, would also have offered to take her in—such orphan cousins or wards are found in many a bourgeois Spanish family—if she had seemed to desire it. But she did not desire it; and I don't know how long her life according to nature, to virtue, and to Rousseau might have continued, but for an accident that I almost blush to record, because it seems invented. Yet it was real, and is referred to in my father's letter of 1888, already quoted.

That solitude, at once tragic and protective, was one day disturbed by a fresh arrival. Batang had remained without a governor; but at last a new governor, a young man, was sent out from Manila. Now two white persons, a young man and a young lady without a chaperon, alone together on a tropical island formed an idyllic but dangerous picture; and it became necessary for that

young lady in order to avoid scandal to return to a corrupt civilization. Thus the life of pure virtue, as I might show if I were
Hegel, by its inner ironical dialectic transformed itself into conventional life; and fate laughed at the antithesis that prudence
and decorum opposed to its decrees: because, though my mother
proudly turned her back on that young intruder, and went to live
with friends in Manila, he nevertheless was destined, many years
later, to become her second husband and my father.

The friends with whom she took refuge were a Creole family
in Manila, for I think the head of it was not a government official
but a merchant or land owner long established independently in
the country. His name was Iparraguirre, a Basque name rich in
resounding r's, and carrying my fancy, I don't know by what
association, to the antipodal seafaring peoples of Carthage and of
Japan. The Basque element is an original but essential element
in the Spanish race; it is sound, it is needed; but divorced from
Castile it would lose itself like those other ancient peoples with
strange languages that are driven to the uttermost coasts of all
continents, to hibernate there without distinction or glory: Lap-
landers, North American Indians, Highlanders, Welshmen, Bre-
tons, and one might be tempted to add, Irishmen, Basques, and
Norwegians. Here a distinction seems to be requisite; for the
Norwegians may seem to be, geographically, a primitive people
driven to the uttermost verge of the habitable earth, yet biologi-
cally they are a fountainhead and source of population, rather
than a forlorn remnant. They multiply and migrate; and though
they are not great conquerors (for their home strength and perhaps their moral development is not firm enough for that) they
become a valuable ingredient in other countries and peoples.
This is or may be the case with the Scotch also, and with the
Irish; and I like to think that it is true of the Basques. I have
known South Americans of distinction who bore the names of
Irazusta and Irarrázabal; as if something Magian or Carthaginian
could resound at the limits of the new world. However, if the
Basques are to propagate their virtues it must not be in the

tropics; and in the family of Iparraguirre there was only one child, Victorina, who became my mother's second intimate and lifelong friend; so much so that afterwards, in Madrid, where Doña Victorina had gone with her husband, Don Toribio de la Escalera, who had been an officer in the Spanish army, the two families lived together for a time; and we have always regarded Mercedes, Doña Victorina's only child, as one of our family.

As I remember Doña Victorina she was a diminutive wizened old woman so round-shouldered and sunken in front as to seem a hunchback; but it was not her spine that was bent but her shoulder-blades that were curved forward, making her little convex back rounded and hard like that of some black insect. My mother too had the right shoulder-blade somewhat bent forward and protruding a little behind, which she said was the effect of continually stretching the arm round the frame of her embroidery; but if that were the cause, Doña Victorina must have embroidered with both hands at once. Nevertheless this little dark lady made a pleasant impression; she was lively, witty, affectionate, interested in everything and everybody, and her bright eye and suggestion of a smile—never laughter—made you feel that she wished you well but had no illusions about you. I can understand that her vivacity in repose—for like my mother she never moved about or did anything—should have made her a perfect companion for my mother, a link with the gay world, as Susana was later, that never pulled you or attempted to drag you into it. Doña Victorina was entertaining, she knew everybody and had known everybody, whereas my mother, if left to herself was silent and sad.

It was Doña Victorina who received me when I first came into this world, and wrapped me in a soft brown shawl that she and Mercedes have often shown me, and which Mercedes still keeps at the foot of her bed, to be pulled up at night in case of need. They must be good shawls and good friends that have lasted in daily use for eighty years.

Doña Victorina was pious, and this, it might seem, would have proved an obstacle to such an intimate friendship with my mother;

yet it did not. There are many kinds of piety. I imagine that Doña
Victorina's was of the ancient, unquestioning customary kind, remote from all argument or propaganda; emotional and sincerely
felt, but only as the crises of life are felt emotionally, deaths,
births, weddings, fêtes, and travels. So you went to Mass or to a
novena, punctually and with the appropriate sentiment, in the
appropriate dress (always black); and you returned to your other
employments and thoughts with the same serenity and simplicity.
It all was one woof; the appointed dutiful, watchful, shrewd, and
passionate life of woman. My mother skipped the piety: it was
not in her private tradition; but piety in others did not offend her,
and the mere absence of it in her did not offend any one.

For the orphan living with the Iparraguirres dancing could
hardly have been again the chief of social pleasures. It was too
warm for much dancing in Manila; but people drove out in the
late afternoon and went round and round the promenade, to look
at one another and take the air. When the Angelus bell rang, all
the carriages stopped, the men took off their hats and the ladies,
if they liked, whispered an *Ave Maria*. But there were some houses
where people gathered for a *tertulia*, a daily *salon* or reception; and
I suppose there were occasional official balls. Anyhow, young people could make eyes at each other and marriages could be arranged.
My mother always spoke contemptuously of love-making and
match-making: yet she herself was twice married, and not by
any simple concatenation of circumstances but in spite of serious
obstacles. Passion may inspire determination in a Romeo and a
Juliet; in my mother I think determination rather took passion's
place. She decided what was best, and then defied all difficulties
in doing it. Now it was certainly not best, or even possible to
remain forever a guest of the Iparraguirres. Victorina any day
might be married and what would the orphaned Josefina do then?
Go to Montevideo to keep house for her uncle, the parish priest?
Wouldn't it be wiser and more natural herself to marry? Certainly
not any one of those Creole youths or Spanish officials who in
the first place did not particularly court her, and in the second

place were not virtuous. However, there was one wholly exceptional young man in Manila, tall, blond, aquiline, blue-eyed, an
American, a Protestant, and unmistakably virtuous. And that
young man, probably as little passionate as herself, and as little
trustful of the Spanish young women as she was of the Spanish
young men, could not but be visited by kindred thoughts. Was
not this grave, silent, proud orphan wholly unlike the other young
girls? Was she not blue-eyed like himself? Did she not speak
English? Had she not lived in Virginia, which if not as reassuring
as Boston, still was in the United States? And as he found on
inquiry, if she was not a Protestant, at least she was no bigoted
Catholic, but a stern, philosophical, virtuous soul. Was she not
courage personified, and had she not suddenly found herself
alone and penniless and, like Benjamin Franklin, made her own
way in the world? Was she not a worthy, a safe, a suitable, even
an exceptionally noble and heroic person to marry? And was it
not safer, more suitable and more virtuous for a merchant in the
Far East to be married to a foreigner than not to be married at all?

Such convergent reflections found ways of expressing themselves, and the logical conclusion was easily drawn. A virtuous
marriage meant safety and peace for him in his old bonds, and
it meant safety and peace for her, who had no dread of novelty,
in new bonds rationally chosen. By all means, they would be married; but there was an obstacle. No legal marriage was then possible in Manila except in the Church; and the Church there had
not the privilege of granting dispensation for a marriage to a
non-Catholic. Everybody, including the Archbishop, was sympathetic and free from prejudice; but a petition would have to be
sent to Rome for a special license. This would involve long delay,
perhaps a year, and of course some expense; and much worse, I
am sure, from my mother's point of view, it would involve a conspicuous act of submission to ecclesiastical authority, such as her
pride and her liberal principles would never submit to. Yet it
would have been useless to take extreme measures, and to declare
that she was a non-Catholic herself; there was no non-Catholic

marriage possible within Spanish jurisdiction. I am not sure whether her free principles would have gone so far as to justify her in eloping, and going to live with George Sturgis unmarried. Perhaps not: whether such a course would have seemed to her nobly virtuous, or not virtuous at all, but disreputable, I cannot say. She was capable of taking either view. It was he, perhaps, who might have blushed at such an idea; not only a foreign but an illegitimate union to be reported to Boston! However, a brief voyage to China, not more than ten days, might have sufficed to make that union legitimate, and to remove all reproach or legal impediment from any possible children. But accident offered a simpler means of effecting this purpose. There happened at that time, April, 1849, to be a British man-of-war at anchor in Manila Bay. The deck of that ship was British territory, and of course there was a chaplain, who being a jolly tar, would not object to marrying a Unitarian to a Papist. Indeed, although the thing was not then fashionable, he might have contended that theologically he was a Catholic, that he stood in the true Apostolic succession, and was blessing a truly Catholic marriage. In any case, the ceremony and the certificate of marriage under British law were legal; and we may imagine the wedding party, the bride and bridegroom, all the Iparraguirres, all the members of the House of Russell and Sturgis, and the nearer friends of both, setting out in the ship's cutter, manned by its double row of sailors, and flying the white ensign, to the frigate, and cautiously but joyfully climbing the ladder up the great ship's side. And perhaps, if the Captain was jovial, as he doubtless was, there may have been a glass of wine, with a little speech, after the ceremony.

This important event—important even for me, since it set the background for my whole life—occurred on the 22nd of April, 1849, chosen by George Sturgis for being the thirty-second anniversary of his birth. This choice of his birthday for his wedding is characteristic; as was also his sanguine assertion, only half facetious, that his son Victor, because born in the Tremont House in Boston, would some day be President of the United States.

Such fancies are in the tone of the Sturgis mind, inclined to pleasantry that is too trivial to be so heartily enjoyed; and these jester's jests are apt to have some sad echo. That future President of the United States did not live to be two years old, and his confident father had preceded him to the grave.

When this double bereavement fell on my mother, eight years after her marriage, she was already deadened to sorrow and resigned to living on resolutely in a world that could no longer please her or wound her deeply. Ten months after the wedding she had given birth to a beautiful boy, blue-eyed like his parents, fair, and destined to have yellow hair though at first quite bald; and his nature at once showed itself no less engaging than his appearance; for when only fifteen months later he found he had a little sister, who sometimes couldn't help calling away their mother's attention to herself, he, far from being jealous, was most tolerant and kind, and would even give the baby his toys, although she was too small to appreciate them. The contrast between the two babies was marked, and had a lasting influence in our family. Susana, the second child, was in the first place only a girl, and although my mother had all due respect and affection for her own sex, and, as I have said, was more attached to her women friends, to one or two of them, than even to her two husbands, yet she had no artificial illusions about womenkind, their rights, or their virtues. They were, in most things, inferior to men; she would have preferred to be a man. So that the fact that Susana was only a girl while Pepín was a boy instituted the first point of inferiority in her. Then curiously, she didn't have blue eyes, like her parents, but only hazel eyes and a great lot of brown hair; as if nature had wished to mark the fact that she was not at all angelic, like her brother, but belonged to a lower, much lower, moral species. And as she grew up, she showed no signs of unselfishness, but on the contrary a lively desire to have her own way, and to take the lead in everything. Our mother actually had to defend the too self-sacrificing Pepín, and later the too self-sacrificing Josefina, from Susana's prepotency. Because the curious part of it was, that not only poor little Josefina later, but even Pepín seemed *to like* doing as Susana wished, and *to imitate* her; which was a dangerous tendency that would have to be suppressed. However, not much suppression of Susana was necessary in those years; the great occasion presented itself only many years later, in regard to me; for Josefina was so tepid and had so few resources and so little initiative, that in regard to her it was almost a blessing that Susana should be there to take the lead.

Until the age of two Pepín had seemed to be in perfect health, even if rather gentle and oldish for a baby; but at that age signs of fading away began to appear, and became slowly more pronounced. No remedies, no care, no change of residence could arrest them, and seven months later the perfect child died.

There is an oval miniature of Pepín in a low-neck green frock like a lady's; he appears wide awake, pale, with very thin fair hair. This miniature was set in a circle of pearls and worn in the old days by my mother as a brooch, to pin a lace shawl over her bosom.

Was the death of this child due only to the effects of a tropical climate? I am not in a position to judge: but none of his brothers and sisters had a strong constitution. Even Susana, who seemed to be the most vigorous, was not rightly put together; and Robert, who seemed normal and commonplace, had a latent contradiction in his nature. I may return to this subject later. If I am right in suspecting that, eugenically, my mother and her first husband were not well matched, and that there was something hybrid in all their children, that latent weakness would only have reinforced the often fatal effect of a tropical climate on children of European race. That little Victor should have succumbed also is not to be wondered at: born in Boston, he was subjected to a long sea voyage to Manila, to a season of that climate, and then to an agitated long journey by sea and land to London, where he decided that he had seen enough of this world, and escaped from it at the age of one year and seven months. Perhaps, on the other hand, these voyages and this speedy removal to a temperate if trying climate—"bracing," Bostonians call it—may have saved the other three children from a gradual decline or relaxation of fiber, if not from an early death.

The loss of her first-born did not affect my mother as it would any mother, especially a Spanish mother. There were no violent fits of lamentation, no floods of tears, no exaggerated cult of the grave or relics of the departed. Especially in a woman who has or is expecting other children, as was the case here, such wild sorrow has its period: the present and the future soon begin to gain healthily upon the past. But with my mother this event was crucial. It made a radical revolution in her heart. It established there a reign of silent despair, permanent, devastating, ruffled perhaps by fresh events on the surface, but always dark and heavy beneath, like the depths of the sea. Her husband, with his sanguine disposition and American optimism, couldn't understand it. He wrote worried letters home, expressing his fears for her life or her reason. He didn't see the strength of this coldness. Her health was not affected. She continued to bear children at frequent intervals—five in seven years. She did not neglect her appearance, her embroidery, her friends, or her flowers. She spoke little, but she never had been loquacious: and when, in a brief interval between babies, he proposed a voyage to Boston, to present her and the children to his family, she readily agreed. This marriage for him had been extremely happy. He described his domestic bliss in glowing terms in his letters. Was it not a happy marriage for her also? Of course it was. Why then this deadly calm, this strange indifference? Why these silent steps, grave bows, and few words, such as people exchange at a funeral?

Many Spanish women live in this way the life of a Mater Dolorosa, and are devout for that reason to Our Lady of the Seven Sorrows, with seven swords fixed in her heart. They give a religious or pictorial turn to their despair; but at bottom they have the same experience that my mother congealed into a stoical philosophy. She knew that her father's positivism and humanism and thirst for progress had a black lining; and she had the courage to wear his mantle with the black side out. Let the world see the truth of its own madness. She at least would not pretend not to see it.

However, let me not exaggerate. This second life, this mystic unmasking of the commonplace and the obvious, was not explicit in my mother. She didn't know what her real philosophy was: her verbal philosophy remained the most trite and superficial positivism. Her depth was entirely psychic, passionately dispassionate, intensely determined and cold; but her intelligence had no depth. It was borrowed, and borrowed not from the best sources, but from the intellectual fashions of her father's time. Therefore, in her outward life and actions, she showed a persistent attachment to persons and to principles that really meant very little to her. This paradox must be accepted and understood if we are to explain the two apparently contrary bonds with which now, in this first voyage to Boston, she outwardly bound herself. One was her attachment to the whole Sturgis family, much more hearty than her attachment to her husband personally, of whom she never spoke with enthusiasm or even with deference. The other was the unwilling but somehow inescapable bond with my father.

For by a second curious chance, or perhaps by an unconscious or even conscious attraction, my father was one of the passengers in the same clipper ship, *Fearless*, that took her and her husband with their little children Susana, Josefina, and Roberto, in the record time of ninety days from Manila to Boston. He was on his way to Spain on leave, for the sake of his health; and by taking this roundabout course not only had a chance of visiting New England, New York and Niagara Falls, but of getting a glimpse of England also, and yet reaching Spain no later than those who had set sail for it directly at the time of his departure from Manila. For from New York to Liverpool there was already a line of steamers.

There is an unusually enthusiastic letter of my father's describing the lovely scene in some genteel suburb of Boston—very likely the same Roxbury that seemed so shabby thirty years later, when we lived there. It was a Sunday morning, and under the arching trees between their neatly painted separate and comfortable wooden dwellings, the happy citizens and their well-dressed wives and children walked with a quiet dignity arm in arm to church. It seemed the perfection of human existence, at last realized on earth. Whether if my father had understood the spoken language and had followed those model citizens into their meeting-house, he would have been as much edified by their mentality as he was by their aspect, I do not know; but his impressions on his second visit to the United States were rather different. From 1856 to 1872, from a rural suburb to a half-built quarter of the town, from summer to winter, from the "flowering of New England" to its industrialization, from the prime of his own life to its decline, many things no doubt had changed to lower the key of his judgment. But I was surprised, knowing his earlier impressions, by something he said when, towards the end of his life, I showed him some comic verses I had just scrawled comparing America with England, in which I satirized the American man, but paid a gallant compliment to the ladies. And he said, "No. The women there are just as second-rate as the men." Did he—he was so apprehensive—take that passing compliment of mine too seriously and think that I might be in love and meditating marriage with an American? Or had his earlier view itself been colored by amorous sentiments awakened during that recent voyage in an American ship by an interesting young mother, seen and conversed with for ninety days on deck and at table? Perhaps it is rash to identify in any case the moral color of a memory with the moral color originally proper to the fact remembered. Sunday morning in Roxbury, by a lucky chance, may once have seemed ideal, and that impression, while warm, may have been recorded in a letter; and some decades later the memory of that same scene, qualified by later discoveries, may have looked mediocre or even ridiculous, like the clothes that were the fashion thirty years ago. Even if Roxbury and the Puritan Sunday had proved elevating to behold

by the stranger, they might mean boredom in a slum to the native
unable to escape from them. Which of these judgments shall we
retain? My philosophy would retain both, each proper to the ideal
essence then present to the spirit; but it would discount both, and
smile at both, as absolute assertions about that poor, material,
ever changing congeries of accidents which was Roxbury in fact,
or those unrecoverable manifold feelings which truly echoed
and re-echoed through the emptiness of a New England Sunday.

What Boston first thought of my mother or she of Boston I
can only infer from their relations in later years; these relations
were always friendly and theoretically cordial, but never close.
Indeed, when she first arrived in Boston she was expecting another child. It was born there, in the hotel that stood in Tremont
Street directly north of the graveyard adjoining the Park Street
church. I remember this *Tremont House* clearly. It had rounded
red-brick bay windows like bastions, and the glass in some of the
square windowpanes had turned violet, a sign of venerable age.
In 1856 it may have passed for a fashionable place, being near
the rural Common yet not far from State Street and the center
of business. The principal churches were scattered round it—the
Park Street Church, the Old South King's Chapel, and St. Paul's
—while round the corner the eye was caught by the State House
with its classic dome, model for all Capitols in the New World.
And almost opposite was the theatre, called the Museum, because
before entering it your cultured mind was refreshed by the sight
of a choice collection of plaster antiques, including the Apollo
Belvedere, as well as by cases of stuffed birds and mammals that
surrounded the grand entrance hall.

Such was the enlightened center of Boston in the 1850's; and
there were gentle lights really burning in some of those houses,
with no exaggeration of their range or brilliance: Ticknors, Park-
mans, Longfellows and Lowells with their various modest and
mature minds. I came too late to gather much of that quiet spirit
of colonial culture, that felt itself to be secondary and a bit remote from its sources, and yet was proud of this very remoteness,

which gave it the privilege of being universal and just. In my time this spirit lingered only in Professor Norton, but saddened by the sense of being a survival. I also knew Lowell, in his last phase; I once shook hands with Longfellow at a garden party in 1881; and I often saw Dr. Holmes, who was our neighbor in Beacon Street: but Emerson I never saw.

All this was nothing to my mother, who was too proud to pretend to care for what didn't concern her. That which she saw and prized in Boston was only what the Sturgises represented: wealth, kindness, honesty, and a general air of being competent and at home in the world. They belonged to the aristocracy of commerce, the only one my mother respected and identified with the aristocracy of virtue. The titular nobility of Spain and other European countries, which she knew only by hearsay, was only the aristocracy of undeserved privilege and luxurious vice. It was detestable; it was also out of reach; and she felt doubly virtuous, being cut off from it physically as well as morally. In Boston her friends were at the top, where they deserved to be; and although her friendship with them was little more than nominal, she was content to be counted among them; and this feeling made her heroic resolution to break away from all her associations and go to live in America very much easier than it might have seemed. Climatically, socially, intellectually she was moving into a strange world, but morally she felt she was moving into her true sphere. It was the sphere of her principles and her imagination. She soon found that in practice she could play no part in it; but that did not change her theoretical conviction that it was the *right* place to live in. There the mighty had fallen from their seat, and the righteous had been filled with good things.

A superstitious person might have been alarmed at the omens and accompaniments of this first visit to Boston; for Old Nathaniel, her father-in-law, whom they presumably went to see, died soon after their arrival, and George Sturgis, her husband, died soon after their return to Manila not only prematurely and unexpectedly, for he was scarcely forty, but in the midst of a disastrous commercial venture, which left the widow with inadequate means. My mother, however, had not a vestige of superstition; and her courage and coolness, her quick and intrepid action, on this occasion contrasted oddly with the utter apathy and despair that had overcome her on the death of Pepín. The pathetic but not uncommon loss of an infant had paralyzed her; the loss of a young husband, the prospect of a complicated journey half round the world, alone with four little children, and the prospect of life in a strange society and a strange climate in reduced circumstances, seemed to revive her energies and to make her more alert and self-possessed than ever.

Yet such a crisis had occurred once before, on the death of her father, when she had no experience and no resources, which this time was not the case: for now she was not penniless: her brother-in-law Robert gave her a present of ten thousand dollars to help her over the crisis and she had recently made the acquaintance of the whole Sturgis family in Boston, where a share, one-eleventh, of her father-in-law's estate remained for her support. She would have to give up her easy colonial life with numerous servants and old friends, and with nothing exacted of her except the usual charities. Yet she was not in the least perturbed. I almost think that she was relieved, liberated, happy to abandon burdensome superfluities and reduce her life to the essentials; and as to the demands that her new environment would make on her, perhaps she did not foresee them, and in any case she had ample strength to resist them. The admiration she aroused at this time was well deserved but not very intelligent. People supposed her to be bearing up under a terrible sorrow and cutting herself off from the dearest ties, in order to do her duty by her children; but the fact was that the most tragic events now could not move her deeply, and the most radical outward changes could disturb her inner life and daily habits very little. She had undergone a veritable conversion, a sweeping surrender of all earthly demands or attachments; she retained her judgments and her standards, but without hope. I am confident of this, because at about the same age I underwent a similar transformation, less obviously, because in my case there were no outer events to occasion it, except the sheer passage of time, the end of youth and friendship, the sense of being harnessed for life like a beast of burden. It did not upset me, as the revolution in her circumstances did not upset my mother; but it separated the inner self from the outer, and rendered external things comparatively indifferent. I recorded this conversion in my Platonizing sonnets; my mother expressed it silently in the subsequent fifty years of her life.

If clearness about things produces a fundamental despair, a fundamental despair in turn produces a remarkable clearness or even playfulness about ordinary matters. That tragic journey of the young widow with her four little orphans to the antipodes was planned and carried out in rather a lordly way. She would not go again in that nasty little clipper ship *Fearless,* or the like of her, where the passengers were cooped up for three months like the poultry under the benches on deck; she would go grandly, overland, or when possible by steam packet. She believed in progress. On her way, she would visit her eldest and richest brother-in-law in London. And she would travel with two maids and quantities of luggage. When travel was still difficult it was still pompous. She carried not only all her personal belongings, shawls, laces, fans, fancy costumes, and family heirlooms, but chessmen and chessboards, Chinese lacquer tables, and models of native Philippine houses in glass cases, with their glass trees, fruits, animals, and human figures. She even took with her, to look after the baby, a little Chinese slave, *Juana la China,* whom she had bought and had had christened and of course liberated. She believed in progress, and she was making one.

The visit to her brother-in-law Russell in London no doubt left its mark on her mind. It set the standard of propriety and elegance for her in the way of living in Northern and Anglo-Saxon countries. It combined, with the tropical charms of Manila, to make Spain, for instance, seem to her most inferior. Possibly it set the standard too high: because after that heroic effort to settle down in Boston she does not seem to have taken root there; and three years later, at the outbreak of the American Civil War, she left Boston again for Spain. It was not to be more than a temporary visit; her Boston house was merely let, and she meant soon to return to it. Yet she was away for eight years. During those three years in Boston, 1858–1861, she had an English governess for the children, a Miss Drew, whose correct British locutions, such as "make haste" instead of "hurry up," I sometimes detected in my sisters, when they spoke English; she had a French maid for herself in addition to Juana, the Chinese girl: in spite of her hatred of priests and indifference to religion, she took a pew in the Catholic pro-Cathedral in Castle Street—an almost disreputable quarter for true Bostonians to be seen in; and she seems to have made only one personal friend, an old maiden lady who was a neighbor and sometimes sat with her over their fancy-work. In fine, I gather that from the first my mother lived in Boston as she did in my time, entrenched in her armchair in her corner between the window and the fire, with a novel or a piece of embroidery to occupy her mind, expecting no visits, receiving them formally and almost silently if they came, going out for a stroll in good weather to take the sun and air, watching our movements and the servants authoritatively but as it were, from a distance, and seldom interfering, and in all things preserving her dignity and also her leisure. Perhaps she resented the tendency, meant for kindness, to assimilate and absorb her, and she emphasized her separateness in self-defense, as I had to do afterwards in personal and intellectual matters. Boston was a nice place with very nice people in it; but it was an excellent point of vantage from which to start out, if you belonged there, rather than a desirable point to arrive at if you were born in some other place. It was a moral and intellectual nursery, always busy applying first principles to trifles.

Was my mother cloyed with too much Boston, was she really troubled by anti-slavery agitation and war, or was she merely attracted by the idea of seeing her friend Victorina again, who had followed her husband to Madrid? I confess that none of these reasons seem to me sufficient to explain, in so calm a person, such a disturbing and unnecessary journey. However, the journey took place; and in 1862 my mother and her three children were living in Madrid with Don Toribio, Doña Victorina and the little Mercedes, then five or six years old. I remember this joint household very well, as it was re-established some years later, when I had come into the world. In Spain Santa Claus is nobly and religiously replaced by the Three Kings or Wise Men of the East that brought presents to the Infant Jesus; and in the absence of chimneys (except in the kitchen) children hang out their stockings or place their shoes on the balcony with which every window not on the ground floor is provided. It was *el dia de reyes* and we had not forgotten to put out our shoes on the night before; the good Kings had taken the hint and left something for each of us; but what was our glee that Don Toribio who had foolishly put out his big shoe also, found nothing in it but a raw potato!

In Madrid there was naturally a circle of retired or transferred officials and military men who had served in the Philippines, and also liked to renew old acquaintance and recall common experiences. Among these retired officials, at that moment, was my father. Don Toribio and Doña Victorina of course knew "Santayana," as they always called him. Without being a society man, he was liked for his wit and for his well-informed conversation. He spoke little—he was very prudent—but he spoke well. It was inevitable that he and my mother should meet again. If I were writing a novel and not a history I should be tempted to invent here a whole series of incidents and conversations that might have occurred during those ninety days in the clipper ship *Fearless* six years before, and to indicate how the scattered little impulses then awakened, now, when all checks to free expression were removed, could gather head, combine their currents, and become an irrepressible force. But I have no evidence as to what really may have brought these two most rational persons, under no illusion about each other or their mutual position and commitments, to think of such an irrational marriage. It was so ill-advised a union that only passion would seem to justify it; yet passion was not the cause. I say so with assurance because there is not only the fact of their ages, nearly forty and nearly fifty, respectively, but there are my mother's verses, kept in secret and sent to my father twenty-five years later, when it was likely that the two would never meet again; and there are also certain expressions of my father's about love and marriage, which it would not be proper for me to repeat, but which show that my mother, a widow who had had five children, could not have been the object, for him, of an irresistible love. It was an irresistible *dæmonic* force, a drift of circumstances and propensities, as in one more throw at dice, or one more picture to paint. Things on the whole *drove* them to that action; but both he and she performed it unwillingly and with full prescience of the difficulties in store. My mother's verses are melancholy and sentimental, containing nothing specific, but the tone is that of renunciation. It is *impossible,* she feels, to entertain the idea that nevertheless has presented itself and has seemed tempting. The lines seem to have been written when her mind was still undecided, as if to encourage herself to resist and to give up the project. It still remains obscure what the irrational force was that nevertheless carried the day.

CHAPTER IV

THE STURGISES

FOR my purposes the Sturgis family begins with the children of Nathaniel Russell Sturgis of Mount Vernon Street, Boston, who died in 1856. These children were twelve in number, like those of my paternal grandfather in Valladolid; but two died in childhood and five others had disappeared before I was taken to America; although their children often come into my story, and cast more or less reflected light on their departed parents. It is only by reflected light that I am able to picture the old gentleman, on a rainy Sunday afternoon, sitting far apart with his newspaper, while Susan Parkman his wife read the Bible aloud to the children; but the reflected ray comes from a sure source, from Sarah, the eighth of those children, afterwards Mrs. Francis George Shaw, mother of the Robert Gould Shaw, Colonel of a negro regiment raised in Massachusetts, whose monument stands at the edge of the Common opposite the State House in Boston. She was aunt to my brother and sisters, and by a pleasant arrangement that at once was established I too called her "Aunt Sarah," and repeatedly stayed at her house in Staten Island or in New York. The family were Unitarian, but apparently with varying degrees of radicalness and fervor; and it was with a twinkling eye and great gusto that "Aunt Sarah," who was a woman of spirit and warm convictions, told me the story. Her mother, she said, was reading about Jonah and the Whale; and her father, whose people came from Cape Cod and who knew what's what about whaling, put down his paper—what political gazette or commercial bulletin could he have been perusing in 1825?—and said solemnly: "Susan, do you

56

expect the children to believe that nonsense?" "I thought," Aunt Sarah confided to me, "I thought, George, that my father was a wicked man."

If the father was wicked, at least the eldest son, whom we called "Uncle Russell," was virtue personified—I don't mean moral virtue only, but *virtù* of every description. Unfortunately it is again only by reflected light that I ever saw him, although several of his children or grandchildren were among my best friends, and he was prominent among the lares and penates worshipped in our own household. For both my father and my mother seemed to think him the perfection of manhood, as exalted as he was kind, a center of dazzling wealth and exquisite benefactions. His career had begun in the East, in Manila and China; but somehow from there he passed to England, and eventually became a partner, at one time I think senior partner, of Baring Brothers in London. He was twice married and had two distinct families, two sons and a daughter married to Bostonians and honestly though gently American, and three other sons and a daughter brought up and settled in England, and, although their mother was American, perfectly English. I knew, more or less intimately, all these seven establishments: in two of them, one in England and one in America, I was a frequent guest; and as this relation lasted for half a lifetime, I had the melancholy pleasure of watching them in their early glory and in their gradual obscuration, dispersion and decline. This theme will recur often: it has become a *leit-motif* in my view of life; and the first great, slow, tremendous variation upon it was made by the splendid Russell Sturgis himself. Of his great days I have seen many traces; all his children's households were at first prosperous, fresh, luxurious, recognizable copies of the parental grandeur; but the reflection paled, as the sun itself descended. Perhaps Russell Sturgis remained too long at his post, or perhaps other greater circumstances altered the fortunes of Baring Brothers; but everybody knows that after being for years, with the Rothschilds, the greatest banking house in the world, it got into difficulties, was rescued by the goodwill of the Government, but sank into comparative obscurity. When I was first in London, in 1887, my mother had instructed me to pay my respects in her name to our great "Uncle Russell"; and after I had been there a week or two, learned the ropes, got suitable clothes, and found myself alone and at leisure, I called one afternoon, at the right hour, at the mansion in Carlton House Terrace where the old gentleman still lived. The air of the great house, even externally, was rather cold and abandoned, but after I had rung the bell twice, a dignified old butler opened the door a little. When I asked for Mr. Sturgis and offered my card, the man explained civilly, in a sort of sick-room whisper, that Mr. Sturgis didn't see anyone, that he was not very well, but that I might see Mr. Henry Sturgis. When I said I would see Mr. Henry Sturgis, the butler seemed surprised. Mr. Henry Sturgis didn't live there; and he gave me an address in Marylebone where I might call upon him.

That was the nearest I ever got to "Uncle Russell"; but I learned from discreet hints dropped by his son Henry, when I saw him some days later, that it was not simple old age or simple illness that kept his father in seclusion. The distinguished head of all the Sturgises, who had united great abilities to the good looks, affability, sound sense, and kindness common to the whole tribe, no longer possessed those abilities. He in whom the not too brilliant intellect of the family had been focused and concentrated, had lost it. It would be no pleasure now, his son had said, for him to see me or for me to see him. That was the melancholy report I had to send to my mother.

I am sorry, in opening this family picture gallery, to turn in this way my first and most imposing portrait to the wall: but they are all to be works of my own brush, not done by the fashionable painters or photographers of those old days; and no living image of Russell Sturgis is in my possession. But I can give him a name, in lieu of a portrait, and will call him and his generation the Great Merchants: a type that in America has since been replaced by that of great business men or millionaires, building up their fortunes at home; whereas it was part of the romance and tragedy of those Great Merchants that they amassed their fortunes abroad, in a poetic blue-water phase of commercial development that passed away with them, and made their careers and virtues impossible for their children.

Nathaniel's second son, Henry, repeated the success of his brother Russell on a smaller scale, and ended with a more decided reverse, which however he barely lived to experience. He had not been long dead when I first reached Boston in 1872, and his stately house, which I passed daily on the way to school, was pointed out to me with a certain funereal reverence. He was also far less fortunate than Russell in his children: most of them died before him; the ominous word dissipated was whispered, or positively hissed, by the ladies when they felt obliged to mention some of them. Only two survived, Fred, who was a doctor in New York and whom we seldom saw, and Nena, who on the contrary seemed more like one of us than any other of the Sturgises. Not that we saw her often, for she was an expatriate, having just enough money to live in decent pensions in Europe, like so many English and American spinsters: but that only increased our points of contact, which were initially numerous. Besides being a Sturgis she was, like my brother and sisters, an East Indian; lively, erratic, and as her name, Nena, suggests, with something pseudo-Spanish or Creole about her. Her mother had been born of British parents in India, and I believe had lived there most of her life; at any rate, she was exotic, and Nena too seemed exotic in Boston, like ourselves. She even pretended to know a little Spanish picked up from her father. He, like his brothers, had been at one time or another connected with the house of Russell and Sturgis in Manila, of which an uncle of theirs had been a co-founder; and they had taken kindly to the place and its lazy opulence, as had my mother also. Their easy Spanish exempted her from having to dig up her little old-fashioned English phrases, as she had to do in conversation with the other Sturgises. Nena was Spanish at least in having *dis-*

posición, the inclination to assume accomplishments without much training; she composed and sang and even published some "Songs of the Pyrenees," in a language which was certainly neither Spanish nor French. Eventually, at a mature age, she married a cultivated Englishman named Middlemore who wrote for the *Saturday Review.* They both loved Italy, ultimately became Catholics, and died romantically within a few days of each other. I stayed with them for a weekend in 1887 in a pleasant house they had taken in the English country; that was shortly before their conversion and death, for they put off pledging themselves about the other world until they were about to enter it, and discover whether they were right or wrong. From my room I heard them discussing in the passage whether I was so much of a Catholic as to require fish on Fridays. "No," said the intuitive Nena, "he is a *philosophe.*" Philosophical indifference she assumed in me also in another direction, when she had her legs massaged in the drawing room in my presence—and this in the nineteenth century. She was forty-three and I twenty-three, ages that might make such a liberty innocent, or very dangerous. In fine she was *corriente* and *despreocupada* (it seems as if only Spanish epithets could fit her); I mean that she had no nonsense about her, was a man's woman, and a good sort. With one degree more of beauty and several degrees more of wealth she might have cut a charming figure in society.

A curious thing was that, with this sympathy between us and Nena and with my mother's admiration for the Sturgis character and ethics, Nena's detested stepmother, the *bête-noire* and stage villain of the whole Sturgis comedy, should have been a special friend of ours. "Aunt Lizzie," as we called this formidable lady, was a tall strong woman of fifty or more, with black hair and bushy eyebrows that met over her nose, and a bass voice; in which it was impressive to hear her tell how her brother, an unemployed clergyman with whom she had a lawsuit, had attempted to poison her, all for the sake of the wretched pittance that remained to her. She had also attempted to break her admirable husband's will, but to no purpose; her reduced circumstances obliged her to live about in boarding houses or with poor relations, no doubt souring her high temper and making her a dangerous enemy. She was a native of Worcester, Mass., and not a self-restrained Bostonian. She seemed mysterious and sordid, like some gaunt ghostly figure from Hawthorne's desolate New England. My mother alone was able to retain her favor; so much so that our house was filled, if not beautified, by remnants of the pictures and furniture from "Uncle Henry's" dismantled house in Beacon Street. This loan was welcome to my mother who, without having any knowledge or taste in matters of fine art, was accustomed to a certain air of luxury in her surroundings; and it saved "Aunt Lizzie" the cost of storage. For it would have been against her principles to *sell* anything: everything that once was legally hers she held forever with a grasp of iron. She even hinted, or actually proposed, coming to live with us, of course as a paying-guest; but this was too much. My mother above all things loved liberty, self-government, and silence; things not to be preserved where "Aunt Lizzie" was enthroned. It would have been an offense to the other Sturgises, and a constraint to ourselves. We should have had to speak English at table, as if we were not at home. We should also have had to double up, at least my sisters would have had to share the same room; and our domestic economy, however modest otherwise, provided that each of us should possess his or her private room as a castle. It might be small, like my narrow one-windowed den at the top of the house, but it should be sacred. I doubt whether this practice is altogether wholesome in youth. Animals are born and bred in litters. Solitude grows blessed and peaceful only in old age.

This habit of privacy turned our house, quite unintentionally, into a little monastery. In a monastery there is strict community in externals, in hours, food, manners, and mode of dress, while in theory and sometimes in fact each member remains inwardly a hermit, and silent in his thoughts and affections. The system suited me perfectly, since nature had framed me for a recluse and only the contrary force of circumstances kept me for many years from complete retirement; but that system perhaps had an unfortunate influence on my brother and sisters who would have been happier and more truly themselves if they had been carried along, body and soul, by an irresistible social medium. They instinctively sought such a medium, perhaps thought they had found it, but were never really unified or inwardly content. They had not the requisite inner clearness and force, such as my mother and I had, to thrive on a deliberate moral independence and a profound solitude.

I think I half understood why my mother was faithful to that objectionable virago, our "Aunt Lizzie." My mother was faithful to everything she once accepted—faithful, that is, within limits, as she was even to my father. This was part of her fidelity to herself. She might seldom or never see her oldest and best friends; she didn't need them; but she always remembered and cherished them as they had first figured in her life, as they ought to prove, if they in their turn would only remain faithful to what she had believed them to be. Now she had deliberately and forever accepted all the Sturgises: not so much because they were her husband's family as because, being his family, they made her husband himself much more acceptable than he would have been individually: for individually the virtuous George Sturgis was rather negative. The simplicity of the Sturgis mind was decidedly marked in him; whereas in Henry, and of course in Russell, if it was present at all, it had assumed the noble characters of integrity, decision, and benevolence. Now "Aunt Lizzie" was Henry's widow; she belonged to the great generation; she had been once accepted, and she should never be disowned. How should the Sturgises be offended, when it was for their sake that she was treated decently? My mother never cooled towards any of them because they hated "Aunt Lizzie" and why should she cool towards "Aunt Lizzie" because she hated *them*? Besides, there was perhaps a certain bond between the sisters-in-law in their common poverty and isolation. For my mother, though she never had any lawsuits or quarrels and was no doubt esteemed by all her first husband's people, was inevitably neglected by them. They came to see her, if at all, once or twice a year, for a visit of ten minutes. It was not their fault. She had nothing to tell them, they had to make talk: how many children their children already had; how sad that so-and-so had died; what a pity that so-and-so had failed, and had been obliged to move to a smaller house; but how bravely and cheerfully everybody put up with everything. And so, good-bye, they must be off; and they were so glad to find her looking so well. With "Aunt Lizzie" conversation had more substance. There was a common background; and to hear long accounts of the misdeeds of one's relations and one's own trials was something to which my mother must have been accustomed in Spain and in Manila. It was the staple of feminine confabulations; and, given my mother's perfect passivity, it was like hearing a novel read aloud: and my mother read many novels. They helped to pass away the time, and required no answer. Anyhow, friends the two sisters-in-law remained to the end. In her will, the Dragon left all those terrible yet space-filling mid-Victorian pictures and sofas and stuffed little armchairs and Chinese dovetailing tea tables to my mother, to live with until death.

Rarest of our Sturgis visitors but most picturesque was "Uncle Samuel," third son of old Nathaniel of Mount Vernon Street, and of Susan Parkman, his wife. Perhaps he called only once, perhaps twice; the dear gentleman was not often let out from Somerville, where he resided in private apartments at the Insane Asylum.* Sound commonsense people, roseate optimists, as the Sturgises were, they were too Bostonian not to have at least one mad member, even in the Great Merchant generation; and "Uncle Samuel's" was an appropriately mild case. He seemed, in these lucid intervals when he was allowed to go visiting, most amiable, dignified, and even happy. Indeed, why should he not

* Later removed to Danvers.

have been secretly a philosopher, saner than any of us, like Hamlet laughing at all the world and pretending to be mad in order to be free to laugh at it unmolested? But no: such complexities, as I have already hinted, were far from the Sturgis mind. It was straightforward, believed in what it saw, and in what sounded right. It had just enough rope to go once round the intelligible world; to go round it twice, like a philosopher, was beyond the Sturgises. Had "Uncle Samuel" attempted such duplicity, I am sure he would have become much madder than he was. It was rather simplicity that perhaps he had carried a little too far; so far, that the moral comfort of not apprehending too much had passed into the practical inconvenience of apprehending too little. At any rate, he visibly took excellent care of his person, if not of his affairs. He was a tall, handsome, courtly old gentleman, beautifully dressed in the style of his first youth. The change in men's fashions had not been radical enough to render his figure ridiculous; I remember only one singular detail. His long-tailed coat, cut like what is now worn for full dress in the evening, was double breasted and buttoned in front; and a thin line of white waistcoat peeped out beneath it. Beau Brummel might have approved, but comment must have been caused in Beacon Street. In his conversation there was nothing especially queer. We smiled on one another; explained our state of health, remarked upon the beautiful weather, so summer-like for the season, till finally, smiling even more pleasantly, he rose, extended his hand to us all in the right order, said he was pleased to have found my mother looking so well, which compliment she of course returned amid our approving murmurs. She thanked him for his visit; my sisters and I accompanied him to the front door, and stood there while he went down the steps, and as he turned into the street beyond the little grass-plot, he once more elaborately took off his very tall top hat, and sent us a parting smile.

My mother certainly had reason to be flattered by the courtesy of such a visit. If her mad but punctilious brother-in-law had extended his unaccustomed walk to one of the last houses in the

Mill Dam, to pay his respects to the foreign and remarried widow of a younger brother whom he had hardly known, save as a young boy, was not this a proof of the esteem in which the Sturgis family had held her from the beginning? That esteem had surmounted a very just initial prejudice against foreign marriages; and the surprise of finding the Spanish stranger so firm and courageous and consistent in her actions, and in her independence, had survived in this shattered mind, as it might not have survived if overlaid by years of commonplace acquaintance.

I leave what more I may have to tell about these elder branches of the Sturgis tree until I come to the part some of them played in my own life; as I leave also the fruits that ripened on the ninth branch. This was that of "Papa George," as I might call my mother's first husband, father of my brother and sisters, who was, as it were, my stepfather by anticipation and after whom I was named. This rather odd fact was due to the original innocent sentiment of my sister Susana, who as the reader may remember was my godmother, and in that capacity had a nominal right to give me a name. She could just remember her father, having been six years old when he died, and it was she, apparently, who suggested that I should be called Jorge, a rather unusual but not unknown name in Spain. That my father should have smiled and made no objection, I can understand, in view of his modesty and ironical turn of mind. He thought his predecessor a good soul, but a simpleton; and somehow his expectation about me, perhaps in order not to count on too much and then be disappointed, seems to have been that I should be a simpleton too. He liked to aim low, not trusting his star, and perhaps calling me Jorge in memory of "Papa George" was a subtle sign of such resignation. When I first returned to Spain in 1883, and we went out together for our first walk, he pointed out to me the first donkeys we came across, and said: "¿Reconoces los compañeros de tu infancia? Do you recognize the companions of your infancy?" I recognized them. But it was not I that ever played with donkeys. It was my brother Robert, Robert *Sturgis*, who had once had a donkey for a pet in his childhood. I reminded my father of this, and we laughed about it.

A more puzzling point would be to ask why my mother saw no objection to calling me Jorge after her first husband. Might not my father resent it? No doubt he said he didn't in the least; but wasn't there some indelicacy on her own part? She was passive, very passive unless her path were crossed; and her path in the matter of children had been crossed once for all by the death of her first-born. I too might have been named José, after her own father, or *Pepín*, her pet-name for that lamented child. But no, that would have been sacrilege. I think in my early childhood she sometimes felt a certain analogy between her lost darling and me, who was her first-born by her second marriage, after five years of widowhood; but the illusion was soon dispelled. I was too inferior; and to institute any such comparison would have damned me at once. Why then establish this strange link with the past by calling me Jorge? Anyhow, Susana had her way—she often did—and there was something prophetic about this mingling of Sturgis traditions with my little person. Jorge, translated back into George, has become a part of my *nom de plume*.

I should hardly mention the tenth child of old Nathaniel at all, or her branch of the family tree, not a luxuriant one and unknown to me save for one sprout; but this one had a peculiarity that impressed my young mind. Her name was Amy White; a spare, active, intelligent spinster, a little older than my sisters, and like any other friendly spinster, save for a horrid secret about her: she had a red hand. She always wore a glove, of course (this was Boston), and I never was permitted to see the offending member: but my sisters had once seen it, when they were children, and Amy, to prove that she could be naughty if she liked, had pulled off her glove and driven away all the little girls playing in Boylston Place by brandishing her crimson hand in their faces. Of course, it was not other people's blood that had stained it, but only her own; it was an enormous birthmark; but the suggestion

of gore remained, and a vague affinity to *The Scarlet Letter*. Poor
Amy White had no other distinction; and though she lived to
old age, we soon lost sight of her. Obscurity—we were obscure,
too—hid us from one another. If she had been rich this matter
of the red hand might have kept her an old maid, partly out of
pride on her part, partly out of a slight disinclination in shallow
wooers. There were many rich old maids in Boston; some of them
remained single precisely because they were rich, and had no
need of marriage to give them all the comforts and luxuries of a
home; and they were little hunted for their money. A poor young
man, vaguely amorous (for mad love was improbable), would
rather turn to a helpful poor young woman who would be attached to him, than to a luxurious rich one, with her fine friends
and family ethics, who would keep him in leash like a poodle.
Had Amy been rich, I say, she might have remained single with
a good grace. She could have become soft and gracious; she could
have been surrounded by books, friends and flowers; she could
have busied herself with charities or with some favorite learned
specialty, like Miss Grace Norton with Montaigne. The red hand
wouldn't have mattered then; the glove, properly varied and always clean, would even have seemed a mark of distinction, like
the ribbon of an order. Red-handed and poor, however, she
couldn't be an attractive figure or a happy woman. She was not
perceptibly soured; yet a chill wind of difficulty, of misfortune, of
solitude played about her, at least in the mind of other people.

James, eleventh and penultimate child of old Nathaniel, like
all his brothers, except silly Samuel, was a man of business and
though he belonged to the generation of the Great Merchants,
he was not one of them. If he went a-fishing for to catch a whale,
it was, like Simple Simon, in home waters; yet he was often
wrecked, having no judgment, and remained as sanguine as ever,
and unsinkable. He would have done better in a government
office, if any self-respecting Bostonian in those days had ever
thought of a government career. Not only the civil service was
taboo, but also the army and navy (except of course during the

Civil War and temporarily); and it is significant that none of the
Sturgises of that generation were professional men, lawyers, doctors, or clergymen. One of Russell's sons, John, of the American
branch, became an architect under the sign of Ruskin; it was he
who built the pseudo-Italian terracotta and brick Museum of
Fine Art in Copley Square, never completed, and soon afterwards pulled down. A grandson of Russell's, Clipston, later
adopted the same profession, as well as High Church Anglican
sentiments; and two of his younger brothers were at one time or
another masters at the Groton School: but all this was under
strong English influence and in another phase of New England
culture. Of Russell's English sons, one was occasionally a Glad-
stonian Member of Parliament, and the other two occasionally
wrote novels, but they all were unmistakably gentlemen of leisure.
The glamour of the Great Merchants was gone, in spite of their
father's glory: the glory of a sunset, perhaps, and to be admired
without being imitated. But in Boston, in the middle of the nineteenth century, no one who was ambitious, energetic, or even rich
thought of anything but making a fortune; the glamour was all
in that direction. The Adamses were not, and always said they
were not, Bostonians; and the orators, clergymen and historians
of the day, as well as the poets, though respected and admired,
never dominated the community: they were ornaments and perhaps dangers. The great affair, the aristocratic path to success and
power was business.

"Uncle James," whose head was full of projects, confidently
took that path, and though he sometimes slipped and "failed,"
he never failed finally. He would start afresh and begin to make
money; there was always some speculation that could help him to
do that, and renew in him the sense of prosperity. He was not
a mere Micawber; he really prospered at times. For safety, he had
a nice home-keeping unfashionable wife with a small fortune of
her own which evidently he was prevented from managing: and
whenever he was bankrupt, they moved to a smaller house in
some side street, and lived on the wife's income until business

looked up again, when the family would come out once more into the social sunshine.

I bore "Uncle James" a grudge. In the first place I didn't like him: and the world is rather sharply divided for me into the people I like and the people I don't like. Philosophy and charity counsel me to correct this caprice, and I don't theoretically build on it; but it persists in my inner feeling, and it is not wholly arbitrary. I dislike the people I dislike for some reason; they offend some natural ideal within me. For I do not either like or dislike people interestedly but absolutely disinterestedly, artistically, erotically: and thus their harmony or disharmony with my psychic impulse has its human importance. After all I am a man: what I like and dislike probably is, fundamentally, what any honest reflective person would like or dislike. "Uncle James" never offended me personally or did me any intentional harm; he would have been kind to me, like all the Sturgises, if there had been occasion; nevertheless I didn't like him. He had a full round beard, and I cannot like that. A long white, or gray, or even yellow beard, especially if clean, forked or blown into strands, is suitable for Michelangelo's Moses or Charon in his bark, or even for God the Father: but a round short full beard like Saint Peter's is vulgar. That keynote was taken up in "Uncle James" by his commonplace talk, his hurry, his bustling unperceptive manners. How inferior to "Uncle Samuel," who was so elegantly mad! But no wonder; James was some fifteen years younger, the world had grown commoner, and he had passed his life making and losing money. Only success, great success, can ennoble that; a success that debouches into something that is not money-getting. Moreover, "Uncle James" was cordial. That is the well-meant American substitute for being amiable; but it won't do. It is being amiable on principle and about nothing in particular; whereas true amiability presupposes discernment, tact, a sense for what other people really feel and want. To be cordial is like roughing a man's head to jolly him up, or kissing a child that doesn't ask to be kissed. You are relieved when it's over.

However, all this may be silly prejudice on my part. My real grievance touches something more positive. "Uncle James" was the only Sturgis of the first generation surviving in Boston during the 1870's and 1880's. It was to him that my mother inevitably turned for advice in money matters. In domestic economy she was firmness personified, never miscalculated her resources or left a debt unpaid (as I never did); but about investments and general business she knew absolutely nothing. "Uncle James," on the contrary, thought he knew everything. Just before the panic of 1873 he was sure of a boom: real estate, especially in the Back Bay and on the water-side of Beacon Street, was rising and rising in value. Now the house in which my mother lived, and which James himself, very likely, had chosen for her in 1858, when she first went to live in Boston, was in the depths of Boylston Place. That spot, genteelly retired in the '50's, had become unsuitable for two young girls about to enter society; several of the houses had become boarding houses, or something even worse. On the other hand business was flooding Boylston Street, just at the head of Boylston Place, and could not fail to run down that little slope and flood Boylston Place also. Let my mother move from Boylston Place but not sell her house, No. 17, because what with the business flowing down (in his imagination) from the busy street above, and the boarding houses requiring just such central but retired spots to flourish in, that property would prove a bonanza: the rent could be increased with every new lease. It would be perfectly safe, therefore, to put a slight mortgage on that house, and with the ready money so secured—say $10,000—buy cheap for $25,000 a very nice new little house on the water-side of Beacon Street, just the place socially for the girls, even if it was one of the last houses on the Mill Dam, surrounded by empty, half-flooded lots, and swept all winter by icy winds. Of course this $25,000 house couldn't be bought for only $10,000; it would be necessary to put a little mortgage, say $15,000, on this house also. But that was only a momentary affair; when the value of the house had risen, it could be sold, and the mortgage on both houses paid off, leaving enough to buy a new and better house elsewhere. The girls would both be happily married then and something different, perhaps in Longwood, would then suit my mother best for her old age.

Why didn't my mother consult some wiser friend before agreeing to this transaction? How could she, so prudent in her own affairs, not shudder at the thought of that double mortgage? Apparently she was simply deceived; or perhaps she, too, was allured by the idea of greater elegance, or (more likely) by the sense of the *necessity or duty* of living where she ought to live for her children's welfare. Why else should she have come to Boston or to America at all? And wouldn't it be unthinkable that she should have left Spain, where with her income she could live very well, in the style of the country, and where Susana already had had several suitors, in order to live in a disreputable back alley in Boston? I call it disreputable dramatically, as my mother would have called it if she had understood: but it was simply Bohemian. Vercelli's Italian restaurant was there in my time, and the Tavern Club, the only club I ever belonged to in Boston; and I frequented both, until they became stuffy and tiresome, and I preferred the Napoli in the North End, which was more genuinely Italian. However, "Uncle James" was right in thinking that it was now a place where "nobody lived"; and this was a reason for selling the Boylston Place house, though not for mortgaging it, and much less for buying another that absorbed half my mother's capital and was an ugly comfortless narrow mean slice of a house, built for speculation.

In the year 1872 there was a great fire in Boston. I well remember the night in which my brother Robert—who was then clerk in "Uncle James's" office and had the keys to it—was called up in the small hours by "Uncle James" himself; they must rush in a cab to get all the papers out of the safe: the fire was gaining ground in the business quarter, the post office was in flames, State Street threatened; just look out of the window and see the glare. Robert, who was then nineteen years old, awoke with difficulty, took some time to understand, but then got ready in the twinkling of an eye, because like all American youths he loved nothing better than "going to a fire." When he was gone, I too got out of bed and looked out of the window. I could see a suffused light in the night sky, but no real beautiful flames; and I went back to bed philosophically. How much "Uncle James" lost by the fire, I don't know. India Building in State Street, in which my mother had a share and which now, if the Boylston Street house were unlet, became the sole source of her income, luckily was not burned; but the ravage was impressive, and Robert took me to look at it, full of the contagious excitement and even pride felt by the Bostonians at having had such a big fire. People wouldn't speak of the Chicago fire any more; they would say the Boston fire. Unluckily for Chicago, Boston had had a more recent fire; and more unluckily in my opinion Boston had no Wren to rebuild the town. That was the era of an architectural medley of styles imitated from picture-books by professional speculators and amateur artists.

It never rains but it pours, and that same year 1872 was marked by one of those periodical crises that now are well known and expected, but that then seemed an inexplicable cataclysm, contrary to the certainty of perpetual progress and prosperity proper to the nineteenth century and to America. It was a financial deluge. Everybody suddenly felt poor: business unexpectedly shrank; Uncle Jameses failed in every family. Hard times came, especially (with those two mortgages and the deflation increasing their relative amount) to my mother and to us. The Beacon Street house could not be sold or let until nine years later, and the Boylston Place house, though usually well let, was even longer on our hands. It was not sold until Robert, having ceased to work in other people's offices, took to administering property, which he did admirably, getting us all out of our penury into gradually increasing comfort, as his son has continued to do by the wisdom of his investments. But the predicament at first was so serious for us that "Uncle James" (himself no doubt ruined)

evidently felt ashamed of having got my mother into such difficulties, and wrote to his brother Russell in London. Russell at
once responded to the appeal, and promised my mother an allowance of £100 a year, which he inserted in his will, so that she
enjoyed it until her death in 1912: a real benefit to us all and
particularly to me. This sum, my mother always regarded as her
own, not her first husband's or her children's; and later it came
to devolve upon me, as a regular allowance.

As none of the great generation were professional men or
government officials or political figures, so none were bachelors or
old maids—except merry Samuel, who I daresay would have married a dozen times had he been at liberty. This was patriarchal,
and characteristic of a prosperous, ambitious, enterprising race.
But now we come to a novel fact: "Uncle James" had two very
presentable sons, Charley and Frank, apparently in good health
and of good habits; yet they remained single until their deaths
at the age of sixty-four and sixty-nine. Why so? I can suggest
only one cause: poverty. Not pauperism of course: they were
always well-fed, well-dressed and well-lodged; and I suppose they
(with their sister) divided their mother's little fortune between
them in the end, and had just enough to live on in modest
bachelor apartments or some secondary club. But they were poor
for their class and for their friends. They couldn't establish a
household of the sort they would have liked. Yet that was
not all. They apparently had nothing to do. Whether perhaps
Frank, who certainly went to College, also studied law, I don't
know, but I never heard that he practised it and as to Charley,
his elder brother (who had a round beard like his father) he
never was known to do anything but potter about in the New
England back country and shoot birds. There was a distinct class
of these gentlemen tramps, young men no longer young, who
wouldn't settle down, who disliked polite society and the genteel
conventions, but hadn't enough intelligence or enough conceit to
think themselves transcendentalists or poets, in the style of Thor-
eau or of Walt Whitman. That is what they would have wished

to be, but they were too well-bred, too citified. Why didn't they go to live in Europe? Frank, especially, had a suggestion about him of being a possible artist or wit: why didn't he paint or write or do something? It was the failure of nerve, the sense of spent momentum, of being sons of Great Merchants, but without either need or opportunity for enterprise, and without money enough to be important men about town. Superfluous persons who felt themselves superfluous: dry branches of the green family tree.

Nothing withered, however, about their sister Susie, one of the five Susie Sturgises of that epoch, all handsome women, but none more agreeably handsome than this one, called Susie Mac-Burney and Susie Williams successively after her two husbands. When I knew her best she was a woman between fifty and sixty, stout, placid, intelligent, without an affectation or a prejudice, adding a grain of malice to the Sturgis affability, without meaning or doing the least unkindness. I felt that she had something of the Spanish feeling, So Catholic or so Moorish, that nothing in this world is of terrible importance. Everything happens, and we had better take it all as easily or as resignedly as possible. But this without a shadow of religion. Morally, therefore, she may not have been complete; but physically and socially she was completeness itself, and friendliness and understanding. She was not awed by Boston. Her first marriage was disapproved, her husband being an outsider and considered unreliable; but she weathered whatever domestic storms may have ensued, and didn't mind. Her second husband was like her father, a man with a checkered business career; but he too survived all storms, and seemed the healthier and happier for them. They appeared to be well enough off. In her motherliness there was something queenly, she moved well, she spoke well, and her freedom from prejudice never descended to vulgarity or loss of dignity. Her mother's modest solid nature had excluded in her the worst of her father's foibles, while the Sturgis warmth and amiability had been added to make her a charming woman.

CHAPTER V

MY SISTER SUSANA

I KNEW the Sturgis clan in two ways, first at home, since my half-brother and half-sisters were characteristic Sturgises in their different directions, and then as friends freely chosen for personal reasons, where our nominal relationship merely furnished an occasion for discovering some real affinity. Of my personal friends among the Sturgises I will speak as they turn up: for these were all social friendships with fixed periods and circumstances, not friendships of the spirit. But the Sturgis influence flooding me at home was primordial and I might almost say pre-natal. It imposed on me my Christian name, and it gave me my second mother or godmother, who, by virtue of her remarkable Sturgis warmth and initiative, was I think the greatest power, and certainly the strongest affection, in my life. This bond, added to the fact that she was my sister, makes any attempt to describe her embarrassing for me and perhaps unbecoming. Yet she must be described, else this narrative would miss its object. I intend my recollections to be fragmentary, but only by excluding things that are of no importance, or all-too-human and well-known to every one in his own person; not at all fragmentary in the sense of leaving out the bull's-eye from my target. Let me tell then the story of Susana's life and thereby allow her, as far as possible, to describe herself.

I have mentioned how, even in early childhood, when she had an older brother, she took the lead; and this became a matter of course when she was the eldest and also far more lively, wide-awake and competent than her brother and sister. In their lessons and in their games she ruled the roost. In Boylston Place, when she was from six to nine years of age, she was the Captain of all the children that played in the street; and if this practice seems not very genteel, we must remember that in Boston, local society was both select and democratic, given an acceptable quarter of the town; and that, as Boylston Place ran downhill, it afforded in winter an irresistible chance for "coasting," that is, for tobogganing with single or even with double or longer sleds. There were big boys in the neighborhood who naturally assumed the duty of steering; but Susana remained the arbiter of what should be done, and how. For a little Spanish girl, fresh from tropical Manila, to command in this winter sport shows her easy adaptability, her gift of inspiring confidence, and the willingness with which people spontaneously caught her enthusiasms.

Her enthusiasms sometimes were rather extraordinary. It was not only others that caught them from her, she herself caught them like a disease and was greatly their victim; because they were all far from expressing her whole nature, or even its fundamental needs. Her religion was the chief instance of this; but the trait appeared earlier. In the summer of 1863, when I had announced my intention to come into this world but had not yet made my appearance, the family lodged at La Granja, the small imitation of Versailles not far from the Escurial, where Queen Isabella and her Court spent the season; and the public were not excluded from the park where the Queen took her daily drive. Naturally when she passed, people took off their hats or curtsied, and sometimes a group might even raise a discreet cheer. Now for some inexplicable reason, Susana was captivated by this little ceremony: she would not for the world miss seeing the Queen drive by, and she would be the first to run forward, wave her handkerchief, and cry: ¡Viva la Reina! As this happened repeatedly, the Queen noticed it, and inquired: ¿Quien es esta niña, que se ha enamorado de mí? "Who is this child that has fallen in love with me?" Isabella was not unaccustomed to have people, not children, protest that they loved her; but one of Susana's Sturgis characteristics was that she showed her feelings in her face often without knowing it; and the élan of her movements and the light in her eye were

unmistakable evidences of her emotions. She *was* in love with the
Queen. How and why was a mystery. Isabella was a stout and not
beautiful woman with a bad complexion; but she was frank,
amiable, hearty, and easygoing (like the Sturgises) and there
was the glamour of her station, her coach, her guards, and her
gracious smiles. Then there was a family in Don Toribio's circle
who held some position at court: *Doña Primitiva*, widow of a
General Orà who had been executed for some *pronunciamiento* or
conspiracy, and her daughter *Milagros*, a young woman of bold
spirit who smoked cigars and was said to go about at night dressed
as a man, so as to see "life." These ladies naturally retailed much
Court gossip, which Susana may have listened to, and they,
being in favor with the Queen, would naturally tend to describe
her generous and regal qualities rather than those that might
have seemed too primitively human. At any rate, Susana's enthusiasm continued, until one day the Queen stopped her carriage,
beckoned to Susana, asked her her name, and after a few amiable
words, said good-bye with some vague reference to the future.

Nothing more occurred, I believe, at La Granja; but later in
Madrid it was arranged that Doña Primitiva should take Susana
to the Palace to be formally received by the Queen. It would
have been indispensable, in ordinary circumstances, that my
mother should have accompanied her daughter and been received
also; but my mother's state of health served as an excuse. For my
mother never under any circumstances would have gone to kiss
a Queen's hand, and such a Queen too, so little virtuous or stoical;
and the odd thing is that she should have allowed Susana to go.
But it was like my mother to let things take their course, provided
she was not personally involved in the proceedings. She hated
royalties as she hated priests, but it did not ruffle her, it rather
entertained her, that her friends and even her daughter should
be interested in such follies, and should have so much to tell
about them. After all, it was more vivid than a printed novel,
especially as Susana was a good mimic and would act out for us
at home all that she might have seen and heard abroad.

This policy of *laissez-faire* had unpleasant consequences in this case, as in many others; for some years later, when we had moved to Avila, a virtual invitation came through the Marqués de Novaliches for Susana to become a lady-in-waiting to the Infanta Isabel, who was of the same age; and my mother was so enraged that she refused to see Novaliches at all, pretended to be ill, and left it to my poor father to explain and to make excuses: that for the moment Susana's mother was ill, that she was about to start with her daughters for the United States, and that the project of Susana's figuring at Court was incompatible with the plans of the family and with their modest resources. Susana, I presume, knew nothing of this proposal until long afterwards; and I never heard her express any regret that it was not accepted. But my father, who had dutiful feelings towards Novaliches, was placed in an awkward position; and my mother herself was embittered and made uncomfortable. This incident, as well as the attentions of several young men courting Susana, no doubt hastened my mother's resolve to escape to Boston, and fostered a certain distrust and resentment that was latent in her towards Susana. Susana, she felt, was not loyal to her; she preferred other people and other principles. Unluckily, escaping to Boston did not correct this disloyalty. From the snares of dissolute courts and undesirable lovers Susana fell into those of the Jesuits and of religious enthusiasm.

She had always warmed towards religious doctrines and practices, as she had warmed towards anything interesting and vivid, such as children's games, social pleasures, or a reigning Queen in her brilliant equipage. She was abundantly alive, and all these were spontaneous ways of giving shape to life and of enjoying it intensely. This enjoyment, in her case as in mine, always had in it a touch of comedy. In regard to Queen Isabella this touch of satire became conscious in time or even dominant, and while Susana never lost her sympathy with that Queen and with all royalties, she saw and admitted their weaknesses and laughed at her own pleasure in those vanities. Thus she rendered her pleasure double, and rendered it pure. But in respect to religion she fought against all dramatic insight or transcendental laughter. She felt the laughter coming round the corner, and she attempted to run away from it, to condemn it in herself as a diabolical temptation. It was a sad business to have to be absolutely solemn, convinced, and fanatical, against her nature and to the ruin of her possible happiness.

From the age of fifteen to eighteen, when we lived in Avila, Susana had rather a limited field in which to display her adaptability, but she seems to have dominated it easily, and to have been happy in it. There was a small, modest, and grave provincial society, Avila being the quietest and most unspoiled of provincial capitals. *Tertulias* gathered together the local worthies and officials, and the town contained half a dozen presentable young men. There was a Casino, with a café on the ground floor, and upstairs a billiard room and a dancing hall, with a small stage. Here an inner circle, called *El Chenique,* sometimes performed amateur plays. These plays and occasional dances seem to have been the principal amusement for the young people. Susana took a leading part in them; yet I should hardly have become aware of it by her own report, because she seemed to have forgotten those early years, but our sister Josefina remembered them vividly, could recall all the people's names, and could recite the greater portion of the plays they acted, which were in verse. Josefina, who was two years younger than Susana, and most timid and dull, took little or no part in those gaieties; but she was always present at them, as she couldn't be left alone at home, and her silent mind, having nothing else to occupy it, retained every detail of her sister's doings and sayings. She and I in after years could thus reconstruct whole farces, *La Casa de Campo* and *Las Hijas de Elena* in which Susana, who had completely forgotten them, had played the heroine. Yet the impressions of those years, though overlaid, were not destroyed. When life in America had proved a failure for her, in society, at home, and in the convent where she had been a novice, Susana returned instinctively to Avila,

renewed old acquaintance with one or two quiet devout ladies of
the place, lived in my father's poor man's house, and eventually
married one of those presentable young men (now a widower
with six children) whom she had danced with at *El Chenique.*

America affected Susana exactly as it affected me. The people,
principally the admirably kind and civilized Bostonians who became our friends, excited our interest, attached our affection and
won our complete confidence. We laughed with them and not at
them, and we thought and judged as they did on current and
social matters; but beneath and in the end there was a chasm.
It was only with friends of the heart, chosen friends, friends who
at bottom had the same religion or philosophy with ourselves, that
this chasm could be bridged; and for Susana, in this direction, it
was requisite that her friends should be Catholics. Now, when
she found herself again in Boston at the age of eighteen, none
of the Sturgises or their friends were Catholics; but at first that
seemed not to matter, and she plunged heartily into that society,
as it was in her nature to do. Yet her view of the Sturgis family
and of Boston in general, as she unfolded it to us merrily at
home, though friendly and kindly, was frankly comic; and none
of her cousins, female or male, became intimate friends of hers
or admirers. It took time—this was Boston—for the admirers and
intimate friends to appear. There was a great obstacle to be surmounted: our comparative poverty. Susana couldn't dress or
travel as the rest did; she couldn't invite anybody to the house.
There were two sets of people, however, with whom this obstacle
didn't count: the very rich and self-satisfied, who might even be
attracted by an interesting young friend to help and protect; and
the semi-foreign Catholic families that were discovered to exist
even in polite Boston. To these two classes Susana's true and
lasting friendships were confined.

Of the highly placed, patronizing and somewhat older friends
the most important was Miss Sara Lowell. (It was essential to
leave out the *h* in Sarah or rather to transfer it to the first syllable
and to call the lady *Sahra.*) Her traditions and standards were of

the highest, and as the youngest and favorite child of a rich father, alone with him at home, she was mistress of establishments both in town and country. With Susana she could discuss all her other friends freely, as to a fresh, uninformed, and sympathetic audience. The two would sleep in the same bed, so as to have perfect privacy and endless time for confabulation. And somehow the religious question, that must have arisen in passing conscientious and ultimate judgments on everything and everybody, seems never to have disturbed this unclouded intimacy. Miss Lowell was of course a Unitarian, and an ornament of King's Chapel; but she was a woman of the world; and I suspect that she smiled to herself a little about the proprieties, thought them expedient but not indispensable or eternal; and a few amiable pagan myths repeated, or devotions practised, by a younger and less well-educated companion far from displeasing her may have seemed to her engaging. They indicated the need of something beyond reason; a need that all reasonable people must end by feeling. Miss Lowell in the end felt their need in her own life; and when everybody had understood that she meant to remain single, being perfectly happy in her virgin state and finding nobody worthy of her hand, she suddenly announced her engagement to a widower as rich as herself. This widower had two sons, no longer little children; and the story reached me (the reader may imagine through what channel) that one day one of the boys by chance caught sight of his stepmother before the long glass in her dressing-room, and exclaimed—those being the days of exuberant bosoms and bustles—"But mama, you are all ups and downs!" And when the lady, who was short and plump, said he was unkind, he protested: "I am not unkind. I like it." From this domestic scene I gather that the accomplished Sara, being a sensible woman, valued the ups and downs in her person, as well as the ups, and never downs, in her fortune.

The foreign Catholic families that became Susana's closest friends in Boston were two in number, the Homers and the Iasigis. The language in both families was French, although English inevitably tended to intrude more and more into their conversation, as it did in our own house, until in the end, for instance, I always spoke English with my brother Robert, and sometimes with Susana, although never with my mother or with my sister Josefina. This was particularly true of the Homers, because the head of that family was a pure American, so that at table—apart from whisperings among the ladies—the official language was English. Susana and I often had luncheon or early dinner at the Homers on Sundays, and as a boy I knew that household very well. There were four daughters, the eldest a little younger than Susana, and the youngest a little younger than I, but no boys; and as Mr. Homer always disappeared when we rose from table, the atmosphere of the house was thoroughly feminine, Catholic, and foreign.

In *The Last Puritan,* the Boscovitz family is drawn in part after the Homers. Mrs. Homer was a native of Gibraltar where her father and later her brother held the practically hereditary post of American Consul; but her mother came from Marseilles and she herself had been educated in a French convent. She had been married off to "Homer" as she always called him in the French fashion, because he was well off, and had been carried away to Boston helplessly, where she lived like a lap-dog in a cushioned basket, with her brood of daughters, her little belongings, and her devotions to occupy her mind. She was a great comfort to Susana, a link with the genuine, human, Mediterranean non-hypocritical world; and Susana in turn must have been an enlivening influence in that too domestic circle.

In blood the Iasigis were far more exotic than the Homers, since the father was a Turk and the mother nominally a Greek, but in language, religion, aspect, and breeding entirely French. Her mother at least must have been a Frenchwoman somehow married in Smyrna, from which the family came. I was not at home among them. The ladies for the most part became pious old maids or pious mothers; only one came later within my range. She had married a young Bostonian who had dipped into Bohemian life in France and Germany, learned to speak those languages with a deceptive fluency, and studied a little music. He could well return to Boston as an art critic, and as a friend (since he was not rich enough to be a patron) of all artists, musicians, and actors. He and his good-natured agreeable wife held open house on Sunday evenings (when theatres and concert halls were closed); there was beer with pretzels, and all artistic or European-ized Boston from Mrs. Gardner down, frequented those easy re-ceptions. I remember speaking there with the prima donnas Sembrich and Emma Eames and with Madame Paderewska. I asked the latter about the fidelity of the men in Poland to the Church; and she said that they all *had* to remain good Catholics, because a soul lost to the Church meant a soul lost to Poland. This Eastern way of identifying religion with nationality gave me a useful hint for the interpretation of both.

These things befell after Susana's time in Boston. For her the Iasigis and the Homers were friendly households, nests of mar-riageable girls, where she could break away from the restraints of polite hypocrisy and could take comfort in feeling that her religion was no anomaly but perfectly natural, traditional, and a matter of course. It was the Bostonians who were eccentric and self-banished from the great human caravan. I found the same comfort in ancient literature and philosophy, which carried me beyond the Church and beneath its foundations. It is all a *Santa Maria sopra Minerva*. But towards Boston and Protestantism Su-sana and I had exactly the same feelings.

I recognize now that the ripest and most settled circles in Boston were difficult for us to move in because of our poverty and lack of early friendships in that society. It was a little like the aristocracy in England, shy and secluded from strangers, but immensely simple and gentle when once you were inside. It was very difficult, for instance, for Susana to go to "parties." She had hardly any suitable clothes; she had to incur each time a relatively large expense in hired carriages, gloves and hairdresser; and she was not as accomplished or as well informed about Boston history and people as were the leading families. Then, as she grew older, she had none of those political or artistic enthusiasms that might bring the older young ladies together. And as to the men—and one went to "parties" to be seen by the men—I suspect that Susana found them dull. She was accustomed to be made love to, and they didn't make love; not unless they deliberately intended to propose marriage. But very few, hardly any of them, intended to do that for the present. Society thus became a skirmish at very long range in a very wide field, with little danger of wounds, and no danger at all of death. Was it worth while?

I am not sure that in all those years in Beacon Street, when she was between twenty and thirty, she received a single express offer of marriage. She had admirers; but none of them such as she could seriously encourage. The best of them, a young architect terribly marked by the smallpox, was poor; and though matters went far enough for her to read Ruskin's *Stones of Venice* (which I profited by, and built my love of architecture upon) poverty on both sides made further progress impossible: and there would have been another difficulty to overcome, namely, the difference in religion. Religion was gaining on her with the fading of youth. Without having had, I believe, any serious disappointment in love—for she did not love men, she loved only their attentions—spinsterhood was certainly leaving her heart unemployed, and even her women friends were growing less communicative, less intimate, more preoccupied with their other affairs.

There was only religion to fill the void; and this had a disastrous effect in our household. Josefina had always followed Susana, up to a certain point, in this as in other things, but mechanically and without a spark of emotion. There was no danger in that quarter. But I was a boy, becoming adolescent, and I naturally inclined to live in the imagination. That I should catch Susana's interest in architecture, and spend my afternoons drawing plans of palaces and fronts of cathedrals, was all to the good; it occupied my young mind harmlessly; but that I should love images and church functions and the mysteries of theology was dangerous and morbid: and who was to blame for it but Susana? A conflict against Susana and against Catholicism thereupon filled our household, divided it, and ended by a separation of all parties, morally and even materially, and the separate entrenchment of each combatant in his own camp.

That Susana, being my godmother, deliberately took me in hand from the first day of my arrival in Boston, and in teaching me English and Mother Goose taught me also my prayers in English and my advanced catechism—for I already knew the elements of Christian Doctrine and Sacred History—is certain; but I think there was a complete blindness on my mother's part in supposing that any deep or permanent attachment to religious faith in my case, could be achieved by Susana: and that for the reason that Susana was herself without it. I understood what she taught me very much better than she did, and I had a much greater affinity than she to a religious life. She tried it and couldn't bear it; I could have borne it gladly if I had wished to try it.

There was another difference. She thought religion a matter of fact, like the geography of the Fiji Islands and the ways of the natives there; and as those were reported to be so grand and so captivating she was anxious to be convinced that the reports were true and that she might ultimately go and live in those Islands. Now I was aware, at first instinctively and soon quite clearly on historical and psychological grounds, that religion and all philosophy of that kind was *invented*. It was all conceived and worked out inwardly, imaginatively, for moral reasons; I could have invented or helped to invent it myself, if I had gone in for it; and I could have accepted it and enlarged it by my own insights if like all original religious souls I had fancied myself inspired. Such invention need not be dishonest, if it is taken for a revelation. But you can't go for the proof or confirmation of it to the Fiji Islands, or to any other part of the existing universe; you must place it, and live by it, on quite another plane. In a word, I was a spontaneous modernist in theology and philosophy: but not being pledged, either socially or superstitiously, to any sect or tradition, I was spared the torments of those poor Catholic priests or those limping Anglicans who think they can be at once modernists and believers. They can be only amateurs, at best connoisseurs, in religion. The rest for them will only be a belated masquerade.

Thus I, who was the nominal prize at stake, came out of this family quarrel without feeling a blow, and my mother, if a little hardened and embittered, was not much changed by it. But for Susana it was tragic; though perhaps not worse, perhaps more satisfactory on the whole, than it would have been to vegetate and wither, an impecunious old maid in self-satisfied Boston.

The crisis came on slowly, and was never sharply terminated. It did not leave a scar but an ailment; and it kept passing, to the end of Susana's long life, through various phases.

In 1876 "Uncle Robert," head of the Philadelphia Sturgises died; and the widow invited Susana to spend a few weeks with her, to cheer her up and keep her company. This was a somewhat unexpected proof of liking from a quarter that had never seemed sympathetic. While "Uncle Robert" showed a traditional good-will towards us (including me, for he gave me my first nice book, a well-illustrated copy of Robinson Crusoe), "Aunt Susie," his wife, seemed too much preoccupied with her clothes, her babies, and her gaieties to take more than a perfunctory notice of her husband's poor relations. But Susana had the gift of inspiring confidence; she was a Sturgis; she was young, available, and a person in need of being befriended. This visit to Philadelphia resulted in a lasting affection on Susana's part not so much towards her Aunt as to the youngest of the children, Maisie, with whom for years afterwards, from Spain, she carried on a desultory correspondence. And the visit had another consequence that helped, as it were, to color a little more pleasantly the sunset of Susana's day in Boston. "Aunt Susie" sent her two trunks full of her almost new dresses, rather gay dresses, useless for a widow in mourning; and these dresses, in lingering adaptations and transformations, helped to furnish Susana's wardrobe for several years. I remember them well to this day. The best was the salmon-colored dress, as we called it, although at night it seemed only a brilliant yellow; it was elaborate with a looped overskirt, yellow satin bow-knots and scalloped edges, and a wealth all over it of little lace flounces. There were other gowns, less ornate and good for daily use, that outlasted the fashions; and there were some that never were worn at all, because Susana's interest in society had begun to flag, and she had at best but little pleasure in dress. She wished to look well of course; but the how and why of it escaped her. Neither she nor Josefina were good at needlework. Had they resisted their mother's lessons and example, or had nothing been done to initiate them into these arts? I think both causes cooperated; and it was a pity in many ways.

The first five years that we lived in Roxbury, which included my undergraduate days at Harvard, were the darkest in Susana's life. She was between thirty and thirty-five years of age; her Boston sewing-circle, her Boston parties, were things of the past; there was sullen disunion and hostility at home; and there were no new interests. She read and re-read the works of Santa Teresa; she conceived plans of offering up her life in sacrifice for the salvation (which seemed unlikely) of the rest of the family: and she considered whether she might not have a vocation to tread in Santa Teresa's footsteps. Her confessor was Father Fulton, head of the Jesuit College attached to the Church of the Immaculate Conception, where we usually went to high mass on Sundays— Susana and I only, because Josefina, thoroughly frightened by our mother's intense hostility to the Church, had given up going. Father Fulton, who belonged, I believe, to a Maryland Catholic family, had a rather philosophical mind; a little sleepy, like his half-closed eyes, perhaps quite healthy, as his sallow complexion and heavy cheeks were not quite healthy. He admired the metaphysics of Coleridge, and perhaps understood it better than he did the feminine heart. There is a curious cruelty mixed sometimes with American shrewdness and humor. The sharp mind finds things queer, crooked, perverse; it puns about them; and it doesn't see why they shouldn't be expected and commanded to be quite other than they are; but all this without much hope of mending them, and a sardonic grin. My old teacher Royce had something of this perverse idealism, and I suspect there was something of it in Father Fulton. Didn't he see that Susana's imaginary vocation was false? He probably saw no reason why, *a priori,* it should not have been true; and he didn't positively dissuade her from testing it. When the test was applied, he advised her not to persist; but this experiment had involved untold conflicts, doubts, vacillations, and disappointments, which might have been avoided by a little more wisdom.

I remember one day, coming home with Susana from church, I said I thought I was better fitted than she for the cloister; and she replied: "You have *one* of the things required. You are *detached.*" This was her way of expressing the fact that she lacked this necessary element. She lacked it so completely that she was most unhappy in going to the Convent of her own free will, and quite happy (according to my mother) in coming out of it (against her will, according to her own account), by the advice or injunctions of her superiors. I accompanied her to Baltimore; there was no simplicity, no ease, in her way of entering the convent or of being received there. She was too old, thirty-four, and too full of old memories and attachments to be happy in a round of mystical devotions; she was tired, and became sleepless. She insisted in her letters, and in her talk to the end of her life, that she loved our mother very much. These protestations seemed to me very strange; she *couldn't* love our mother very much: only enough to suffer, as I did not, from her hostility. Perhaps this morbid love (for there was something cowed or cowardly about it) was hypnotic and allied to forgotten experiences; perhaps it was only a verbal cloak for Susana's love of people in general, and her craving to be loved. In any case, it was a symptom of her radical unfitness for an ascetic regimen.

She had been for three months in the convent as what they called a Postulant, dressed in her own clothes but following the routine of the community, and had grown much attached to the

Mother Superior and to the Mistress of the Novices, when she became a Novice herself, having her hair cut, and wearing the nun's habit with a white veil in lieu of the black one. Talking with my cousin Elvira and me some years later in Avila, she said that this attachment, especially to the Mistress of Novices (who acted, I suppose, as a sort of female confessor or spiritual director), was the strongest she had ever felt in her life; and this assertion, making due allowances for dramatic exaggeration, seems to me interesting. It shows that she had never been much in love with any of her admirers, nor with her future husband, who was then courting her once more; and that her love for our mother had never been spontaneous, but a sort of unwilling and resentful love, a sense of subjection to an irrational influence. I saw a letter or two written afterwards by this nun to Susana; they were commonplace, pious, motherly letters; but motherly affection was new to Susana, and especially a motherly affection extending to spiritual troubles and needs, and bringing spiritual consolation. If when a girl she could fall in love at sight with a commonplace Queen, for being motherly and amiable, it is intelligible that as an unhappy woman she should have fallen in love with a gentle nun, for being wise and motherly. It is a wonderful thing to come upon intelligence and a guiding hand in the realm of spirit.

In spite of these affectionate ties and precisely because of this intelligent guidance, before six months of novitiate were over it was agreed that Susana should leave the convent. Then our mother did a very kind thing such as her usual manner would not have led us to expect: she with Josefina left Robert alone in the house with one servant (I was at College) and went to spend the winter in a boarding house at Baltimore, so that Susana should not have to return home directly, and might have the relief of a wholly new scene and new faces.

When they came back to Boston I was on the point of leaving for Avila and for an indefinite student life in Germany. I could not observe Susana's conduct or moods; but I believe she lived almost in seclusion, saw none of her old friends, and during the next winter decided to return to Spain, at least for some years, where she could live with Doña Victorina and with my father, alternately. This was practicable, because when Robert reached his majority, the trust that my mother had established on the occasion of her second marriage terminated, and her Sturgis children came into their money. It was a most modest sum, at that time only a few hundred dollars a year; but this was enough to get on with in Spain, living with old friends, and contributing a little to the household expenses.

I went to meet her in September, 1887, at Gibraltar, and returned with her to Avila; and in the winter she joined Doña Victorina and Mercedes in Madrid. But she still had, as it were, one foot in the stirrup. Could she live on in this way, as paying guest at other people's houses, forever? Would she return to dreary Roxbury? Could she persuade our mother to move back to Spain and reunite the family? Only one circumstance was favorable. Robert had taken charge of the family property and was doing very well in his investments. Without venturing on what is called speculation, he bought and sold safe investments with excellent judgment. The Beacon Street house had long been sold. The houses in Boylston Place and India Building were sold at good prices, and the family income increased steadily, until it became ten times what it had been in the beginning. Had Susana foreseen this development, which would have enabled her to set up a comfortable establishment of her own in Spain, she might have been content to do so. She had friends enough, and would have made many more; and the current affairs of the world, political and social, would have kept her mind occupied and her wits sharp.

But how could this favorable turn of fortune be foreseen? She was simply a little better off, but still had only a slender income; and she was alone. Unfortunately, not being a Sturgis, I had no share in the family trust, and had to earn my living; otherwise Susana and I at that time, about 1890, could have joined forces and lived very happily together, by preference in Avila. There are nice old houses there, one of which we could have restored and turned into a dignified and peaceful residence: and both summer and winter there, in one's own house with a few modern conveniences, are pleasant and healthy.

But the gods otherwise decreed: and Susana decided to marry her old admirer, Celedonio Sastre, in spite of his crusty old provincial habits and his six children. Her married life forms another chapter, which I need not write separately. Glimpses enough of it will come in the course of my own visits: for Avila never ceased to be a place of frequent pilgrimage for me so long as Susana was alive.

Old age—she lived to be seventy-seven, as Josefina did also—changed her character very little: perhaps time did not change her at all, but only brought out more clearly—worldly respect and timidity being gone—her frank and sensible humanity. This had been veiled by untoward circumstances, and sophisticated intellectually. Poverty and religion had long constrained and misled her. I do not mean for a moment that it was incongruous for her to be a believing Catholic. It was not only congruous with her temperament, but essential to her breeding and background and to the place she filled in the world. Why else should her good American relations have turned to her and hugged her in their troubles? Catholicism is the most human of religions, if taken humanly: it is paganism spiritually transformed and made metaphysical. It corresponds most adequately to the various exigencies of moral life, with just the needed dose of wisdom, sublimity, and illusion. Only it should be accepted humanly, traditionally, as part of an unquestioned order, a moral heritage, like one's language and family life, leaving religious controversy to the synods and metaphysical speculation to the schools. The synods and the schools make enormous assumptions, and perhaps reason on them correctly: that is a question of art and technique with which the layman had better not meddle. But as to the need or importance of those assumptions each man and each society decides afresh, and instinctively; because the controversies that agitate the public are inevitably superficial, making contrary and hasty assumptions of their own, without knowing it.

Susana's misfortune was that her instinctive and ardent sympathy with Catholic and Spanish conventions was crossed by controversy and strained speculatively, when she had no capacity for speculation; so that instead of finding peace and a secret symbolic life in religion, she turned religion into a problem and a torment. She became fanatical against her natural good sense, and worried about the salvation of her friends and relations as if that were not in God's hands, and as if the salvation of souls were a physical event, like the saving or drowning of passengers in a shipwreck. That was exactly how the early Christians conceived it, so that her zeal was strictly orthodox; but this only shows how orthodoxy must be taken with a grain of salt, to keep it beneficent and prevent it from turning into madness. The pity was that both in religion and in family life circumstances should have suppressed and embittered the native warmth of her nature, her need of being impassioned. She needed to be carried away, to be ravished; and since the days of being ravished by irresistible bold men were gone, she dreamt of being ravished, like Santa Teresa, by sacrifice and prayer. But Susana was not made either for prayer or for sacrifice, but decidedly like the other Sturgises, for that natural joyous enthusiasm and kindness which are their own reward. Before sacrifice and prayer can be self-rewarding a revolution has to be worked in the soul; and though Susana knew of this, she never experienced it in her own person. It would have required her to key her nature up to a note that it was incapable of sustaining.

I have said nothing of Susana's appearance and physique, yet what is more important in life than our bodies or in the world than what we look like? And not only for a woman. The crusty old Hobbes observes that good looks are a power even in a man, since they predispose women and strangers in his favor. But women and strangers are not all fools; and there is something unprejudiced and disinterested in a first impression that runs deeper than any labored or conventional judgment. Body, character and mind are formed together by that single hereditary organizing power which the ancients called the psyche or soul; so that however much the mind or the body may be distorted by accidental influences, at bottom they must always correspond; and the innocent eye often catches this profound identity. We are arrested by a beautiful body because the sight of it quickens in ourselves the same vital principle that fashioned that body. And so too any deformity or distortion offends us in beings akin to ourselves, and ways of life contrary to ours seem to us monstrous even to look upon, like the wallowing hippopotamus opening a vast mouth half as large as himself. Chaos is fertile in monsters destroyed as soon as they appear; but definite species establish and perpetuate themselves unchanged where the seasons revolve steadily and the very enemies of life are so constant that means of defense may be prepared against them. In the human family it is an open question how far inbreeding will perfect or debilitate a type, and how far half-breeds may form new and healthy races.

I like to muse on this theory apropos of my brother and sisters and of the American melting-pot in general. My mother's first marriage seems not to have been eugenically a perfect match. Of five children two died in infancy and of the other three only Susana could be compared to her ancestors in vital fiber; and yet even in her an odd constitutional disharmony was visible to the eye. She had elements of pure beauty, but neither her face nor her figure was well composed. Most arresting were her large clear eyes, between hazel and green, and *à fleur de tête,* with delicately pencilled almost invisible eyebrows much higher up; and this effect of aristocratic innocence was reinforced by the high smooth forehead; so that when she was a young girl she could have posed in a *tableau vivant* for *La Belle Jardinière.* Yet those beautiful eyes were rather too close together, and that calm forehead was too narrow; the oval of the face, in time, became decidedly pear-shaped; and if the little mouth went perfectly with the eyes, the nose that intervened was too long and pointed, and too flat under the forehead. Altogether this countenance, when animated, arrested and held people's attention. In a Victorian epoch when ladies were not made up, it was conspicuous for a youthful white and ruddy complexion and a great liveliness, because those Madonna-like eyes surprised you by their subtle changes in expression, their involuntary unaffected confession of eagerness, intelligence, or fun. In conversation everything was fused into a vivid personality, but in repose you couldn't help wishing that so many good points had been combined differently.

It was especially in her figure that the disharmony was obvious. Above the waist Susana was slender, as if designed by the same hand as her eyebrows; but if the upper half of her figure imitated Raphael the lower half most successfully imitated Rubens. She had very small hands and feet, quite Spanish, with short fingers proper for a dumpy woman; yet she was tall, American in her movements, and entirely without our mother's deftness and grace. She and her sister would never dance: they were conscious of doing it so badly that they refused to do it. As Susana grew older her weight became too great for her small feet, walking tired her and soon grew painful. For a time after her marriage she had a small Victoria in which she could drive, but in the end she ceased to go out, even to church, and set up a chapel at home, where a Dominican from the great monastery of Santo Tomás, in the valley beneath her windows, might come to say Mass on Sundays and feast days, and give her Communion.

The imperfections I could not help seeing in Susana and the points—very few—on which we did not sympathize, were a source of unhappiness to me, for she occupied a niche in my pantheon where I could never place any other creature. I remember how seriously my father upset me one day, after Susana had returned to Spain and had lived with him for a season, when he said: "Ah, Susanita, whom we thought the world of, so exceptional, so sprightly, so perfect, now she has become a woman like any other woman." There was truth, I couldn't deny it, in this judgment, but there was no charity. Susana was still herself; we are always ourselves at bottom, however disfigured by the incrustations of life. She had been defeated by unhappy circumstances, forced out of her native element, denied the breathing space necessary to her nature; and charity will always judge a soul, not by what it has succeeded in fashioning externally, not by the body or the words or the works that are the wreckage of its voyage, but by the elements of light and love that this soul infused into that inevitable tragedy.

CHAPTER VI

AVILA *

AVILA became by chance the headquarters of my family in Spain; we had no hereditary bond with that ancient and noble town. The first of us to go there was my uncle Santiago, sent no doubt by his official superiors, as a sort of punishment, to the worst of government posts. I fear he was rather a merry and lazy fellow, given to drink, and not useful in the office; yet his chiefs had the virtues as well as the vices of nepotism; and if advancement went automatically to their relations and to persons recommended by the big-wigs, still room was made for the ne'er-do-wells also in the smallest and dullest of provincial capitals. My father lighted on Avila because his brother was there; and the place recommended itself on acquaintance for being in the Old Castile of his youth, healthy, tranquil, and cheap. My mother too was willing to go and live there when, in 1866, she agreed to postpone her return to America. At least the town was accessible, being on the main line between Madrid and Paris, habitable in summer as well as in winter, and safely remote from the Court, from fashion, and from corrupt society. After three years she was finally able to escape with her daughters; yet unsuspected associations remained in their young minds with unsuspected virtues in that place, so that both eventually returned to live and die there; and there they both are buried.

As for me, I was scarcely three years old when we moved to Avila and I was nearly seventy when it ceased to be the center of my deepest legal and affectionate ties. That these ties, albeit

---

* Pronounced *Ah'vilah*, from the Latin *Abŭla*, from which the official Spanish adjective, *abulense*.

the deepest, should have left me so remarkably free was a happy circumstance for my philosophy. It taught me to possess without being possessed, yet it gave me a most firm and distinctive station. For the freest spirit must have some birthplace, some *locus standi* from which to view the world and some innate passion by which to judge it. Spirit must always be the spirit of some body. Now the chance that made me an exiled Spaniard and linked me in particular to Avila (rather let us say than to Reus) was singularly fortunate. The austere inspiration of these mountains, these battlemented city walls and these dark churches could not have been more chivalrous or grander; yet the place was too old, shrunken, barren and high-and-dry to impose its limitations on a travelling mind: it was a mountain top and not a prison. Standing there, the spirit was situated, challenged, instructed; it was not controlled.

The same thing, by another happy chance, might be said of my other principal point of attachment, namely Boston and Harvard College. The extreme contrast between the two centers and the two influences became itself a blessing: it rendered flagrant the limitations and the contingency of both. Granted that I was to awake in Spain in the nineteenth century, I could have found myself in no place less degraded than Avila; and granted that I was to be educated in America and to earn my bread there, I could have fallen on no place friendlier than Harvard. In each of these places there was a maximum of air, of space, of suggestion; in each there was a minimum of deceptiveness and of the power to enslave. The dignity of Avila was too obsolete, too inopportune, to do more than stimulate an imagination already awakened, and lend reality to history; while at Harvard a wealth of books and much generous intellectual sincerity went with such spiritual penury and moral confusion as to offer nothing but a lottery ticket or a chance at the grab-bag to the orphan mind. You had to bring a firm soul to this World's Fair; you had to escape from this merry-go-round, if you would make sense of anything or come to know your own mind.

In quality Avila is essentially an *oppidum,* a walled city, a cathedral town, all grandeur and granite; yet it is so small as to seem in the country. Step out of one of the lofty gates and you are at once amid wheat fields or on rocky and windy moors. At this altitude primitive bald nature has coexisted for ages with the tightest and most fortified civilization, ecclesiastical and military. Here no one need hanker after *rus in urbe*; he has the opposite, which is almost an equivalent. He has what we might call *urbs ruri,* or rather *oppidum in agris. Urbs ruri* would be a good name for some great English country house with its park, and its subject farms and villages; for in the mansion there would be all the social amenities and sophistication of London, and yet looking about the eye would see nothing but emerald lawns and blue horizons, while at the gates the thinly peopled country would lie open to all lordly sports, from hunting and shooting down to driving, walking and golf. Avila, on the contrary, is an instance of *oppidum in agris*; not a private seat to which the great retire for pleasure and quietness, but a defensible eminence, perhaps with an ancient place of pilgrimage in it, where the country people have collected and walled in their granaries, leaving an open space in the midst for their meetings and fairs. Here in time the surrounding landlords will build themselves town houses, and perhaps come habitually to live, without surrendering their farms or neglecting their farming interests. They will form the ruling class, the *patres conscripti,* of the little republic, the typical ancient town, with its local religion and its gradually developing political eloquence.

Very likely the original pre-Roman *Abula* was a town of this kind; but that native simplicity has not survived the passage of migrations and conquests armed with alien imperial force, or with the force of immensely contagious militant religions. After the Romans and the Visigoths, the Moors swept over this region, but have left no such traces of their arts as may be seen at the not very distant Toledo. The great walls, the glorious crown of Avila, might have looked much as they do now in the Moorish epoch, for they are such as prevailed during the whole Byzantine millennium, from the fourth to the fourteenth century; but in their present form they belong to Christian times. There is a sweep and unity in their plan that indicate royal government and national resources; this had become a stronghold of kings against rival kings. and with this two new features, foreign to the ancient city, impressed themselves on Avila, and still, in their decay, lend it its dominant character: the seats of the nobility and those of the clergy. In my day several great families still had houses in Avila, to which some of them sometimes returned. Oñate, Superunda, Santa Marta, Parcent; but aristocratic families from different provinces and kingdoms had long intermarried, so that each great title might go with estates scattered all over Spain; and estates in the province of Avila, or palaces in the town, were not likely to be those of most importance to the family or favorite places for them of residence. Many great houses were therefore neglected, or turned into public offices or private apartments. Better preserved even if somewhat shrunken and depopulated were the convents and churches. The former Jesuit College, built into the walls and replacing the upper part of them over the *Rastro*, had become the Bishop's Palace; and many monasteries and convents, rather hidden behind blank walls, occupied large mysterious spaces in the town or choice positions in the suburbs. Avila was a distinctly clerical town, with Santa Teresa for its native patron and chief glory.

Yet the fundamental realities are still in evidence. The town walls, for all their massiveness, do not shut out the country from the eye. At every turn, through one of the city gates, or over some bastion, the broad valley remains visible with its checker-board of ploughed fields and straggling poplars lining the straight roads, or clustered along the shallow pools by the river; and at night, in the not too distant mountains, the shepherds' fires twinkle like nether stars. Or if the townspeople are too busy and nearsighted to remember the country, the country every Friday morning invades the town, and fills the market place with rustics and rustic wares.

At dawn they ride in from their villages in groups, on their trembling little donkeys, the man or woman perched on the hind quarters, behind the four-pocketed wicker saddlebags brimming with scarlet tomatoes, bright green and red peppers, lettuce and yellow chick-peas or clod-colored potatoes. In my time the peasant costumes, though tending to disappear, were still prevalent: the men in broad black hats, short jackets, bright sashes and leather greaves, attached like armor over their knee-breeches and blue stockings; and the women bell-like in their wealth of brilliant flannel petticoats, worn one over another, and the topmost on occasion pulled up to serve as a shawl, and protect the many-colored kerchiefs covering their heads and shoulders. Nor was garden produce all that these self-sufficing peasants brought to market: there were also home-made garments in plenty, such as *alpargatas*, or canvas shoes with rope soles, and country crockery, *botijos* and *cantaros*, shining in their newness, and no less smooth and rotund than the gorgeous melons and watermelons of midsummer.

No danger that such a town should think itself self-supporting like a capitalist, or existing by divine right to rule and instruct the world. The country has created the city, built it up at the crossroads between one threshing-ground and another, where the bridge crossed the river, and the riding paths met, leading beyond the valley to the neighboring market towns. From the country each city still draws its wealth and sustenance, as well as the fresh hands required for its multiplying trades, the servants for its great houses, and the young soldiers to be enlisted, by force or by bribes, in its feuds and conquests.

Markets and fairs were dwarfed at Avila, however, by the religious feasts, doubtless much decayed in my day, yet still imposing. I remember the procession of Corpus Christi, wonderful in my childish eyes. And this not at all on account of the *gigantones*, grotesque cardboard and cambric giants that formed the comic part of the show. These were monstrous primitive caricatures such as the raw mind loves, originally no doubt often obscene, and were still allowed to precede or to follow the religious pageant, like an

Aristophanic farce after three tragedies. No: farce and even ob-
scenity fall flat in early childhood; it is lovely marvels that entrance. Yet it was hardly the theological mystery that impressed
me, the Eucharist as a means of grace: that too requires experience
to comprehend it, and a second mind. The lóvely mystery glittered
on its own spectacular plane, the wonder was intrinsic to it, like
that of the stars. To have explained would have cheapened it.
At the age of six or seven I could feel the happy excitement of
this feast, without words to express it or ideas to justify it; but
had words and ideas been at my command they would have been
like those that come to the French writer Alain on such an occasion. The occasion creates emotion, and the emotion creates intuitions to focus it and to lend it form. Was not this the festival
of the summer solstice? Did not the summer sun and the June
roses fill it with light and fragrance? Was not everybody happy
and gaily dressed? Did not tapestries and damasks hang from the
balconies, or where they were lacking, at least some gay coverlet or
shawl or tablecloth? Did not gold thread and tinsel shine everywhere from vestments and banners? Were not the sun's rays
doubly reflected from the golden monstrance that seemed to
imitate them? And as the Host approached, borne high in a silver
shrine amid lights and flowers, did not doves let loose from some
window soar and circle in the upper air, while handfuls of rose-
leaves fluttered down like snowflakes on the procession? And the
Host itself, the mystic center of all this joy, what was it but the bread
of life, white wheaten bread sublimated into the pure principle of
eternal happiness? For although hidden from the eye, the red wine
that can turn to blood was not absent from the heart, and every
holiday influence seemed fused together in this sacrament of
union.

All this might be conceived to be the latent burden of my
childish wonder, if the eventual poet who gave form to it had no
further experience and no contrary inspiration: it is all that Alain
cares to note, whose philosophy is rich in casual intuitions, but
without foundations or results. What a pagan satirist might recog-

nize in this pageant might be only the echo of some cult of the
sun and the harvest, of golden Apollo and golden Ceres, with some
reminiscences of Bacchus. We might even go a step further and
see here only a prelude to the *Pervigilium Veneris* with its unfor-
gettable refrain: *Cras amet qui nunquam amavit, quique amavit
cras amet.* But that would be to take a false turn in the reading of
history, a turn that, at the crossroads, history did not take. To
reach Corpus Christi moral evolution had to move in the opposite
direction. These little boys and little girls dressed in white, fresh
from their first communion, are not simply preparing to make love,
and tomorrow to sing *Little Roger Coming Home from the Fair.*
Very likely some of them will do so, but it will not be in continu-
ation of this ceremony: they will do it rebelliously, sullenly, or
sneakingly, perfectly aware of their change of front. This feast
commemorates the institution of the Eucharist on the eve of the
Passion. It was moved from Maundy Thursday only because too
much overshadowed there by Calvary still to come; whereas now,
after Pentecost, it could be celebrated joyfully, and be felt to be an
initiation into a happy but transfigured life; a sacrament of love,
indeed, but of a love made selfless by renunciation and sacrifice.
The sun, the banners, the rose-leaves, the young children, are not
out of place in this feast; they rhyme with the new joy and innocence to be achieved; the purity of nature harmonizing perfectly,
while it lasts, with a chastened purity of spirit.

Those to whom such things seem nonsense must be puzzled
at the vogue that the cult of the Sacrament has acquired in the
present conceited but distracted age: it seems incongruous with
dominant industrialism and with opinion controlled by the daily
press. Perhaps it is a safety valve, a self-defensive movement of he
human psyche, threatened with absolute servitude, like that of the
working ants.

The rich, the polite, the well-informed about everything, would
perhaps see more in the other feast that I chiefly remember at
Avila: an autumn feast, the apotheosis of a reforming and literary
woman. Santa Teresa is not buried there, her heart alone is kept

as a relic in the chapel built over the room in which she was born; and her beautiful image, an image almost identified with her now by local sentiment, stands or rather kneels over the same altar. It is a wooden image, moveable and fit to be carried in procession: only the attitude and the face and hands manifest the artist; the rest is dressed in the Carmelite habit, modified by a gorgeous mantle, a golden nimbus and many jewels. Yet the sculptor and the saint triumph over these accessories, and we see the enraptured nun, pale and heroic, lifted from the earth by the power of faith and love. Yet Santa Teresa was eminently sane; she was considerate of circumstances, of particular cases, of human weakness and the humors of fate; she was distinctly modern. She can appeal to the pragmatist in the believer: a dangerous tendency, it seems to me, that carries religion into politics and, almost inevitably, coarsens religion itself into a sort of celestial politics and diplomacy. One world is enough to my feeling, and I should wish religion to digest and transmute this life into ultimate spiritual terms rather than commit us to fresh risks, ambitions, and love-affairs in a life to come. But my impulsive half-American sister was an ardent disciple of Santa Teresa; and something unsatisfactory in Susana's piety perhaps prejudices my judgment in respect to the perfection of her model. Religion in Susana seemed to remain always strained, and did not sweeten her old age. Did she perhaps doubt the truth of her faith, and did she assert it so persistently precisely because, at heart, she doubted it? Santa Teresa had no such secret unrest; but perhaps she would not have escaped it had she breathed for twenty years an American atmosphere. Fixity of tradition, of custom, of language is perhaps a prerequisite to complete harmony in life and mind. Variety in these matters is a lesson to the philosopher and drives him into the cold arms of reason; but it confuses the poet and the saint, and embitters society.

In Avila, in these processions of Santa Teresa, there were charming survivals of popular naïveté, worthy of the middle ages. The Saint was too great, the crowds too large, for everything to go on in her own church: ten days before the feast she was borne to the Cathedral, where the image of the Virgin Mary was brought out from her chapel to welcome the pilgrim; and the two statues, one to the right and the other to the left of the high altar, presided over the ensuing Novena. When this was finished, another procession was formed to carry the Saint back to her own home; but such was her ascendency in heaven as well as on earth, that the Virgin Mary herself could not forbear to accompany her parting guest at least halfway on the journey. At the appointed place, an open square where the eye could extend for some distance, the procession halted. Santa Teresa, who preceded (ecclesiastical etiquette requiring that the greatest shall come last), then turned completely round, and made three deep obeisances to the Queen of Heaven, who amid the delighted whispers and gratified vanity of the crowd actually made an obeisance in return, and then majestically moved away towards the Cathedral; whereupon the Saint resumed her homeward progress. So much for popular piety: but the pious also have their little human dissensions. At another hour there was another procession, by a rival confraternity carrying a different newly bought image of Saint Teresa, in the style of Saint Sulpice. And why? Because the regular Confraternity of Santa Teresa, whose property the old venerable image was, was said to be in the hands of rich men and ecclesiastics; and the artisans had seceded and formed a different confraternity of their own, with a modern pink-and-white image, plain painted stucco without silks or jewels, that they liked better.

To confirmed pedestrians like my father and me the friendly if rugged visage of Avila appeared more in its environs than within its walls. Each time that, coming from Paris in the 1880's and 1890's after my second night in the train, the dawn warned me that I must be approaching my destination, it was always with a beating heart that I looked for the names of the last stations, Arévalo, then Mingorría; after which, at any moment, I might expect to see on the right, sloping down gently towards the bed of the invisible river, the perfect walls of Avila, every bastion shining clear in the level rays of the sun, with the cathedral tower in the midst rising only a little above the line of the battlements, and no less imperturbably solid and grave. The stone in that level sunlight took on a golden tint, beautiful and almost joyful against the blackish rocks and arid slopes of the descending hills, only relieved here and there by fringes of poplars or dark green oaks. The landscape near Avila (that, I suppose, of an extinct glacier) is too austere to be beautiful, too dry and barren; yet it reveals eloquently the stone skeleton of the earth; not a dead skeleton like the mountains of the moon but like the mountains of Greece, vivified at least by the atmosphere, and still rich in fountains and in hidden fields. After all, Castile is not so high and dry as Arabia, which also has its green spots; the whole Spanish table-land slopes gently westward and south-westward towards Portugal and the Atlantic, whence come its rains and where its rivers debouch without impediment. Avila sits on the very tip of a tongue of high land stretching in this direction; and its peculiar picturesqueness depends on the circumstance that, although situated among the northern foothills of the Castilian sierras, it does not look northward but southward towards those very mountains, from a parallel minor spur. Being more often cold than warm, it has turned its face and opened its windows to the sun. From the promenade of the Rastro or from my brother-in-law's house on the crest of the same southern slope, the eye consequently dominates the pleasanter and more humane aspect of the country. At one's feet lie the roofs of a picturesque suburb, not without its churches and belfries; in the fields beyond rises the great monastery of Santo Tomás; you see the long straight roads, sometimes lined with trees, that cross the broad valley, and you may even catch a glimpse of the river, although in summer it is little more than a string of pools, with a little water trickling from one to another, or hiding among heaps of stones and stretches of sand. Beyond all this, to close the vista, rise the sharp peaks of the Sierra de Avila, and the more distant and massive Sierra de Gredos, both alike purple to the eye, and as it were liquefied by excess of light.

In this direction there was an interesting goal for a long walk in cool weather; and a walk is pleasanter when it is directed to some specific spot, where one may stop, look about, and rest a little before turning satisfied homewards. This was the Hermitage of Our Lady of Sonsolès, a large stone chapel with a farmhouse attached, built on an eminence at the foot of the sierras, with a grove of trees before it, a fountain, and some stone benches. In my father's day we seldom visited it, because my visits then fell in midsummer, and the walk across the whole valley was long and dusty in the sun; but later, when I could stay with my sister in the autumn, I could walk there alone, or sometimes accompanied by my brother-in-law, who however rode his mule, while I and his son Rafael (my usual companion) went on foot.

Celedonio, middle-aged and heavy, didn't come on my account, although he pretended to do so. He came on a religious pilgrimage. My fondness for this excursion served only as a hint to his secret conscience, that perhaps he had neglected Our Lady of Sonsolès too long. On these occasions it was therefore in order to enter the Chapel, and to kneel for a while in prayer, or as if praying, before the miraculous image. My brother-in-law's piety was of a primitive, prudential and chthonic kind, not at all theological. He with his whole family marched dutifully together to confession and communion once a year, at the Easter season, according to the precept of the Church, and he went to Mass on Sundays, unless something prevented; but he would have nothing to do with modern devotions, or the people who, as he said, *se comían a Dios*, gobbled up God, every day. Religion to his mind was and ought to be a formality, like calling on the authorities, respecting the written law, and keeping up the ancient dignity of Church and State. One mustn't offend the powers that be: and these powers, according to his agricultural sense of cause and effect, were mysterious and multiform. Our Lady of Sonsolès was one of them. He carried in his waistcoat pocket a small silver reproduction of her image and as Sonsolès was visible from the windows of his dining room, before sitting down at table, he invariably went to the window, as if to examine the look of the weather, pulled the little image out of his pocket, lifted (as if to scratch his head) the cap he always wore in the house, muttered a word or two in the direction of Sonsolès, and kissed the tiny amulet before slipping it back into its hiding place. This was his private grace before meat, good for his whole household, well known to everybody, but never spoken of.

On occasion, however, Celedonio would tell us about the miracles worked by this particular *numen*. One was commemorated by the votive model of a seventeenth-century ship that we might all see hanging from the rafters of the Chapel at Sonsolès, and depicted in the large painting on one of the walls. Some one in a storm at sea had invoked the aid of Our Lady under this advocation and had been saved from shipwreck. Had I been quite at ease in Celedonio's company (as I never was) I might have asked him whether he thought that, if this mariner had invoked, say, Our Lady of the Pillar instead of Our Lady of Sonsolès, he would have been less likely to escape. And if he had hesitated, I then could have aired my own strictly orthodox theology and said that the intercession of the Virgin Mary would of course be equally efficacious under whatever name she was invoked; but that the prayer, in each person, might be more spontaneous and trustful, and therefore worthier of being heard, if it were associated with the favors and the cultus familiar to him at home. Celedonio would have (or should have) congratulated me on this explanation; but he would certainly have thought me a dangerous person if I had asked whether, if that mariner had invoked not the Virgin Mary but Castor and Pollux, he might have been no less earnest and no less worthy of his reward. Whatever name we may invoke, is not prayer always essentially addressed to whatsoever real power we may depend upon to liberate us from the troubles that pursue us? Superstition may variously deceive the fancy; it never changes the allegiance of the heart, which I suppose is all that matters from a spiritual point of view.

Celedonio's allegiance, at least in his old age, was solidly prudential, and such as befitted a farmer, a lawyer, an administrator, and a *pater familias*. Perhaps in his youth he had had dreams. He had been in love with Susana, a love apparently never quite extinguished; for he had hung opposite his desk, where he could see it whenever he looked up from his papers or stopped to light a cigarette, an oil painting of Susana, at the age of fifteen, holding me in her arms, done in those early days by my father, after a photograph; and there were certain romantic vistas in his mind concerning Spanish history, and in particular concerning this shrine of Sonsolès. He vouched personally for a modern miracle—proving its sanctity. A certain person, whom at first he named, but who later became vague and might ultimately have been identified by tradition with himself, was one day riding across the valley when he was overtaken by a violent thunderstorm, and imprudently took shelter under a solitary oak by the wayside. The oak was struck and riven by lightning; the horse was killed, and the rider's clothes burned: yet the man had raised his eyes towards Our Lady of Sonsolès, had invoked her protection, and had miraculously escaped.

Without counting on miraculous favors, I too felt a genuine sanctity, a pagan sanctity, hanging about Sonsolès. Nothing forbidding, nothing ominous, but a sort of invisible sympathy of all things with man, when he takes his place gladly among them. The sanctuary was old, simple, solid, nobly placed on the hillside, with an enclosed grove before it, and a stone fountain, from which the water flowed in paved channels among the trees, keeping the grass green in the shady places. Chapel, farmhouse, and barns were contiguous along one side of the enclosure, all equally familiar possessions, ancestral, and tended with equal prudence and care. Poultry, a dog and a cat, even a stray pig or two formed a happy family. Not useless near a temple, any more than the donkeys and sheep in the background; for this was a place of pilgrimage, travellers must be refreshed, and there was even a rude space serving as a bull-ring at the yearly feast when a fair was held, with great concourse from the neighboring villages. From these coarse pleasures and hubbub in the hot sunlight, and from these troubles of the poor, it was all the more grateful to slip for a moment into the darkness of the cool oratory, and visit the Virgin in her placid unearthly splendor. The universe, our own souls, then revealed to us another dimension, besides those of our labors and sorrows.

The chapel was a perfect little temple, dark and windowless save for some opening in the roof. No modern ceiling or plastered walls or wooden flooring, but only rough stone everywhere and bare rafters; yet the shrine was ornate, and the image of Our Lady of Sonsolès, rather less than life-size, stood magnificently dressed and crowned, her white and gold mantle and rich veil being piously worked and renewed on occasion by Celedonio's daughter and other young ladies of Avila. "Sonsolès" means, or may mean, *they are suns*; and the place has a coat of arms or at least an emblem, rudely sculptured here and there on the stone, representing three faces of Sol, encircled by rays, like so many monstrances; for such symbols have transferable applications, and what depicts visible radiance may also indicate the diffusion of divine grace.

At heart Avila itself only repeats on a grander scale this same religious and human theme; only that the rustic setting has disappeared, and repentant paganism has become more Byzantine, more mediæval, enclosed and overshadowed as it is by such high military and monastic bulwarks. The place in my time was in part ruinous and neglected, reduced to 6,000 inhabitants from the 30,000 it is said to have had in its day. Almost half the area that slopes down to the river from what might be called the upper town was deserted within its circle of battlements and towers; there appeared only heaps of rubbish, a few nondescript huts, and some enclosures where occasional stray pigs and poultry might be encountered. Even in the upper part many old mansions and chapels were closed; sometimes only the great door, with a wrought-iron balcony over it, attested their ancient dignity. Yet dignity was not absent from the good people that remained, leading a simple, serious, monotonous provincial life, narrowed by poverty and overhung more obviously than busier places seem to be by the shadow of illness, sorrow, and death. Almost all the women appeared to be in mourning, and the older men also. There was nothing forced or affected in this: people were simply resigned to the realities of mother nature and of human nature; and in its simplicity their existence was deeply civilized, not by modern conveniences but by moral tradition. "It is the custom," they would explain half apologetically, half proudly to the stranger when any little ceremony or courtesy was mentioned peculiar to the place. If things were not the custom, what reason could there be for doing them? What reason could there be for living, if it were not the custom to live, to suffer, and to die? Frankly, Avila was sad; but for me it was a great relief to hear that things were the custom, and not that they were right or necessary, or that I ought to do them.

How much respect did these grave, disillusioned, limited people of Avila have for their conventions, and in particular for their religion? Not much, I think, at bottom; but nothing else was practically within their range; and if something else had been possible for them, would it have been better? The more intelligent of them would have doubted this, and resigned themselves to their daily round. What they had and what they thought was at least "the custom"; they could live and express themselves on those assumptions. Their inner man, in bowing to usage, could preserve its dignity. In breaking away, as the demagogues and cheap intellectuals wished them to do, they would have fallen into mental confusion and moral anarchy. Their lives would have been no better, and their judgments much worse. They could never, at the time when I knew them, have come to feel at home in a society where nothing was any longer "the custom," either in opinion or in conduct. Everything in Avila, the walls, the streets, the churches, the language, still bore witness to a faded but abiding civilization; and it was not impossible for me to heighten and vivify the picture, as I projected it into the past, and turn it into a proud, distinct and uncompromising power, such as a corrupt world would have to respect and to fear.

Every tourist with a guide book may learn that in Avila the
Cathedral, San Vicente, Santo Tomás, and the Chapel of Monsén
Rubí are notable monuments in which the whole troubled history
of Gothic architecture might be studied, if there were not elsewhere so many purer examples of each of those phases. Architecture, especially Gothic, was a passion of my youth, when I
searched and analyzed everything of the kind that I spied anywhere, and a pinnacle or the tracery of a window arrested my eye
as if it had promised to be Helen in all her glory. But that illusion
is gone, and Avila was not a place to encourage it. On the contrary, it is a place where I have felt the profounder power of unintended harmonies, of accidents, not happy in themselves, that
merge into a background for happiness—I speak of happiness for
a philosopher who can live happy in the intellect, amid the lovely
promise and quick ruin of all other happiness. Lovely promise and
quick ruin are seen nowhere better than in Gothic architecture, all
exuberance, freedom, and instability, "vaulting ambition" in stone,
original sin thinking it could glorify repentance. Oriental luxury
invaded classic art in Byzantium; and the purely aesthetic and
geometrical glory of this art appears better when the Christian
occasion for it does not exist, as among the Moslems. It could then
supply a myriad of lovely settings for poetry, for love, and for un-
bridled imagination, all without imposing a moral on the ara-
besques of creation. And for religion it could leave the empty and
silent dome, where the solitary mind might settle its account with
the universe. Our Gothic on the contrary became insatiably lavish
in ornament and in all sorts of distracting curiosities; and I like it
best when the hand of time or of chastisement has intervened in
that orgy, which tended to become tiresome, and has introduced
a new style, a different taste, an imperious broom, sweeping away
half those golden cobwebs. Sometimes the incongruous addition is
more beautiful than the background on which it intrudes; and
many a Gothic church would lose its charm if you removed the
renaissance tombs or the baroque porches. After all, it was only
by the force of its own restlessness that Gothic was superseded.

This irony of progress was illustrated in my time even in the Cathedral of Avila. There were formerly magnificent red damask hangings round the chancel and choir. They covered the wall beneath the triforium and the upper half of the arches into the aisles, the lower half being screened by the no less magnificent wrought-iron and brass railings. They made the whole inner space warm to the eye and nobly secluded to the heart. The sanctuary then seemed something like a throne room and audience chamber for the Most High. It was regal without loss of sublimity or mystical suggestion, since the vault still soared far above this earthly luxury, and vast somber spaces remained open in the direction of the nave and of either transept. Nor was the public cut off as in eastern churches from viewing the ceremonies. Room was left for them between the sanctuary and choir; for the Spanish practice of placing the choir west of the transepts allow the laity to flood the very center of the scene of worship. It is the favorite station for the officially devout, benches being sometimes provided there; while the unpretending Christian can still see and hear everything from the aisles, without being observed among the observers. These intimacies and charms of divine worship are missed by the superior critics who deplore such intrusion of the choir into the nave. That the tunnel of a long nave is thereby blocked seems to them an aesthetic sacrilege; but to me it seems a devotional advantage, and even a poetic one; because a partial veiling of beauty often enhances it, and the screens that enclose the choir, without interrupting the continuity of the clerestory and the vault, diversify the scene beneath, and supply appropriate places for monuments and altars. Therefore to a more Catholic age those red damask hangings seemed an appropriate ornament for a church, and they lent to the Cathedral of Avila, which is rather cold and severe, a special humanity and splendor. Nevertheless, some years ago, the Chapter sold the whole to an American for twenty thousand dollars. They said that the damask was rotting, that they needed the money for structural repairs in the fabric of the Cathe-

dral itself, and that without the damask the architecture of the
church would appear to more advantage.

These excuses seem to me as lamentable morally as the loss of
the hangings is æsthetically. No doubt those hangings needed over-
hauling; but if the silk were rotting, would any shrewd Chicago
millionaire or his careful wife want them in their bright new
home? No doubt the government architects that direct repairs in
national monuments did not always act as the Chapter would have
wished, if they acted at all; and no doubt twenty thousand dollars,
to be spent as they directed, was an unprecedented temptation to
the bishop and canons. But if any of them said that to remove so
great an ornament to the cultus would better reveal the beauties of
the edifice, he must have been a sad Catholic and a false lover of
the arts. Churches are built for prayer, not to exhibit the history
of architecture; and it was a sound instinct in Christian times to
assume that all richness and beauty might be laid at the foot of the
Cross. Nothing that man naturally loves need go unconsecrated, if
only it be sacrificed in part and in part redeemed. Moreover, it is
not true that the damask hid anything worth looking at. The
Cathedral of Avila is noble, but no part except the apse is particularly original or interesting. The student could examine every
detail sufficiently before, while to the poet the bare stone walls—
for there is much flat empty surface here without any riot of sculptured niches, windows, or galleries—seem now exposed to too
much light, common, comfortless, bleak and discouraging. The
vandalism that has devastated the interior of almost all churches
elsewhere had now begun to attack them even in Spain. They
were becoming sepulchres for the religion that built them.

This church, faded and neglected but still glorious, was the last
in which I have been able to hear mass with inward satisfaction.
For one thing, there was no sermon in the morning. To separate
the Mass from the sermon shows a genuine respect for both. The
liturgy and the eventual discourse are alike assumed to be worth
attending to, each for its own sake. Then, at the High Mass here,

the rite was performed honestly, simply, in less than an hour, as a
traditional ceremony, without any affectation of personal devotion
or unction. It was the ancient Church still living. The little aco-
lytes scampered about as if at play, swung their heavy silver
censers with gusto, and let the chains rattle and the great puffs of
smoke escape at each high turn of the pendulum, as if pleasure
and duty had never been better matched. The music was rough,
gusty, and not very classical, but at least brief; and like all the rest
it was not offered to the public for admiration but performed
simply to conform, as well as might be or was usual, to the pre-
scriptions of the liturgy. Here was ancient priestly religion, as
acceptable to the truly intelligent as their native language or their
accidental governments, not because miraculously right or perfect
but because ingrained in all their traditions, part of the soil and
substance of their only possible life, to be transmitted with the
inevitable variations to the next generation, if this generation is
not to be wholly disinherited and barbarous.

I did not feel at all disinherited, although never a partaker in
those rites. I respect them, I like them, and I refuse to use them
for any baser purpose. They celebrate inevitable human passions
and joyful hopes; and I shed no tears if those hopes and passions
in myself have had their day. Why envy illusions? Insight is not
only calmer, but more sympathetic and charitable, because each
passion or hope when alive sees hateful enemies in every other
passion and hope, whereas insight sees in each the good to which it
aspires. In pure religion and in art all these rival goods may be
celebrated without contradiction or disloyalty; for after all it is only
the profane that expect art and religion to serve their private passions. Those who have passed the *pons asinorum* in the inner life
know that the function of art and religion is precisely to transfigure
those private passions so that, far from being served, they may all
serve religion and art.

It was not, however, for the High Mass on Sundays that I most
often visited the Cathedral, or lingered there with the most pleasure. Any day at any hour, to make a short cut from street to street

or to escape from the sun at the hot hours, I could traverse the dark
cool aisles, or sit for a while in the transept, measuring the vaults
with the eye, and examining the rather nondescript stained glass
or the agreeable if somewhat obscure paintings in the great gilded
reredos, or the charming twin pulpits, or the sculptures in some old
altar or tomb. Enough scent of wax and of incense clung to the
walls to preserve the atmosphere of the cultus, and the focus of it,
where some old man or old woman might be seen kneeling in
prayer, was usually some modern shrine; this was still a living
church, not a museum or a ruin. That circumstance, like Avila
itself, pleased and consoled me. Everything profound, everything
beautiful had not yet vanished from the world.

CHAPTER VII

EARLY MEMORIES

OF EARLY childhood I have some stray images, detached
and undatable, called up occasionally for no reason,
after the fashion of dreams. Indeed, sometimes I suspect that they may be fragments of old dreams, and
not genuine recollections; but in that case, where did the old
dreams come from? For autobiography it might be no less pertinent, and even more telling, to report them if they were dreams
than if they were true memories, because they would show how
my young mind grew, what objects impressed it, and on what
themes it played its first variations.

These images are all visual. I remember the *sota de copas* or
knave of cups in the Spanish cards, with which I was playing on
the floor, when I got entangled in my little frock, which had a
pattern of white and blue checks; and I can see the corner of the
room, our *antesala*, where I was crawling, and the nurse who
helped me up. I also remember sitting in my mother's lap, rather
sleepy, and playing with a clasp that could run up and down the
two strands of her long gold chain, made of flexible scales; she
wore a large lace collar, and had on a silk gown which she called
el vestido de los seis colores, because the black background was
sprinkled with minute six-petalled flowers, each petal of a different
color, white, green, yellow, brown, red and blue. Clothes and colors
evidently had a great fascination for me: the emphasis may have
been partly borrowed and verbal, because I heard the women constantly talking *chiffons*; but the interest was congenial. I have
always been attentive to clothes, and careful about my own; and in
those days of innocence, it was by no means indifferent to me
whether with my white summer dress I wore the plain everyday

blue sash, which I despised, or the glossy and fresh silk tartan, that made me feel more like myself. Yet I retain a memory, that must have been much earlier, of quite another kind. One evening, before putting me to bed, my mother carried me to the window, sitting on her arm, and pulled back the *visillo* or lace curtain that hung close to the glass. Above the tower of the Oñate house opposite, one bright steady star was shining. My mother pointed it out to me, and said: *"Detrás de ese lucero está Pepín."* Pepín, her lamented first-born, was behind that star. At the time, this announcement neither surprised nor impressed me; but something about my mother's tone and manner must have fixed her words mechanically in my memory. She seldom spoke unnecessarily, and was never emotional; but here was some profound association with her past that, for a moment, had spread its aura about me.

Another set of memories can be dated as not later than my third year, because they introduce my brother Robert, who left Avila when I was three and he was twelve. We occupied the same little room behind our mother's and next to the schoolroom; and I remember our pillow fights, or rather games, because Robert had a tender heart and was nice to his baby-brother. He was forbidden to purloin any part of my food, but might stick out his tongue in the hope, not always disappointed, that with my fork I might delicately place a morsel upon it. It was a feat of equilibrium on my part, as well as of magnanimity, and I remember it for both reasons. Also the crisp potato omelette, fried in oil, that I had for supper, and that I still pine for and seldom obtain; and the napkin, white on the black and red table cover, on which the feast was spread. The first toy I can remember was also in Robert's time at Avila, for it was given me by his Alsatian tutor, Herr Schmidt: a velvety gray mouse that could be wound up to run across the floor. And finally I can remember distinctly the occasion of Robert's departure. We all went to the station to see him off; for my father was taking him as far as London, from where his cousin Russell Sturgis (the Evangelical major with the side-whiskers and shapely calves) was to convey him to America to be put to school. But it is not any emotion connected with leave-taking for an indefinite absence that remains in my mind: only the image of young Robert's back, walking before me at a particular corner where we had to go in single file. He wore a long gray coat with a braided mantlet or short cape covering the shoulders; above which I can still see his gray cap and the tightly curling brown hair escaping and bulging out under it. Whether I was actually walking too or was being carried does not appear from the picture. The self in these clear and fixed intuitions remains wholly transcendental and out of sight. It is doing its duty too well to be aware that it is doing it.

That Robert should have had an Alsatian tutor in Avila (who also taught the girls) may seem odd. It was one of those unstable and unsatisfactory compromises that were involved in the circumstances of my parents' marriage. For a time they lived in Madrid, in the flat where I was born: but Madrid has a bad climate, with great heat in summer and cold winds in winter; it made a second residence necessary for the hot months, and was expensive and, for my mother, socially distasteful. Moreover, she had to go back to Boston; my father knew it, but kept finding reasons for putting the thing off. Finally, very characteristically, my mother took the law into her own hands, secretly made all the arrangements and one afternoon escaped with all of us, save my father, in the express train for Paris. There my father's remonstrances reached her. They were so eloquent, or backed by such threats of action (since he had a right at least to retain *me*), that we all finally returned. It had been agreed that we should live in Avila. But what education could Robert or the girls receive there? None! Therefore a private tutor was imperative, and somehow a young Alsatian was found who seemed to possess all the requirements. French and German were native languages for him, he spoke a little English, and would soon learn Spanish. His demands were modest and his character apparently excellent. So Herr Schmidt was installed as a boarder with a poor widow who lived on the ground floor, and there were daily lessons in the sunny little room at the back of the house which became the schoolroom. I don't know what idealistic cobwebs the German Minerva might have spun there had not her labors been interrupted; but presently a German Cupid had flown in over the flowerpots in the open window, and tangled those learned threads. For although this was before the Franco-Prussian war, young Schmidt showed all the sentimentality and push of a pure German; he believed in discipline and thoroughness, and the duty of founding all instruction on German geography, in the native language; so that between the difficult and most clearly articulated names of *Harzgebirge* and *Riesengebirge* he would whisper in Susana's ear: *"Je vous aime avec rage."* She was hardly sixteen, and he had to be sent away, which no doubt he thought a great injustice; for he wrote a long letter explaining his worthiness to be Susana's husband, and his willingness to go to America and establish himself there—on nothing a year.

It was this collapse of superior international education at home that had made it urgent to send at least Robert at once to school in America, and that separated me from my elder brother for the next five years. Two more years elapsed before my mother and sisters also departed. I remember nothing of that interval; but after they went my uncle Santiago, with his wife Maria Josefa and his daughter Antoñita, came to live with us, and a new and distinct chapter begins in my experience. The scene, the persons, the events are still present to me most vividly. I didn't feel deeply or understand what was going on, but somehow the force of it impressed my young mind and established there a sort of criterion or standard of reality. That crowded, strained, disunited, and tragic family life remains for me the type of what life really is: something confused, hideous, and useless. I do not hate it or rebel against it, as people do who think they have been wronged. It caused me no suffering; I was a child carried along as in a baby-carriage through the crowd of strangers; I was neither much bothered nor seriously neglected; and my eyes and ears became accustomed to the unvarnished truth of the world, neither selected for my instruction nor hidden from me for my benefit.

My aunt Maria Josefa was frankly a woman of the people. She was most at home in her kitchen, in a large blue apron that covered most of her skirt; and I shall never forget the genuine fresh taste of the fried peppers and eggs, and the great soft cake or *torta* that came from her hands. She was a native of Jaen, with a strong but pleasant Andalusian accent and exaggerated rhetoric. Her every word was a diminutive or an augmentative, and her every passion flowed out in endless unrestrained litanies of sorrow or endearment. She could hardly read or write, and her simplicity or humility was so great that she would casually observe that her daughter Antoñita had been a *siete mesina* or seven-months child; from which any one could gather the reason for her marriage. For my uncle this marriage had been unintended and undesirable; he was much too young and she was much too common; but having got the poor girl into trouble he nobly made the *amende honorable*; and terrible as the sacrifice would have been if he had had much ability or ambition, as things were it rendered poverty perhaps easier to bear. Poverty was not the only misfortune they had to put up with: but when the worst was over, I found my aunt living in Granada with a brother who was a tanner. This was in the summer of 1893, when I had reached Spain via Gibraltar. My mother and I were in the habit of sending Maria Josefa a small allowance so that she was well received and respected in her brother's household. The tannery occupied the court of an old, possibly a Moorish, house; the skins hung drying from the gallery; and my aunt's brother, in order to do the honors of the city (as I had not been there before, or had no guide book), took me to see the University, which indeed it would not have occurred to me to visit. In the library there was a large globe; and in order to make talk, which rather ran dry between us, I said I would show him the voyage I had just made from America. I was doing so when he asked, "But which is Spain?—What, that little spot? I thought it was this," and he pointed to Africa. It occurred to me that some great wits before him had seen no difference between Africa and Spain; but I didn't go into the intricacies of that opinion. As to my aunt, of course she was then old, fat, and broken, but calm and strangely silent. She had protested enough, and this was the fifth act of her tragedy, all storms subdued and equalized in resignation. Yet one more trial awaited her. Her brother died before her, and she had to retire to her native village near Jaen, from which soon no more answers reached us to our letters.

Not the person, *tia Maria Josefa*, in whose hands my mother could have wished to leave me at the age of five! But my mother's mind was made up and inflexible; it was made up abstractly, in scorn of particulars and of consequences. She had put off her departure only too long, and now she *must* go. Besides, strange as it may seem, she was well disposed towards my father's relations, as they were not towards her. She seldom spoke of them, but when she did it was amiably, even sympathetically. She seems to have trusted Maria Josefa, as one might a devoted old nurse; and this trust was observed, because in relation to me Maria Josefa behaved perfectly. Moreover there was Antoñita, who but for her love-affairs and marriage would have looked after me more playfully than her mother. Antoñita was a nice girl, a friend of Susana's, pretty and with a latent depth of feeling which made people think her not insignificant, in spite of her simplicity and lack of education. My mother had liked her, and helped her to get prettier clothes. But she was ripening into womanhood and preoccupied with love. I remember her first *novio*, or acknowledged lover, the youngest of the Paz brothers, who were among the leading bourgeois families of Avila; and I think there was more between him and Antoñita than the local conventions allowed to *novios*. He came to the house, which is contrary to the rules: *novios* should meet only in public places, in sight of their elders, or talk together at the window, the girl sitting inside the *reja*, or in the balcony, and the young man standing in the street. This was called *pelando la pava*, plucking the turkey, or conjugating the verb *amo*, I love. There was a great attic over a part of the house, accessible from my father's room or studio, where he painted; and from one of the big beams of the roof hung a trapeze, arranged, I suppose, for my benefit. Into that attic the lovers would wander alone, whether to admire my performance, or not suspecting that I might be swinging there, I didn't know. That something was brewing became evident on another occasion. We were sitting one evening or late afternoon in the *café del Inglés* (for the lamps were lighted) when suddenly my aunt got up, evidently very angry, bundled Antoñita and me out of a side door; and once in the adjoining *portal* or *porte cochère*, began violently beating Antoñita with fists and claws, with such a flood of imprecations as only my aunt was capable of. All I could gather was that the poor girl had been looking at somebody; no doubt, as I now conjecture, at young Paz, at another table, making love to another girl. Anyhow, my aunt had worked herself up to such a rage that, being subject to fits, she fell full length with a loud bang on the stone floor. She fell exactly as *prima donnas* and murdered heroes fall on the stage; and apparently as harmlessly, for I heard no more of the whole affair. Relations with Paz were evidently broken off; there were no more trips to the attic, where I did my swinging undisturbed; and presently a very different *novio*, this time meaning business, appeared on the scene.

What brought him to Avila I do not know; probably some great lawsuit, for he was a lawyer, and ostensibly an important person, *bellâtre*, with well-oiled curly black locks and silken side-whiskers and the beginnings of a paunch, on which a conspicuous gold chain with dangling seals marked the equator. He was a widower with two little girls, but still young, not over forty; for people spoke of his brilliant prospects rather than of his brilliant past, and he had a still beautiful mother whom my father and I once visited in Madrid. She received us in her boudoir, or rather in the alcove attached to it, for she was still in bed, but elaborately prepared to receive callers. There were great lace flounces to her sheets, over a red damask coverlet, and she wore a lovely fresh peignoir and little cap, from which two great black braids hung down over her two shoulders, ending in coquettish knots of blue ribbon. What she and my father were talking about I didn't understand, but I felt I had never been in such a luxurious nest before, so much carpeted, so much curtained, so softly upholstered, and so full of religious and other bric-à-brac.

With such a mother, Rafael Vegas must have begun life convinced that he was a distinguished and fashionable person, and that his clients, when he had them, should pay him handsome fees. Nor could he have helped being a ladykiller, having not only the requisite presence and airs, but the requisite temperament; for he was no vulgar libertine, but a genuine lover of the fair sex, who demanded to conquer and to possess his conquests exclusively. He might have liked a harem, but he despised a brothel. His success with the ladies, young and old, was immense and in one sense deserved, since his admiration for them was sincere. That he was truly subject to the tender passion was proved by his courting and marrying two of my pretty and penniless cousins, beginning with Antoñita. Nothing but love could have prompted him in these cases; but to them it seemed a dazzling match, that meant initiation into a higher social sphere, as well as into all the mysteries of untried passion.

The wedding took place secretly in the small hours of the night, because a rowdy custom subjected widowers, on their new bridal night, to a *cencerrada,* or derisive serenade of cow bells, if the date and place of those mysteries could be discovered. Everything was therefore kept as dark as possible; only the immediate family was summoned, and they at the last moment, and only a cup of chocolate offered afterwards to the sleepy company before the newly married pair vanished to some unknown hiding place. I was of course present, and impressed by the strangeness of going out at night into a dark street and a dark empty church, with a knot of people whispering and hastening, with much trepidation, as if on some criminal errand. We were in our ordinary clothes, the bride in black, with a lace mantilla. It was all over in a moment. I was bundled to bed again, and might have thought it a dream, but for the talk afterwards about everything. Rafael's emphatic personal dignity would have suffered sadly had he not escaped the *cence-*

rrada; and he managed it cleverly, by not going on any wedding trip (he may also have been short of money) but establishing himself at once in our house, with his two daughters, in the best front rooms left vacant by my mother and sisters, who were in America. For a day or two, however, bride and bridegroom occupied my bedroom, because it looked out on a tangle of little courts and walled gardens, quite shut off from any street. On the first morning I followed the housemaid there—after all, it was my room—when she took in their breakfast to the happy pair. The two cups of chocolate were on a particularly fresh and well-filled tray, with *azucarillos*; there was a bright brass bed, wholly unknown to me, and a gorgeous red damask coverlet, and great lace flounces to the sheets, like those, or the very same, that on that other occasion, in Madrid, I saw setting off the charms of Rafael's black-browed mother. Rafael and Antoñita lay smiling and rosy on quite separate pillows; they said good morning to the servant and me with unusual good humor, and people all day indulged in witticisms and veiled expressions which I didn't quite understand.

I now had playmates in the house, two well dressed little girls about my own age; but we didn't like one another. It was made clear in every direction that our house and our standard of living were not such as the Vegas expected, and they bore us a grudge for causing them to be lodged and fed so badly. Yet our double or triple *ménage* was kept up for a year or more until an event supervened that brought disaster to my uncle's family and eventually sent my father and me to America.

Antoñita was soon quite obviously in what was called an interesting condition. The place that children come from was no mystery to me, although I was only seven or eight years old. I was already a calm materialist; not that in another direction I was less knowing in theology; and if any one had made the mistake of telling me that babies came in bandboxes from Paris, I am sure I should have scornfully replied that God and not milliners had made me; and that as God was everywhere, it was just as easy for him to make babies in Madrid or even in Avila as in Paris. Yet

Antoñita's baby, that God was undoubtedly making in Avila, was very long in coming to light. She continued more and more strangely to enlarge, until her haggard and unseemly condition, and murmurs and consultations in the family, began to suggest that something was wrong. Perhaps the date for the expected event had been miscalculated; or perhaps some complication prevented nature from bringing it about. At last one evening there was much agitation in the house, with strangers coming in, and long consultations; and I began to hear from Antoñita's room (which was my mother's room back to back with mine, but with no communication) piercing cries and weeping invocations of all the heavenly powers. This presumably lasted all night, since it was still going on when I woke up in the morning; and then there were more consultations with strange doctors and exhibition of surgical instruments. At one moment I remember my aunt bursting into the passage, with a bundle of bloodstained linen in her hands and floods of joyful tears, crying "She is saved, she is saved!" Yet later we children were taken to our neighbor's on the second floor, where we didn't know the people; and on the way out I saw, in a small wooden box that might have held soap or candles, a dead child lying naked, pale yellowish green. Most beautiful, I thought him, and as large and perfectly formed as the Child Jesus in the pictures; except that where the navel ought to be he had a little mound like an acorn, with a long string hanging out of it.

The image of that child, as if made of green alabaster, has remained clear all my life, not as a ghastly object that ought to have been hidden from me, but as the most beautiful of statues, something too beautiful to be alive. And it has suggested to me a theory, doubtless fanciful, yet which I can't think wholly insignificant, concerning the formation of living things. They are all formed in the dark, automatically, protected from interference by what is called experience: experience which indeed would be impossible if there were not first a definite creature to receive it and to react upon it in ways consonant with its inherited nature. This nature has asserted itself in a seed, in an egg, in a womb, where the world couldn't disturb its perfect evolution. Flowers and butterflies come perfect to the light, and many animals are never more beautiful, pure, and courageous than when they first confront the world. But man, and other unhappy mammals, are born helpless and half-shapeless, like unbaked dough; they have not yet become what they meant to be. The receptacle that held them could not feed them long enough, or allow them to attain their full size and strength. They must therefore be cast out into the glare and the cold, to be defeated by a thousand accidents, derailed, distorted, taught and trained to be enemies to themselves, and to prevent themselves from ever existing. No doubt they manage to survive for a time, halt, blind, and misshapen; and sometimes these suppressions or mutilations of what they meant to be adapt them to special environments and give them technical knowledge of many a thing that, if they had been free, they might never have noticed, or observed only poetically, in a careless and lordly way. But every living creature remains miserable and vicious, so long as in serving other things it has to suppress itself: and if that alien world must need be served, the only happy solution and one that nature often finds, would be for the unfit species to perish outright—there is nothing ignoble in perishing—and for a different species to appear whose freedom and happiness would lie in contact with those particular circumstances and mastery over them. I say to myself, therefore, that Antoñita's child was so exceptionally beautiful, and would doubtless have been exceptionally brave and intelligent, because he had profited longer than is usual by the opportunity to grow undisturbed, as all children grow in their sleep; but this advantage, allowed to butterflies and flowers, and to some wild animals, is forbidden to mankind, and he paid for it by his life and by that of his mother.

For she had not really been saved; only a false hope made my aunt think so for a moment; and on Antoñita's death, it would have seemed natural that Rafael and his two little girls should have left us and gone to live elsewhere in their own more luxurious way. But not at all. Primitive human nature in my aunt Maria

Josefa yielded absolutely to every passion in turn, put up with every trial, but survived and clung no less passionately to whatever was left. Her grief on this occasion was violent, but violent only by fits, as when each new visitor came to condole with her, and she had to repeat the whole story, with appropriate floods of tears, sobs and lamentations. She even said at times that now she knew there was no God, because, with all her prayers and vows, no God could have allowed her poor innocent daughter to suffer so horribly to no purpose. Her heart thus unburdened, however, she couldn't but take comfort in that splendid man, her son-in-law, and devote herself to his service and care for his little girls. Rafael therefore not only remained in our house, but became all-important in it, as if my father had not existed. Nor could I be looked after exclusively, when after all I had my own mother to love me, even if a thousand leagues away, and there were those two darlings to rescue from the shock of having lost their second Mama as well as their first one. Moreover my uncle Santiago, though he said little, was beginning to go daft. Not on account of his daughter's death. He used to say, when people expressed their sympathy, that his real loss had come when she was married. I don't think this observation in itself a sign of dementia; but it indicated a general despair and passivity that went with his taking refuge in drink, and finally in idiocy. For idiocy may begin by being partly acted, like Hamlet's madness, in order to mock the facts, until the mockery becomes an automatism, and the facts are lost altogether. Years afterwards, when he was at his worst, he would walk ceaselessly round and round the house, half singing, half moaning, always repeating the same sounds, and crushing a piece of paper in his hand. He had recovered the animal capacity—such an insult to the world!—of still doing his old trick, no matter what might be going on. The marvel is how many individuals and how many governments are able to survive on this system. Perhaps the universe is nothing but an equilibrium of idiocies.

My father was mildness itself on ordinary occasions, but sometimes could be aroused to reveal his hidden and unusually clear

mind, when all his command of terse language and his contempt
for the world would flow out in a surprising and devastating manner. I was not present, but I gathered from stray comments over-
heard afterwards, that he had had an explanation of this sort with
Rafael and Maria Josefa. At any rate, they suddenly left us. My
father and I remained in what seemed that vast house alone with
one little maid servant. Such an arrangement could not be permanent and doubtless was not meant to be so; and presently we
too said farewell to that house forever and to Avila, as far as I was
concerned, for eleven years.

During the three years that I was separated from my mother I
went more or less to school. It was a large darkish room on the
ground floor in the public building directly opposite our house;
but the entrance was not in our street, and I had to go round the
Oñate tower into the lane at the back, where the school door was.
We children stood in *corros* or circles round the teacher—I think
sometimes only an older lad—and recited the lesson after him. I
don't remember any individual questions or answers, nor any reading or writing, yet we did learn somehow to read and write. I had
two books: the *cartilla*, with the alphabet and the different sylla-
bles, with easy words following; and the catechism, perhaps in a
later year. This was itself divided into two parts, one Sacred History, with pictures in it, of which I remember only Moses striking
the rock from which water gushed; and Christian Doctrine, of
which I remember a great deal, virtually everything, because it
was evidently an excellent catechism, so that after learning it I
have been able all my life to distinguish at the first hearing the
sapor haereticus of any dangerous doctrine. Especially present to
me is the very philosophic dogma that God is everywhere, by his
essence, by his presence and by his power: of which, however, the
first clause has always remained obscure to me; for if God is everywhere by his essence, it would seem to follow that everything is
essentially divine—a vulgar pantheism; so that the meaning must
be something very recondite and highly qualified, which escapes
me. But the other two clauses are luminous, and have taught me

from the first to conceive omnificent power and eternal truth: inescapable conceptions in any case, quite apart from any doctrines of historical Judaism or Christianity. I have reasserted them, in my mature philosophy, in my notions of the realm of matter and the realm of truth: notions which I am happy to have imbibed in childhood by rote in the language of antiquity, and not to have set them up for myself in the Babel of modern speculation. They belong to human sanity, to human orthodoxy; I wish to cling to that, no matter from what source its expression may come, or encumbered with what myths. The myths dissolve: the presuppositions of intelligence remain and are necessarily confirmed by experience, since intelligence awoke precisely when sensibility began to grow relevant to external things.

CHAPTER VIII

I AM TRANSPORTED TO AMERICA

M Y FIRST voyage—if I hadn't been deadly seasick—
might have initiated me into the life of primitive
mariners, for we sailed the high seas in an open boat.
It was a little freight steamer plying from Bilbao to
Cardiff, hardly more than a tug; and though it had a small bridge
and a deck house aft, it was open to the sky forward, and visibly
freighted with reddish earth, which I believed was iron ore. The
Bay of Biscay in such a craft confirmed its bad reputation; but on
the third day there was sunshine and smooth sparkling water, and
I recovered instantly. A quick and complete recovery is characteristic of my ill turns in general, and particularly of seasickness,
which purges the system of its poisons. If I could have secured this
advantage without the horrid prolonged trials that produced it, I
might have gladly become a sailor. I love moving water, I love
ships, I love the sharp definition, the concentrated humanity, the
sublime solitude of life at sea. The dangers of it only make present
to us the peril inherent in all existence, which the stupid, ignorant,
untravelled land-worm never discovers; and the art of it, so mathe-
matical, so exact, so rewarding to intelligence, appeals to courage
and clears the mind of superstition, while filling it with humility
and true religion. Our world is a cockleshell in the midst of over-
whelming forces and everlasting realities; but those forces are cal-
culable and those realities helpful, if we can manage to understand and obey them.

We were in the Bristol Channel, in sight of the Welsh coast;
smooth grassy hillsides, gray-green in the slight mist and dotted
with little white houses. But there was something far more interesting for me to watch; several boats with white sails, probably

small yachts, bending and tacking in the almost imperceptible breeze. A British note: a first hint to me of that brave, free, sporting side of the youthful Anglo-Saxon character which I was later to love so much. For if in most things it is contrast that makes me admire and trust the unspotted young Englishman, in one respect it is affinity; I too love the earth and hate the world. God made the first, and man, with his needs and his jealousies, has made the second.

On landing, an ungainly ridiculous side of this world, and especially of Britain, became suddenly present. We had plumped on a Sunday into a British non-conformist industrial town. Ugliness and desolation could not be more constitutional. Perhaps we lodged in a too modest quarter, too near the port; but nothing was in sight save rows of mean little brick houses all alike, a long straight street wet with the rain, and not a soul stirring. However, the rain ultimately ceased, and on going out for a stroll we came upon a forbidding castle wall, closely skirted by what evidently was the old High Street of the place; and we learned that this was the seat of the Marquis of Bute, the great landlord of that region. Another British note: the living survival of mediæval features, material and moral, in the midst of modern England.

The next day we travelled to Liverpool, where I remember nothing but the docks, with long inclined ways, paved with cobblestones, leading down between great warehouses to the water's edge. There we crept into a small rowboat, that was to convey us to our ship. Several large vessels were riding at anchor in the stream: my father pointed to the ugliest and most dwarfish of them and said that this would be ours. No help for it now, I reflected: but at once my eye was attracted by a line of little flags running from stem to stern, over the top of the two masts. What did that mean? My father explained that dressing the ship in that fashion, although a British vessel, was a compliment courteously paid to the United States, because most of the passengers were Americans, who on that day were celebrating the anniversary of their Declaration of Independence. This incident has fixed the date of my first sailing to America unerringly in my mind: it was the Fourth of July, 1872.

The Cunard Steamship *Samaria* of that date was a vessel of 3000 tons, with a squat red smokestack between two stumpy masts, and a bowsprit like a sailing-ship. Sails were indeed often set, in order, it was said, to steady her, but probably also to help her along; for never was vessel more distinctly an old tub. She stood high, black, and short above the water, looking rusty and almost derelict; however she bore us safely, if not steadily, to Boston in twelve days. I was again terribly seasick most of the time; and my father, if not exactly seasick, being an old sailor, suffered from severe and prolonged indigestion, which he said upset and discouraged him altogether, and spoilt his whole visit to the United States. I, at least, had intervals when I was well and hungry. A nice young woman, Irish she said, took pity on me and tried to entertain me; but we couldn't talk. I didn't know a word of English or she of Spanish; and my father, who read English perfectly, could neither pronounce it nor understand it when spoken; so that with English-speaking people he was reduced to uttering single words, if they could be recognized as he sounded them, or to writing them on a piece of paper. His deafness added to the difficulty, and made it impossible for him to surmount it. Nevertheless my young Irish friend and I got on well enough without a common language: the goodwill in what we might say was always intelligible. I afterwards often saw her family, for they occupied the pew immediately in front of the one in which my sisters and I sat at the Church of the Immaculate Conception; but our acquaintance never went beyond an occasional bow and discreet smile. My particular friend, the young lady, for some reason was never there. I have a dreamy recollection of hearing that she was the invisible contralto that sang with so charming and rich a voice in the choir; I am not sure of it, but in any case I liked to think so.

The day of our arrival was very warm, with the damp suffocating heat of the New England summer; there was naturally some confusion in landing, and everything seemed odd and unaccount-

able. It was a sordid scene. I saw no stone quays, such as I associated with ports, at Bilbao, at Portugálete, and lately on a grand
scale at Liverpool. No docks; only a wooden pier raised precari-
ously on slimy piles, with the stained sea water running under it;
and on it a vast wooden shed, like a barn, filled with merchandise
and strewn with rubbish. America was not yet rich, it was only
growing rich; people worked feverishly for quick returns, and let
the future build for the future. But along came my brother Robert.
I shouldn't have recognized him, nor he me, after those five years:
a youth not yet eighteen, of middle height, with a narrow chest
and sloping shoulders, and a straw hat with a bright blue ribbon:
yet the tightly curling brown hair, quite dry and brittle (we both
grew prematurely bald) was unmistakably Robert's: besides, he
spoke Spanish, and very soon I was quite at home with him. But I
had never seen a man in a straw hat before, and the blue ribbon
didn't please me. Of course I had no idea that blue ribbons might
have a meaning: 'varsity blues, royal blues, the Garter, or the
record in Atlantic crossings or choice champagnes: there was no
question of any of those things in Robert's case. His ribbon was an
accident, a caprice of the hat-makers, seconded by thoughtless taste
in the buyer. I say thoughtless, not to say crude: because I nurse
a sort of moral sense about colors, and in artificial objects a plain
unmitigated blue seems to me vulgar. Robert had pale blue eyes,
innocent and sometimes a little watery. To pale blue my color-
sense makes no objection, nor to dark blue; these have separate
moral qualities proper in their place; and the lightest blue eyes
always possess a mysterious center and several shades in the iris. I
could have positively liked the blueness of Robert's eyes, and even
that of his ribbon, if it had matched them.

Once on terra firma, or rather on the rough planks of the
Cunard wharf, in what resembled the baggage room of a large
station, I looked about for the carriages and horses. Carriages—
anything with wheels—had been my favorite toys. Mine had been
little ones, that I could pull round and round the dining room
table on a string; but more exciting, in Madrid, had been the real

carriages, so smart and shining, with their gay red or yellow wheels, their high-stepping horses, their solemn coachman and groom, and the smiling ladies inside. But what did I see here? I daresay there were vehicles of various sorts; but just in front of me, what first caught and held my attention, was something like a large baby-carriage suspended high in air on four enormous skeleton wheels: Robert called it a buggy. The front wheels were almost as large as the back wheels, with the rims almost touching. Those front wheels were too high to slip under the body of the carriage; in turning, the near tire was apt to scrape against the side with an ominous and unpleasant sound, so that it was impossible for a buggy to face about sharply; this littlest of carriages could make only a great sweep, and was in danger of upsetting at every corner.

Here by chance my eye, at the first moment of my setting foot in the new world, was caught by symbols of Yankee ingenuity and Yankee haste which I couldn't in the least understand but which instinctively pleased and displeased me. I was fascinated by the play of those skeleton wheels, crossing one another like whirling fans in the air, and I was disgusted by such a dirty ramshackle pier for a great steamship line. I think now that the two things expressed the same mentality. That pier served its immediate purpose, for there we were landing safely at it; it hadn't required any great outlay of capital; and what did it matter if it was ugly and couldn't last long? It might last long enough to pay, and enable the Company to build a better one. As for the buggy, its extreme lightness economized force and made speed possible over sandy and ill-kept roads. The modest farmer could go about his errands in it, and the horsey man could race in it with his fast long-tailed pair. Never mind if in the end it turned out to be like some experimental and too ambitious species of insect, that develops an extraordinary organ securing an immediate advantage but leading into fatal dangers. Abstract ingenuity is a self-rewarding sport. The taste for it marks the independence of a shrewd mind not burdened by any too unyielding tradition except precisely this tradition of experimental liberty, making money and losing it, and being happy rather than ashamed of having always to begin afresh.

Robert somehow guided us and despatched our things to Beacon Street; it was a complicated process and a complicated journey, a ferry and two horse cars, besides three short walks, but it was economical, ten cents each for the trip, and twenty-five cents to send the trunk by express: whereas a "hack" (a hired landau) would have cost five dollars. The method of sending luggage by express seemed to us obscure and disquieting. How could we trust all our worldly goods to a stranger, paying him besides in advance, and meekly accept in exchange a coarse brass medal perforated with a number? There was a twin medal perforated with the same number, which the expressman kept; and Robert said he would attach this to our trunk, having taken a note of the address to which that number should be despatched; and the trunk was sure to arrive safely and speedily. Although my own scepticism was not yet fully developed, neither my father nor I were by nature inclined to faith in the unintelligible: however, being born travellers, we were ready in a new country to bow to a new logic and a new ethics; and we trusted Robert and the mysterious order of nature.

Our faith proved entirely justified: and though my father perhaps never felt at home in this system of trust and credit, fearing the confidence tricks of omnipresent rascals, I soon learned to swim happily with my eyes closed on this stream of business convention, which indeed at this moment is supplying me with a comfortable income coming, as far as my direct action or perception goes, from nowhere. But I have meditated on this point, and think I see the principle of it. Life, physical life, would be impossible without bold and risky presumptions about the future and without the opportune course of nature, coming to meet and to reward those presumptions. Millions of seeds, thousands of hopes, are frustrated: but there is enough adaptability in living beings, and enough constancy in things, for some arts to prosper. When these arts have been long established with little remembered change, people think it a matter of course that things should proceed in that way, and are shocked if any accident, as they call it, produces what they call an anomaly; and they never perceive that they are daily building on faith over a sleeping volcano. Now a commercial society at first knows very well the risks it is running; ships sent out never return; stores are burned or pillaged; coin must ring true before it is accepted; and treasure must be kept hidden at home and guarded night and day with fear and trembling. But this state of things is so wasteful that merchants can afford to pay highly for a government that can give them security: and governments supported by trade will then police the country and the sea in the interests of trade, subordinating all other interests. Faith, trust, credit, security are the lifeblood of trade: when strictly protected by courts and prisons, they will reduce the expense of business enormously, and enable the merchant not only to grow rich and remain rich, but to supply the public with endless commodities at reasonable prices. And this is why, on landing in Boston in 1872, my father and I were able safely to commit our trunk to the expressman (police, courts, and prison would have got him instantly if he had stolen it) and could be conveyed from East Boston to Beacon Street at the expense of fifty-five cents instead of five dollars. But we had not the lordly pleasure of driving in our private carriage, or the excitement of carrying swords and pistols, in case bandits should waylay us.

Events looked forward to with trepidation, when at length they occur, often fall flat. I was going to see my mother and sisters again after three years! Husband and wife were to be reunited! Well, when Robert said, "This is our house" and we walked up a little flight of stone steps to a half-open door in a row of doors, belonging to a narrow high house exactly like the house next to it, nobody seemed to inhabit the house or any of the others. It was the dead season, July 16th, and the whole street was deserted. However, before we got to the last step, a second door further in was opened; we were expected; there were faces peering out: Susana and Josefina in white dresses, and, much smaller, my mother wearing a cap and looking very grave. We kissed each other all round, and Susana cried. (We had forgotten to kiss Robert at the wharf.) Why did Susana cry? Was it mere excitement, nerves? Or was she already—she was twenty-one—secretly regretting Spain and her *beaux jours*? They took us into the dining room to show us the "beautiful view" from the back of the house—a great expanse of water, with a low line of nondescript sheds and wooden houses marking the opposite bank. It was Bostonian to show us the view first; but we noticed that this dining room was hung with many oil paintings, little Dutch or classic Italian landscapes, still life, and over the mantelpiece an old portrait: some Elizabethan worthy in a ruff and puffed sleeves, with a large ring on his fat forefinger. My father naturally had begun by examining these pictures, all copies, of course; and we learned that the Elizabethan gentleman was supposed to be Lord Burleigh, but that "Uncle Henry," whose pictures these had been, had bought it because he thought the personage looked like a Sturgis and might have been one of his ancestors. My father must have been amused at this, it was so typical of the Sturgises; but he never spoke of it. As for me, what interested me was to find the large sofa so soft when I sat on it. One might ride on the springs as if on horseback.

It was inevitably Susana who took me in tow and who began to teach me English. I learned some verses by rote, about a bird's nest, out of a brightly colored and highly moral book for young children. They ended, as I pronounced them, as follows:

> You mahsthnoth in play-ee
> Esteal the bords away-ee
> And grieve their mahther's breasth.

The moral of this was wasted on me—I was not a young child—and if I had had an impulse to steal any bird's nest or bird's eggs, or even to climb any tree, it would not have been these nursery rhymes that could have dissuaded me. But I had no such impulse, and no such opportunity, which made this moralizing, like all moralizing, ring hollow in my ears. The lady who said many years later that she envied me for not having a conscience, didn't altogether misread me.* Like my mother I have firmness of character; and I don't understand how a rational creature can be wrong in being or doing what he fundamentally wishes to be or do. He may make a mistake about it, or about the circumstances; or he may be imperfectly integrated, and tossed between contrary desires, not knowing his own nature or what he really wants. Experience and philosophy have taught me that perfect integrity is an ideal never fully realized, that nature is fluid and inwardly chaotic in the last resort, even in the most heroic soul; and I am ashamed and truly repentant if ever I find that I have been dazed and false to myself either in my conduct or in my opinions. In this sense I am not without a conscience; but I accept nobody's precepts traversing my moral freedom.

As to my pronunciation, it improved rapidly and unawares. I then had a good ear and a flexible tongue, and the fact that English was a foreign language to me positively helped me to learn it well and to speak it, for instance, much better than Susana or Robert, or most of the boys in my successive schools. For among our friends and my teachers there were some who spoke excellent English, traditionally or by careful chastening of the Yankee vernacular; and I could easily distinguish the better of my models from the worse. We were expressly taught pronunciation and declamation, and declamatory American speech, in the 1870's, though blatant and sometimes infected with the Calvinistic drawl, still was at bottom noble and pure. The irregularity of English sounds and their subtlety was an interesting challenge: far from irritating, it attracted me, and made me sensitive to its fine shades; so that even before I had heard an English voice or lived in England, my

* This incident is related, with variations, in the *Prologue* to *The Last Puritan.*

English was good. In 1887, Russell * once asked me to join him at his grandmother's, Lady Stanley of Alderley, a great and venerable personage; and after we had exchanged a few phrases, Lady Stanley said, "But how well you speak English!" That is a backhanded compliment that one ordinarily prefers not to hear, since it implies that one evidently speaks like a foreigner: but in this case, as I was considered a Spaniard, it was not rude; and I explained that I had been educated in Boston. "But you haven't an American accent," the lady insisted. I reminded her of the culture of Boston, and protested that all my English was American, as I had been but three days in London. "No," she admitted, "you haven't a *London* accent. You speak like Queen Victoria." Let this stand as early testimony to my English speech: I spoke like Queen Victoria.†

* The name *Russell* in these pages, unless otherwise indicated, designates John Francis Stanley, second Earl Russell. His brother Bertrand, who was also my friend, I venture to call "Bertie."

† At my nicest, perhaps, but not always. And didn't Queen Victoria have a German accent?

CHAPTER IX

NO. 302 BEACON STREET

THE house to which Robert had guided us, although the most commonplace of houses and meanly built for speculation, is perhaps worth describing. We passed the next nine years in it—all the later years of my boyhood; and its character and the life we led there are indelible not only in my memory but no doubt in my character and sentiment. I was unhappy there. At school nothing was imposed on me that I could complain of; there were no grinding tasks and no punishments; but until the last two or three years, when I formed close friendships and awoke to literature, it was all dead routine, and insufficient. A great void remained, which nothing at home could fill. The family was deeply disunited, and each member unhappy for a different reason. One of the boys at school, Davis, who had once come to lunch with us, said afterwards that we seemed to live as if in a boarding house. This was not true at bottom, or at first, because on our Spanish side we formed a true family; but life in America gradually dispersed our interests and our affections. I found my own center later, at Harvard: and then the bond with my mother's house, when Susana had returned to Spain and Robert was married, became pleasant and peaceful. Once or twice I spent a whole summer there, reading in the Public Library near by, and preparing my lectures. But that was no longer in Beacon Street; the scene was more retired, more modest, more suitable. There was no longer the pressure of poverty or of tiresome dissensions.

Our house was, at that time, one of the last on the waterside of Beacon Street, and there was still many a vacant lot east of it, where on passing in sharp wintry weather it was prudent to turn up one's coat collar against the icy blast from the river; as also, for the matter of that, at every cross-street. On the opposite side there were straggling groups of houses running further west along the Mill Dam, under which, at some points, the tide flowed in and out from the Back Bay, the shallow lagoon that originally extended to Boston Neck, turning the town almost into an island. The water in 1872 still came up to Dartmouth Street and to what is now Copley Square. Among the provisional features of this quarter were the frequent empty lots, ten or fifteen feet below the level of the street. These lots were usually enclosed by rough open fences, often broken down at the corners, from which a short cut could be made diagonally to the next street; and by this we school-boys were quick to profit, for a free run on rough ground amid weeds and heaps of rubbish. The architecture of these half-built streets was conventional and commercial; no house of more than five stories, no apartment houses, no fanciful architectural styles, only two or three churches, closed except at the hour for services on Sundays. To go to Mass we had to walk over the Dartmouth Street railway bridge and some distance beyond, into the South End. I liked the spire at the corner of Newbury and Berkeley Street, and often walked that way in order to see it. It looked to my eye, fed on copperplate views of English cathedrals, a bit of genuine Gothic: but the brick Italian Gothic introduced by Ruskin as well as Richardson's personal memories of Provence, left me quite cold, in spite of *The Stones of Venice*. They were indeed absurdly out of place, bastard, and theatrical.

Ours was one of two houses exactly alike; yet as they were only two, we could distinguish ours without looking at the number displayed in large figures on the semicircular glass panel over the front door: for ours was the house to the left, not the one to the right. The pair were a product of that "producer's economy," then beginning to prevail in America, which first creates articles and then attempts to create a demand for them; an economy that has flooded the country with breakfast foods, shaving soaps, poets,

and professors of philosophy. Our twin houses had been designed
to attract the buyer, who might sell his bargain again at a profit if
he didn't find it satisfactory; and this was precisely the ground on
which my mother was persuaded to buy her house, not expecting a
financial crisis and a sudden but prolonged disinclination on the
part of the consumer to buy anything that he didn't need. The
advantages in our house were in the first place social or snobbish,
that it was in Beacon Street and on the better or fashionable
waterside of that street; which also rendered every room initially
attractive, since it had either the sun if in the front, or the view if
in the rear. This view of a vast expanse of water reflecting the sky
was unmistakably impressive, especially when the summer sunset
lit up the scene, and darkness added to distance made the shabby
bank opposite inoffensive. Gorgeous these sunsets often were;
more gorgeous, good Bostonians believed, than any sunsets anywhere else in the world; and my limited experience does not belie
them. The illumination often had a kaleidoscopic quality, with
fiery reds and yellows; but at other hours the seasons and aerial
effects of the Charles River Basin were not remarkable. Moreover,
the grand attraction of the water view was marred by two counter-
effects discovered eventually by enthusiastic purchasers. One was
the immediate foreground, modified but not removed afterwards,
when the embankment was added. Under your nose was a mean
backyard, unpaved, with clothes or at least clotheslines stretched
across it; and mean plank fences divided it from other backyards
of the same description, with an occasional shed or stable to vary
the prospect. Under your nose too—and this was the second coun-
ter-effect—rose now and then the stench from mudflats and sewage
that the sluggish current of the Charles and the sluggish tides that
penetrated to the Basin did not avail to drain properly. However,
this was chiefly noticeable in summer, when Beacon Street people
were expected to be out of town; they made no loud complaints;
and the democracy in general was not yet aroused to the importance of town planning for its own sake. The age was still enam-
ored of *laissez-faire*; and its advantages were indeed undeniable.

For the Government it meant a minimum of work, and for the
public it meant a minimum of government.

Our white elephant offered attractions also for the investor; the
town was rapidly spreading in that direction, land-values were
sure to go up, and the house would become every year more central
and more desirable. Finally, it was a small house, with only two
rooms on each of the principal floors: comfortable and cosy, therefore, for a rich spinster or for an ambitious young married couple;
especially as with its reception room and large dining room on the
ground floor, and its front and back parlors upstairs, it lent itself
to entertaining on a moderate scale. That it had only two decent
bedrooms, one bathroom, and no backstairs, wouldn't matter with
a very small family.

But we happened to be a family of five, demanding five separate
rooms. Entertaining of any description was out of the question for
us, apart from the expense, since our mother didn't pay visits or
go anywhere, or wish for any society; and at that moment she possessed neither the objects nor the money necessary to furnish
decently those superfluous reception rooms. She therefore turned
the front parlor into a bedroom for herself, while my sisters occupied the two good rooms on the second floor, and Robert, the cook,
the housemaid and I had the four small cubicles in the mansard or
French roof. At least, this was the ultimate and normal arrangement; but when my father and I arrived, the family prejudice
against doubling up had to be overcome for the time being. Not,
however, in the case of my father and mother; for she resigned
the front parlor to him and moved to one of the rooms above, the
two girls being crowded into the other, while I was tucked, as a
waif new to the New World, not only into Robert's room but into
his bed, which happened incongruously to be a large double one.
My mother had taken on her furniture from previous tenants or
from "Aunt Lizzie"; and the double beds, not being wanted, had a
tendency to pass out of sight into the upper regions; one falling in
this way to Robert's lot. But this cohabitation with my elder
brother didn't last long; it was contrary to my mother's instinct and

habits; and soon a small bed was provided for me and I was moved
into the adjoining little room, as into my own castle.

The strip of land that our house occupied was nineteen feet
wide, and not far from ten times as long, since it stretched from
the edge of the public road over the "side-walk," broad and paved
with brick, which it was the tenant's duty to keep swept and rea-
sonably free from snow; over the grass plot in front of the house;
and behind the house over a long back-yard, and the alley outside
to the water's edge. The brick façade was meager and graceless;
my architectural fancy often conceived how easily those twin
houses might have been rendered symmetrical, homelike, and even
pleasing, in the Dutch manner, if the two doors had been placed
together in the middle, and if the steps, the little upper platform,
and the steps on either side leading down to the basement had
been combined into one picturesque design. The sash or guillotine
windows too might at least have retained the square panes of the
colonial period, instead of the hideous plate glass that was thought
an "improvement." But the builder was no artist; he made one
drawing for one cheap house, and for economy built two of them,
his capital or his courage not permitting him to build a dozen.

To this unsuitable residence our habits adapted themselves as
well as might be. The small room beside the front door became our
family sitting room. It was sunny and cosy; on cold evenings when
the furnace proved insufficient, it could be at once warmed and
ventilated by lighting the fire; and by day it afforded us the feminine Spanish entertainment of looking out of the window and
watching, a little below our own level, the stray passers-by. It was
here that I sat, close by the window, doing my fancy drawing and
reading, which occupied me much more than my school lessons.
We had one study-hour out of the five at the school in the morning, and that sufficed for most of my preparation; but I took my
Latin book, and one or two others home, where I could read them
aloud to myself, of course in my bedroom, and gather a rhetorical
impression, with little profit to my scholarship.

The back wall of our family sitting room was covered by a large bookcase with glass doors, which contained the eighth edition of the Encyclopaedia Britannica, Lane's *Arabian Nights*, and a lot of old books that nobody opened. But we had a few Spanish books, and could get others from the Boston Public Library. In this way I read Oliver Optic's stories for boys, doting on the seafaring and the oceanic geography; also Abbot's *Lives*, of which I remember *Alexander the Great* and *Mary, Queen of Scots*. We also had Motley's and Prescott's pseudo-Spanish histories; but I knew enough to spew them out of my mouth at the first tasting. The sectarian politics and moralizing of most historians made history an impossible study for me for many years; not ancient history, of course, nor Plutarch's Lives, which we had at school to read from at sight, and not Gibbon, when I came to read him; because although Gibbon's bias is obvious, it is entertaining, and by the time I came to him I was willing to laugh at absurdities whether in Church or State or in philosophic opinion, without feeling that ultimate truth was in the least affected by such accidents or by the derision of worldly wits.

During the first years Susana and Robert would read aloud to us in the evening, at first in Spanish: *Don Quixote* in its entirety (save the *lunares*)* and *El Servilón y el Liberalito* by the pious lady-novelist "Fernan Caballero." Then, because our interesting Spanish books were exhausted, or because Robert, especially, found English easier, they shifted to Shakespeare, and read *Julius Caesar* and *Romeo and Juliet*, of which I remember liking the first and thinking the second inexpressibly silly. There the practice died out. We had no more reading aloud, but Susana and I often read the same books separately. When I became fond of poetry, I tried to interest her in it, but failed. She liked nothing I showed her except Byron's *Don Juan*, because, she said, it was as good as prose.

The walls of this little sitting room were hung exclusively with engravings, most of which had adorned "Uncle Henry's" house. There were official large portraits of Napoleon the Third and the

* Facetious name for the interspersed Tales: literally, *moles*.

Empress Eugénie in their regalia, theatrically posed and very pompous: also an affecting scene in an English churchyard, full of yew and weeping willow, and showing a brave little boy and a sweet little girl, sitting and holding hands on the edge of a newly made grave, strewn with wild flowers; while above their heads, a large white angel in muslin, the spirit of their departed mother, spread her hands and her great wings over them in protection and blessing. To take away the taste of this, like a savory after a milk pudding, there hung near it a framed collection of *Poor Richard's Proverbs,* with quaint little eighteenth-century illustrations for each maxim. I learned most of them by heart, but can remember only *Early to bed and early to rise Makes a man healthy and wealthy and wise* and *Three removes are as bad as a fire.* I wished Franklin had said something crushingly true and materialistic about the Angel Mother and about Napoleon the Third's corsets and waxed mustache; but I was willing to nurse illusions about the Empress Eugénie. She had been the queen of fashion in her day, she was Spanish, and she might be said to look a little like Susana idealized.

The article in our Encyclopaedia on architecture, which I studied persistently, was an excellent corrective to Ruskin, to Ferguson's *History of Architecture,* and to the taste of my time. The illustrations were all plans, elevations, and sections; and the only styles treated were the classic and the "Italian." There were no perspective views. I was thus introduced to the art professionally; and the structural interest became as great for me as the picturesque. Yet as I was never to build anything except in fancy, and even if I had become an architect could never have built great English country seats like those depicted in my text, I turned all these technicalities to imaginative uses. Here were the magnificent houses in which the English nobility lived; I had only to supply the landscape, the costumes, and the characters—and vivid representations of all these were accessible to me—in order to complete the picture, and bring it to life. English high life, before I had seen anything of it—and I have never seen much, except at Oxford and Cambridge—at once established itself in my regard side by side with ancient and with Catholic life as one of the high lights of history. The notion of belittling any one of them—or of belittling any other civilization, because less known to me—never crossed my mind: and as one style of architecture does not prevent the others from being equally beautiful and proper in their time and place; so the whole mental and moral civilization that flourished with that style must be accepted as right and honorable in its day. This principle is applicable to religions and philosophies, in so far as they too are local and temporary; but in so far as the universe and human nature are constant, it is evident that a single system of science will serve to describe them, although the images and language will constantly differ in which that system is expressed. In the last resort, all mutations must help to fill out a single history of things, that doubtless never will be finished or written. There is no vacillation in the truth about vacillations; and in this sense philosophic insight, if humble and sane, is as perennial as its object.

In regard, however, to rival forms of art or civilization, I was directed from the beginning towards impartiality, which does not imply omnivorousness or confusion. All beauties are to be honored, but only one embraced.

CHAPTER X

THE LATIN SCHOOL

WHEN I search my memory for events and feelings belonging to my earlier boyhood in America, from the age of eight to sixteen, I find for the most part a blank. There are only stray images, like those of early childhood, with no sense of any consecutive interest, any affections or sorrows. And yet I know that my feelings in those years were intense, that I was solitary and unhappy, out of humor with everything that surrounded me, and attached only to a persistent dream-life, fed on books of fiction, on architecture and on religion. I was not precocious; I may have had more ability than the average boy, but it was lavished on boyish thoughts; and a certain backwardness, or unwilling acceptance of reality, characterizes my whole life and philosophy, not indeed as a maxim but as a sentiment.

Why have I forgotten all those years? The causes are no doubt physical, but the effects may be expressed in literary terms. The past cannot be re-enacted except in the language and with the contrasts imposed by the present. The feelings of children, in particular, although intense, are not ordinarily long-lived or deeply rooted. We cry desperately or we silently hate, for not being allowed to do this or to have that; but these objects are trifles. If we remember those occasions they would seem to us indifferent; we should be ashamed to confess those feelings, or we should laugh at them with superior airs: as if the things that now preoccupy us, if we outgrew them, could seem to us more momentous. Thus vast portions of the past—almost all our dreams, almost all our particular thoughts and conversations—become unrecoverable. Our accepted, organized, practically compulsory habits shut them out. But these habits themselves will change more or less with time and with circumstances. Even what we still think we remember will be remembered differently; so that a man's memory may almost become the art of continually varying and misrepresenting his past, according to his interests in the present. This, when it is not intentional or dishonest, involves no deception. Things truly wear those aspects to one another. A point of view and a special lighting are not distortions. They are conditions of vision, and spirit can see nothing not focused in some living eye.

Something like this was in Goethe's mind when he entitled his essay on his life *Fiction and Truth* or *Truth and Poetry*; not that any facts were to be reported inaccurately or invented, but that his mature imagination, in which those facts were pictured, could not but veil them in an atmosphere of serenity, dignity, and justice, utterly foreign to his original romantic experience. I am no Goethe; the atmosphere of my aging mind is not Olympian, and in retrospect it cannot help lending to my insignificant contacts with the world some flavors that Goethe's wisdom had washed out, though they were not absent from his younger days: I mean salt, pepper, and pity for mankind.

Of Miss Welchman's Kindergarten in Chestnut Street, my first school in Boston, I remember only that we had cards with holes pricked in them, and colored worsted that we were invited to pass through the holes, making designs to suit our own fancy. I suppose this was calculated to develop artistic originality, not to convince us how trivial that originality is, and how helpless without traditional models. I remember also that I used to walk home with another boy, not so old as I, but also much older than the other children; that there were banks of snow on both sides of the path; and that one day—this must have been in spring for there was a bush with red flowers in his grass plot—he said something very strange as he left me, and ran up the steps into his house. I reported what he had said to Susana, who pronounced it *pantheism*: perhaps it was that those red flowers were opening because God was awakening in them. This shows how far my English had got in that Kindergarten and how we lisped metaphysics there.

The Brimmer School, where I went during the next winter, 1873-1874, was the public grammar school of our city district, although more than a mile from our house, in the depths of the South End. I had to walk the whole level length of Beacon Street, cross the Common, and go some distance downhill in Tremont Street to Common Street, where the school was situated, looking like a police station. It was a poor boys' free school, the roughest I was ever in, where the rattan played an important part, although usually behind the scenes, and where there was an atmosphere of rowdiness and ill-will, requiring all sorts of minor punishments, such as standing in the corner or being detained after school. I don't know what lessens we had, except that there were oral spelling-matches, in which naturally I didn't shine. A word spelt aloud (as some Americans like to do facetiously, instead of pronouncing it) still puzzles me and leaves me dumb. Nevertheless, partly because I was older and bigger than most of the boys, I soon became "monitor," and had my little desk beside the teacher's, a woman, facing the whole class. This distinction was invidious, and there were attempts at chasing me or hooting at me when we got out of school. Only once did it come to blows; and inexpert as I was at fisticuffs, or rather wrestling, I was taller, and managed to hold my own, and make my nasty little enemy sneak away sullenly. And I was not friendless. There was another boy from the West End, Bob Upham by name, with whom I usually crossed the Common; this was the danger-zone, since in the streets there were policemen who understood these things and would stop hostilities. On that occasion Bob Upham behaved according to the strictest rules of honor, standing by me sympathetically, but without interfering, and he afterwards said that the other boy had "Very nearly got me." But I hadn't been at all hurt, and never have had another opportunity to try my hand at the manly art, in which no doubt I should have been a miserable failure.

By a happy chance it was possible to transfer me the next year to a much better school, the historic Latin School, where from the earliest times until my day at least, all well-educated Bostonians had been prepared for College. The School Committee in the City government had that year decided to try an experiment, and establish a preparatory course of two years, to precede the six traditional classes. The experiment was not long continued, but I profited by it, and passed eight full years in the Latin School, thus being more of a Latin School boy than almost anybody else. We were not lodged during those preliminary years in the regular Schoolhouse, but at first in Harrison Avenue, and later in Mason Street. Both these places, as well as the Schoolhouse in Bedford Street, were in a central quarter of the town. I still had to cross the Common, but now to West Street, whence it was but a step to those schoolhouses.

More than once in my life I have crossed a desert in all that regards myself, my thoughts, or my happiness; so that when I look back over those years, I see objects, I see public events, I see *persons and places*, but I don't see myself. My inner life, as I recall it, seems to be concentrated in a few oases, in a few halting-places, *Green Inns*, or Sanctuaries, where the busy traveller stopped to rest, to think, and to be himself. I say the *busy* traveller, because those long stretches of spiritual emptiness were filled with daily actions and feelings, later in my case often with giving lectures and writing books: yet all was done under some mechanical stimulus, the college bell, the desk, the pen, or the chapter planned: old thoughts and old words flowing out duly from the reservoir, until the college bell rang again, and the water was turned off. Of myself in those years I have no recollection; it is as if I hadn't existed, or only as a mechanical sensorium and active apparatus, doing its work under my name. Somnambulistic periods, let me call them; and such a period now seems to begin and to last for two-thirds of my Latin School days.

Certain detached images, with the crude spectral coloring of a child's picture-book, remain from this first somnambulist season. At the school in Harrison Avenue I can see the yellow wainscoting

of the schoolroom, and the yellow desks; and especially I can see
the converging leaden sides of the sink, where on one winter morning the teacher—now a man—sent me to thaw out my ears, frozen
stiff on the way to school. I was to bathe them in cold water;
there was sharp pain and subsequently enormous blisters; but the
accident never recurred, although I resolutely refused all scarves,
pads, or ridiculous cloth rosettes, such as the women recommended
to protect those asinine organs. I found that a little pressure,
applied at the right moment, at once brought the warm blood
coursing back, and prevented trouble. Cold, rain, and wind, unless
there were dust, never spoilt my pleasure in the open air when I
was young; on the contrary, I liked them.

I remember also my first Headmaster at the Latin School, Mr.
Gardner by name: a tall, gaunt figure in some sort of flowing
long coat—of course not a gown—with a diminutive head like the
knob of a mannikin. The insignificant occiput was enlarged, however, as if by a halo, by a great crop of dusty brown hair. Was it
a wig? That suspicion seemed to my mocking young mind curiously comic and exciting. What if it were a wig and should fall
off? What if we hung a hook on an invisible wire over the door, to
catch it as he sailed out? One day on his rounds of inspection the
Headmaster found us having our French lesson. A headmaster
has to pretend to know everything, and the pretense soon becomes
a conviction. Mr. Gardner at once took over the duty of teaching
us his super-French. "The French word *bonne*," he said, "is pronounced in Paris—I have been in Paris myself—exactly as the English word *bun*." Now, I had heard a good deal of French out of
school. There had been the French *bonne* Justine, the Alsatian
tutor who loved *avec rage*, and the Catholic families in Boston
who chatted in French together. And hadn't I inherited from my
sisters *La Jeune Abeille du Parnasse Français* and couldn't I say by
heart:

> *Et ma plus belle couronne*
> *De lilas*
> *Sera à toi, ma bonne,*
> *Si tu me dis où Dieu n'est pas?*

If *bonne* sounds exactly like bun, would Mr. Gardner maintain that *couronne*, save for that first letter, sounds exactly like *you run?* I was sure that it was as ridiculous to call a *bonne* a bun as to call a bun a *bonne*. But apparently headmasters were like that; and I kept my phonetic science to myself with the immense satisfaction of feeling that I knew better than my teacher.

I may add that at that time our French master was not a Frenchman, but a Yankee farmer named Mr. Capen, whom we called Old Cudjo, and who had a physiological method of acquiring a Parisian accent without needing to accompany the Headmaster to Paris. He would open his mouth wide, like the hippopotamus at the Zoo, and would insert a pencil, to point out exactly what parts of the tongue, lips, palate or larynx we should contract or relax in order to emit the pure French sounds of *u, an, en, in, un,* and *on.* Nobody laughed. I think the boys were rather impressed for the moment by the depth of Mr. Capen's science, and the hopelessness of profiting by it. He was not a man to be trifled with. He had a most thunderous way of playing what he called Voluntaries on the piano; and rumor had it that he had stolen a march, under a heavy handicap of years, on his own son, by marrying the girl his son was engaged to.

Scraps of rude, quaint, grotesque humanity: bits of that Dickensian bohemia still surviving in my day in certain old-fashioned places, of which I shall have occasion to speak again. But the image that for me sets the key to them all appeared when we moved to the Bedford Street schoolhouse. It seemed a vast, rattling old shell of a building, bare, shabby, and forlorn to the point of squalor; not exactly dirty, but worn, shaky, and stained deeply in every part by time, weather, and merciless usage. The dingy red brick—and everything in that world was dingy red brick—had none of that plastic irregularity, those soft pink lights and mossy patina that make some old brick walls so beautiful: here all the surfaces remained stark and unyielding, thin and sharp, like impoverished old maids. This house was too modern to be as solid as the Hollis and Stoughton Halls that I afterwards lived in at Harvard; it had been built in a hurry, and not to last long. The windows were much larger, but blank and somber; their cold, glassy expanse with its slender divisions looked comfortless and insecure. When up three or four worn granite steps you entered the door, the interior seemed musty and ill-lighted, but spacious, even mysterious. Each room had four great windows, but the street and the courts at the side and rear were narrow, and overshadowed by warehouses or office-buildings. No blackboard was black; all were indelibly clouded with ingrained layers of old chalk; the more you rubbed it out, the more you rubbed it in. Every desk was stained with generations of ink-spots, cut deeply with initials and scratched drawings. What idle thoughts had been wandering for years through all those empty heads in all those tedious school hours! In the best schools, almost all schooltime is wasted. Now and then something is learned that sticks fast; for the rest the boys are merely given time to grow and are kept from too much mischief.

A ramshackle wooden staircase wound up through the heart of the building to the fourth story, where the Hall was; and down those steep and dangerous curves the avalanche of nail-hoofed boys would come thundering, forty or eighty or two hundred together. However short their legs might be, it was simpler and safer, if not altogether inevitable, to rush down spontaneously with the herd rather than to hold back and be pushed or fall out, or be tramped upon or deserted.

And the teachers, though it is not possible for me now to distinguish them all in memory, were surely not out of keeping with their surroundings: disappointed, shabby-genteel, picturesque old Yankees, with a little bitter humor breaking through their constitutional fatigue. I daresay that for them as for me, and for all the boys who were at all sensitive, the school was a familiar symbol of fatality. They hadn't chosen it, they hadn't wanted it, they didn't particularly like it; they knew no reason why it should be the sort of school it was: but there it stood, there they somehow found themselves entangled; and there was nothing else practicable but to go on there, doing what was expected and imposed upon them. You may say that for the teachers at least, in that age of individual initiative and open careers, a thousand alternatives were, or had been, possible; and you may say that they could not have been altogether insensible of their high vocation and the high vocation of their country to create gradually and securely a better world, a world free from superstition, from needless hatreds, from unjust inequalities, and from devastating misery. Yes: but all that was negative; it consisted of things to be got rid of and avoided, and in America the more obvious of them had actually been escaped. Officially, especially now that slavery had been abolished, everything was all right. Everybody was free. Everybody was at work. Almost everybody could be well educated. Almost everybody was married. Therefore almost everybody was, or ought to be, perfectly happy. But were the teachers at the Latin School, perhaps the best of American schools, happy? Or were the boys? Ah, perhaps we should not ask whether they were happy, for they were not rich, but whether they were not enthusiastically conscious of a great work, an endless glorious struggle and perpetual victory, set before them in the world. And I reply, not for myself, since I don't count, being an alien, but in their name, that they decidedly were conscious of no such thing. They had heard of it; but in their daily lives they were conscious only of hard facts, meagerness, routine, petty commitments, and ideals too distant and vague to be worth mentioning.

Those teachers were stray individuals; they had not yet been standardized by educational departments and pedagogy. Some were like village schoolmasters or drudges; elderly men, like Mr. Capen, with crotchets, but good teachers, knowing their particular book and knowing how to keep order, and neither lax nor cruel. Others, especially Mr. Fiske, afterwards headmaster, and Mr. Groce, were younger, with a more modern education. They might have been college professors; they loved their subjects, Greek and English, and allowed them to color their minds out of school hours. In a word, they were *cultivated* men. I was an unprofitable though not unappreciative pupil to Mr. Fiske, because I didn't learn my Greek properly. That was not his fault. If I could have had him for a private tutor I should have become a good Grecian: it would have added immensely to my life and to my philosophy. But I was only one of forty; I was expected to study dryly, mechanically, without the side-lights and the stimulus of non-verbal interest attached to the words. In Latin, I could supply these side-lights and non-verbal interests out of my own store. Latin was the language of the Church, it was old Spanish. The roots were all my roots. But Greek roots were more often foreign and at first unmeaning; they had to be learned by hammering, to which my indolence was not inclined. And there was another difficulty. My apprehension of words is auricular; I must *hear* what I read. I knew, with small variations, what was the sound of Latin. I had heard it all my life; slovenly and corrupt as the Spanish pronunciation of it may be, at least it is something traditional. But what of Greek pronunciation? How should Homer sound? How should Sophocles? How should Xenophon or Plato? The artificial German Greek that we were taught—without even a proper *o*—was impossible. I tried many years later, when I was in Greece, to learn a little of the modern language, in hopes that it might react on my sense for the ancient texts and make me feel at home in them: but the time was too short, my opportunities limited, and I was too old to be quick in such a matter.

Even as it was, however, I learned a little Greek at School after my fashion, and one day surprised Mr. Fiske by reciting a long speech out of *Œdipus Tyrannus* for my ordinary declamation. He couldn't believe his ears, and afterwards privately congratulated me on my pronunciation of the *o*'s. But that didn't make me master of the Greek vocabulary or the Greek inflections. I didn't *study* enough. I learned and remembered well what I could learn from Mr. Fiske without studying. He was an exceedingly nervous, shy man; evidently suffered at having to address any one, or having to find words in which to express his feelings. His whole body would become tense, he would stand almost on tiptoe, with two or three fingers in the side pocket of his trousers, and the other two or three moving outside, as if reaching for the next word.

These extreme mannerisms occasioned no ridicule: the boys all saw that there was a clear mind and a goodwill behind them; and Mr. Fiske was universally liked and admired. This, although his language was as contorted as his gestures. He always seemed to be translating literally and laboriously from the Greek or the German. When he wished to fix in our minds the meaning of a Greek word he would say, for instance: "χᾰρά̆δρα, a ravine, from which our word *character*, the deeply graven result of long-continued habit." Or "κατᾰρρέω, to flow down, whence our word *catarrh*, copious down-flowings from the upper regions of the head." We didn't laugh, and we remembered.

Very different was dapper Mr. Groce, our teacher of English composition and literature, a little plump man, with a keen, dry, cheerful, yet irritable disposition, a sparkling bird-like eye, and a little black mustache and diminutive chin-beard. I suspect that he was too intelligent to put up patiently with all the conventions. Had he not been a public-school teacher, dependent on the democratic hypocrisies of a government committee, he might have said unconventional things. This inner rebellion kept him from being sentimental, moralistic, or religious in respect to poetry; yet he *understood* perfectly the penumbra of emotion that good and bad poetry alike may drag after them in an untrained mind. He knew how to rescue the structural and rational beauties of a poem from that bog of private feeling. To me this was a timely lesson, for it was precisely sadness and religiosity and grandiloquence that first attracted me in poetry; and perhaps I owe to Mr. Groce the beginnings of a capacity to distinguish the musical and expressive charm of poetry from its moral appeal. At any rate, at sixteen, I composed my first longish poem, in Spenser's measure, after *Childe Harold* and *Adonais*, full of pessimistic, languid, Byronic sentiments, describing the various kinds of superiority that Night has over Day. It got the prize.

That year I won several other prizes, and began to be a personage in my own estimation, because other people, in my little world, began to take notice of me. At home I had never been petted or praised, and my conceit, which was rather disdain for other things than claims for myself, had had only itself to feed upon. Being noticed had a good effect on me in awakening my sympathy in return without, however, either establishing or much modifying my good opinion of myself. Neither praise nor blame has ever done so. On the contrary, if people praise me I almost always feel that they praise me for the wrong things, for things which they impute to me out of their preconceptions, and which are not in me; and the blame often, though not always, has the same source. Yet blame is apt to be more keen-scented than praise; praise is often silly; but blame, though it may be baseless objectively, probably indicates a true perception of divergence from the critic's standards: so that relatively to the critic, it is seldom mistaken.

I have mentioned declamation: that was another stimulus to vanity. Inwardly it was one more dramatic indulgence, one more occasion for fantastically playing a part, and·dreaming awake; as I did in making plans of vast palaces and imaginary islands, where I should one day be monarch, like Sancho Panza; and this slides into the sphere of my youthful religiosity, of which more presently. But, socially considered, declamation was an effort *de se faire valoir*, to make oneself count, to gain a momentary and fictitious ascendency over others. Momentary and fictitious, because our declamation was pure oratory. It had nothing of that political timeliness which characterizes young people's debates in England. With us, the subject matter was legendary, the language learned by rote, stilted and inflated, the thought platitudinous. Apart from the training in mere *elocution* (as indeed it was called) it was practice in feigning, in working up a verbal enthusiasm for any cause, and seeming to prophesy any event. Very useful, no doubt, for future lawyers, politicians, or clergymen—training for that reversible sophistry and propaganda that intoxicates the demagogue and misleads the people.

That prize-day in June, 1880, in the old Boston Music Hall, marked my emergence into public notice. It abolished, or seemed to abolish, my shyness and love of solitude. I could now face any public and speak before it; and this assurance never forsook me afterwards, except when sometimes, in my unwritten lectures or speeches, I found myself out of my element, had nothing to say, or was weary of saying it. In reality I was always out of my element in teaching and in society, and was saying something forced. The dramatic practice of accepting a brief, or developing an argument, helped me for a time. I could be sincere and spontaneous in the logic of my theme, even if the ultimate issue were unreal or problematical; and in reviewing the history of philosophy this critical honesty is enough, and supplies the information and the dialectical training that are officially required. Nevertheless, this was not preaching a gospel. It did not come from the heart. It left the pupil unguided and morally empty, and in the end the teacher felt himself a drudge. My shyness came back in what Hegelians would call a higher form: I was no longer timid or without resource, but rebellious against being roped in and made to play some vulgar trick in a circus. My love of solitude reasserted itself, not that I feared the world, but that I claimed my liberty and my *Lebensraum* beyond it. In solitude it is possible to love mankind; in the world, for one who knows the world, there can be nothing but secret or open war. For those who love war the world is an excellent field, but I am a born cleric or poet. I must see both sides and take neither, in order, ideally, to embrace both, to sing both, and love the different forms that the good and the beautiful wear to different creatures. This comprehensiveness in sympathy by no means implies that good and evil are indistinguishable or dubious. Nature sets definite standards for every living being: the good and the beautiful could not exist otherwise; and the failure or lapse of natural perfection in each is an irreparable evil. But it is, in every case, a ground of sorrow to the spirit, not of rage; for such failure or lapse is fated and involuntary. This sorrow in my case, however, has always been mitigated by the gift of laughter. Laughter helped me both to perceive those defects and to put up with them.

Between the laughing and the weeping philosopher there is no opposition: *the same facts* that make one laugh make one weep. No whole-hearted man, no sane art, can be limited to either mood. In me this combination seems to be readier and more pervasive than in most people. I laugh a great deal, laugh too much, my friends tell me; and those who don't understand me think that this merriment contradicts my disillusioned philosophy. *They*, apparently, would never laugh if they admitted that life is a dream, that men are animated automata, and that the forms of good and beautiful are as various and evanescent as the natural harmonies that produce them. They think they would collapse or turn to stone, or despair and commit suicide. But probably they would do no such thing: they would adapt themselves to the reality, and laugh. They might even feel a new zest in living, join in some bold adventure, become heroes, and think it glorious to die with a smile for the love of something beautiful. They do not perceive that this is exactly what national leaders and religious martyrs have always done, except that their warm imagination has probably deceived them about the material effects of what they were doing.

My lachrymose prize poem about the beauties of darkness was not my only effusion. The habit of scribbling mocking epigrams has accompanied me through life and invaded the margins of my most serious authors. Mockery is the first puerile form of wit, playing with surfaces without sympathy: I abounded in it. During the winter of 1880–1881 our class, then the second class, formed a society to meet once a week in the evening and have a debate. We hired a bare room in Tremont Street, opposite the Common, with a few benches or chairs in it; some one would propose a resolution or advance an opinion, and the discussion would follow. When my turn came, I read a little satire on all our teachers, in verse, saying very much what I have said about them above; only that my account was more complete, included them all, and treated them less kindly. It had a great success, and the boys wanted to have it printed. Printed it was, but not as it originally stood. "Holy Moses," for instance, which was the nickname current for our headmaster, Moses Merrill, was changed to the less irreverent and more exact phrase: "lordly Moses," and many other things were modified. Then the whole was enveloped in a tirade, of a sentimental sort, about the Bedford Street Schoolhouse, which was about to be abandoned for a new building in the South End. A lot of copies were printed, perhaps two or three hundred; and on the day of our Farewell Public Declamation in the Hall, the Headmaster somehow got wind of its existence, and said, "We hear that one of the boys has written a poem about leaving this old Schoolhouse: will he get up and read it." I had a copy in my pocket: I got up, and read the longish sentimental part and then sat down again, leaving out the personalities. For the moment all was well; but other boys and some outsiders got copies; and the disrespectful gibes at the teachers became public under their noses.

It was a day or two before Christmas, and the School was not to meet again for ten days or more: however, after consulting with the family at home, I went to see the Headmaster at his own house, and explained how everything had happened. He wasn't severe; I had been really very complimentary to him, and had come spontaneously to apologize. But he said I had better write to the various teachers, explaining that I had only intended the thing as a private joke, without any thought that it would become public; and that I must particularly apologize to Mr. Chadwick, whom I had spoken of unkindly, and who felt the blow. When School met again, Mr. Merrill made us a long speech; but nothing more happened, and official sentiment towards me was not unfavorably affected. This appeared at the opening of the next term. My class had to elect the Lieutenant Colonel of the Boston School Regiment, the Colonel that year coming from the English High School; and by a majority of one vote they elected Dick Smith, and then me unanimously for Major of our Battalion. But the Headmaster reversed the order, and appointed me Lieutenant Colonel and Dick Smith Major, without giving reasons, at which legal but arbitrary exhibition of favoritism on the Headmaster's part Dick Smith's father took him out of the School; and I became both

Lieutenant Colonel and Major, both offices being almost sine-cures.

These incidents established me during my last year as, in a sense, the leading boy in my school, far as I was from being the head of my class: yet in my irregular way I was not bad at my studies, and got six honorable mentions in my Harvard entrance examinations. This capacity of mine to pass examinations and to win prizes was doubtless what had caused Mr. Merrill to prefer me to Dick Smith for the head of the School Battalion; because Dick Smith was a clean manly boy and a gentleman, but not an intellectual luminary. This sporadic brilliancy of mine seemed to render me a better representative of the School as a whole—a surprising and only momentary phenomenon. In reality I remained there, as I remained later at Harvard for twenty-five years, a stranger at heart; and all the false appearances to the contrary would not have misled anybody (as they did not mislead President Eliot and the intelligent public at Harvard) if *athletics* had been important at that time in the School. Now, although there was, I believe, a baseball team, it was an obscure unofficial affair; else my complete uselessness, either as a performer or as manager in such sports, would have at once set me down for a stray individual of no importance to the life of the place. Not that I had then, or ever, any *ideal* hostility to sport or to polite society or even to politics or trade. As customs, as institutions, as historical dramas, these things interest and please me immensely and excite my imagination to sympathy with this form of them or antipathy to that other form. But I can truly live only in the reaction of the mind upon them in religion, poetry, history, and friendship. If I take a practical part, it is only by putting on a domino for the carnival. I am capable of that impulse, I can feel the fun and the intoxication of it; but the louder the rout the greater the frivolity, and the more complete the relief of stripping off the motley, washing away the paint, and returning to solitude, to silence, and to sincerity.

CHAPTER XI

THE CHURCH OF THE IMMACULATE CONCEPTION

W HEN I began, in this small way, to play a part in the
world and to be absorbed in it, was I awaking from
my childish daydreams—my imaginary architecture
and geography and my imaginary religion—and entering into real life? Or was I being seduced and distracted from my
natural vocation, and caught in the vortex of a foolish dance where
I could neither shine as a reveller nor find satisfaction as a mind?

Now when at an advanced age I look back upon my whole
career, I think I can reply to this question. At bottom there was
no real change, no awakening and no apostasy. There was only a
change in the subject matter on which my fancy worked. I had
new materials for my dreams, and other terms in which to express
my secret aspiration. Instead of being an ineffectual poet I became, at intervals, a mediocre player: in both directions I was
simply the artist. There was ultimately no material issue, in either
case: it all inevitably ended in nothing. But in both cases there
was a passing music of ideas, a dramatic vision, a theme for dialectical insight and laughter; and to decipher that theme, that
vision, and that music was my only possible life.

This is a book of memoirs, not of philosophical argument, and I
have no wish to browbeat the reader into accepting my theory of
myself or of anything else. Let me return at once to my narrative
and let him judge the facts for himself.

In the Boston of my boyhood there were two churches served
by the Jesuits. The more modest one was a parish church for the
German-speaking population, in which the Jesuits were mission-

aries under the direct authority of the Archbishop. Here I used to go sometimes to an early Mass on Sundays, always alone. Mass was said in the basement, low, dark, flat-roofed, and perfectly bare, except for the altar and the Stations of the Cross hung around the walls. But it was filled with a devout, decent crowd, chiefly men; and they sang in unison several German hymns, simply, gladly, and unaffectedly, yet rather musically as if they were singing glees. I thought that here must be the origin of the Protestant practice of psalm-singing: they had knocked off most of the Mass, but kept the popular German accompaniment of a general chorus, as in the Greek tragedies. Yet what a difference between these Catholic effusions, which were not substitutes for the ritual but a private and spontaneous participation in it, and the perfunctory, inaudible pretense at keeping up with the paid quartet that was really performing; where the music was not good enough to be listened to for a concert, and the words too crude and obsoletely doctrinal to express anybody's feelings—at least not in those Unitarian churches which, at that time, I was being taken to against my will. It was in order to find myself for a moment in a religious atmosphere that I got up before dawn on those winter mornings, and took that double walk at a great pace, perhaps over snow, in any case through deserted streets in biting weather. But I liked the communal spirit of those people, devout and unspoiled; I liked their singing, without myself understanding the words; and though the priest turned round after the Gospel and said something in German, it was not a sermon, only a few announcements or admonitions for the coming week; and the strange language lifted me out of time and place, into the universal fold of all pilgrim spirits. I also liked the long double walk, with its slight tang of hardship, I who never had real hardships to bear: and breakfast afterwards seemed better than usual. Walking has always been my sole form of exercise; and then I never went out merely to walk, but only to get to and from school; and here was the same kind of errand, only more voluntary, done with a more concentrated mind.

If later I was taken to some Unitarian Church, it didn't matter. It seemed a little ridiculous, all those good people in their Sunday clothes, so demure, so conscious of one another, not needing in the least to pray or to be prayed for, nor inclined to sing, but liking to flock together once a week, as people in Spain flock to the *paseo*, and glad to hear a sermon like the leading article in some superior newspaper, calculated to confirm the conviction already in them that their bourgeois virtues were quite sufficient and that perhaps in time poor backward races and nations might be led to acquire them.

The other church served by the Jesuits was entirely their own, being attached to their Boston College, and built and managed according to their taste and traditions. It was not a parish, but attracted unattached or inquiring people from any quarter. Jesuit policy did not forbid certain attractions not found in poorer churches. The edifice was not—as often happened in those days— a Protestant meetinghouse turned into a church; nor did it attempt to rival the picturesqueness of an ivy-clad village church in a shady churchyard. It was frankly urban and rectangular, like a hall or a temple without columns, and without tower or belfry. The custom of the country demanded that the interior should be filled with pews, so that there could be no freedom of movement and no true vistas; yet the double row of high Ionic columns was imposing, and there were square vaults over the aisles, and a tunnel vault in the nave, without a clerestory. The whole was plaster or stucco, in my time painted white: nevertheless the ground-glass windows subdued the light, and turned this interior, for the benevolent eye, into an inoffensive harmony in grays. There was florid music: organist and choir attempted the most pretentious masses, Bach, Mozart, Schubert, Verdi, and on occasions threw in Rossini's *Stabat Mater* and Gounod's *Ave Maria*. On the great feasts we even had an orchestra in addition. I liked this rococo music, and I still remember and sing it to myself with pleasure. It *transports*; the means may be at times inferior, but the end is attained. The end is to escape to another world, to live freely for a while in a medium made by us and fit for us to live in. Not all that is artificial is good, because the artifice may escape control and become stupid or even vicious; and much that is natural is good, because we are vitalized by it; but only the artificial can be good expressly.

The adjoining College naturally required a good many teachers, so that a number of priests were available for preaching in the church, some of them, however, not quite masters of the English language. One pale Italian in particular was admirable on difficult points in the religious life, as for instance on the words: *My God, my God, why hast thou abandoned me?* The spiritual aspiration to abandon oneself here corrected the Jesuit's tendency to view salvation as a matter of legal give and take between God and man. We couldn't be saved I know if we didn't exist, and in that sense we must coöperate in our salvation; but the point is to be saved from ourselves morally while physically retaining our personal being and limitations. Tradition, since Plato, calls this method *mortification*; and the secret of it sometimes pierces through the machinery of religious ethics. More frequent and noted preachers, however, were the two successive heads of the College, Father Fulton and Father O'Connor. The latter was a young and very oratorical Irishman, eloquently proclaiming Catholic Truth against all heresies. It is not difficult for a man with a ready tongue and a good memory to pluck moral and theological arguments from the patristic garden. St. Augustine alone will furnish flowers for a thousand good sermons. And this practice of repeating ancient authorities cannot be taxed with laziness. More diligence and more conscience are shown in ransacking the Fathers than in ventilating one's casual notions; and Catholic preachers at least are expected to preach the Gospel, and not some message new to the age. But the Gospel arouses different feelings and meets with different opposition in successive times; and a mind sensitive to these influences can therefore preach it more usefully than if he merely echoed the words of the Gospel itself. Father

Fulton, of whom I have said something as confessor to my sister, was not eloquent; he was not warm; but he could explore the dialectics not only of doctrine but of sentiment; and it was in unravelling the complexities of our divided allegiance that I found him an instructive guide.

There was a feature in the interior of this church that, in my empty head, led to much architectural theorizing. The sanctuary, which was square, had an ordinary double vault lower than that of the nave; so that we were forever faced by two round arches of the same span, one of them two or three yards above the other. The space between them was awkward, and the architect had done nothing to disguise or relieve it. I knew very well that in basilicas the apse is often much lower than the nave; but there the semi-circular apse was not a sanctuary meant to house the altar, but only the head of the choir, round which the clergy had their stalls, with the bishop's or superior's throne in the middle; while the altar stood out in front, under an architectural canopy, and was approached by the priest from his end, looking eastward over the altar, and over the people beyond it; for in the original Christian basilicas in Rome the entrance is at the east end. Moreover, the arch of that apse is not surmounted by another arch, since the nave has a wooden roof, either showing the rafters or closed with a flat ceiling. In either case the arch has a rectangular setting, like a triumphal arch, and the triangles in the corners are adorned with mosaics or frescoes, to which they are admirably adapted. But in chapels or later churches, where the altar is set against a wall, or, as in the Cathedrals, stands at the extreme *chevet* or east end of the choir, the vault is never lower over the chancel or choir than over the nave: on the contrary, it might well be higher—as for instance it is at Le Mans and at Carcassone—with excellent effect and significance; while at St. Peter's the altar with its immense *baldacchino* stands under the vault of Michelangelo's dome, five hundred feet high.

Our local architect, then, whatever his model or reasons, was

guilty of a solecism in designing those two equal, closely super-
posed arches, and that chancel vault lower than his nave: but I
was ready to forgive him in view of the favorable atmosphere that
his interior, as a whole, offered me for meditation. The reredos
contained three paintings, and the side altars in the aisles two
more, all warm in color and acceptable in design—very likely copies
of late Italian masters; their white plaster setting, with grouped
columns, was graceful and pleasantly touched with gold in the
moldings and ornaments; and above was a sensational baroque,
curved pediment, broken in two, with two ecstatic saints kneeling
perilously, but divinely confident, on the inclined upper surface
of the two separated fragments. It was symmetrical, it was decorative, it was full of motion and enthusiasm. It warned me that
there are more things going on in oneself than are dreamt of in
our too economical philosophy.

When you looked, however, a little higher up, you saw things
depicted as going on in heaven which, whatever may go on there,
should not be so depicted on earth. Art, like mind, has its own
categories and grammar for symbolizing realities beyond it, and
makes nonsense if it violates them. Our language cannot control
its objects, yet could not even indicate them if it destroyed itself.
What you saw above the reredos, filling the whole space under
the vault, was a painting, a fresco, I suppose, of the Assumption.
The figure of the Virgin Mary was at the very top, as in Titian's
Assumption, foreshortened, and clothed in the same dark red and
dark blue; a heavy, materialistic, unworthy conception of the subject. Out of place here, too, since this church was not dedicated to
the Assumption, but to the Immaculate Conception. The Assumption is an alleged event; it is conceived to have occurred on earth,
at a particular place and time; so that a treatment like Titian's,
with the foreshortening, and with the drama of wonder and surprise in the crowd of witnesses, is not unjustified; and there the
artist had a superabundant technique to exhibit in painting a great
variety of gesticulating figures, a landscape, and an Italian sky.
The Immaculate Conception, on the contrary, is a theological

idea,* the notion of a human soul created perfect and spotless, with a body subject, like a flower, to the direct, unconscious, unimpeded magic of that soul. Why, then, not have filled this space with the accepted representation of the Immaculate Conception, after the manner of Murillo? An ethereal, girlish, angelic Madonna, clothed with the sun (the image is based on a passage in the Apocalypse), with the moon at her feet and the stars encircling her head, would have filled the center of the composition. Her garments would have been, in texture and color, like the sky and the light clouds; she would have floated as the sun in mid-heaven, and everything would have been tinted and softened by the radiance of a pervasive yet hidden light that she seemed to shed. In that heaven, any number of seraphs and cherubs that the artist could paint or could draw might have flown or soared as in their native element.

Cherubs? Seraphs? No: half a dozen large young women in modest evening gowns (except that their feet were bare), one pure yellow, one sea-green, another terracotta, with correspondingly large wings, like the Angel Mother in our engraving at home, all yearned aesthetically upward: and the central ones seemed anxious

* The non-theological reader must not be misled into thinking that the "Immaculate Conception" refers to the *Incarnation of Christ* without an earthly father, or to what Anglicans improperly call the "Virgin Birth." There is indeed a Catholic doctrine of the *perpetual* virginity of Mary, the *birth* of Christ being no less miraculous than his incarnation; a doctrine that my first Spanish catechism beautifully expressed by saying that the Child Jesus passed from his mother's bosom into her arms as a ray of sunlight passes through a pane of glass, without breaking or staining it. This might properly be called the "Virgin Birth," and is entirely distinct from the doctrine of the Incarnation contained in the Creed, and a later refinement upon it. The doctrine of the "Immaculate Conception," on the other hand, asserts that *the soul of the Virgin Mary herself* (though she was begotten and born like other people, except that her parents were unusually old) *did not inherit original sin from Adam,* being exempted by prevenient grace, in view of the redemption to be worked by her Son. As an inscription on her monument in the Piazza di Spagna in Rome has it, *Sanctificavit tabernaculum suum Altissimus,* the Most High had sanctified his tabernacle.

to hold up the Madonna, as if she were not levitating of her own accord. I don't know what models, if any, this composition may have followed, but it didn't please me. I was glad when on feast days a canopy with red and white hangings was set up to hide it, and to turn the altar, with all its lights and flowers, into a sort of throne. Regal and priestly grandeur, even dimly suggested, has always impressed me. In Egypt, in those colossal temples and profound sanctuaries, I envied the priests that once officiated there, faithful to immemorial traditions, and learned in mysterious conventions. It was somnambulism, but in a noble setting, healthful, protective, capable of perpetuating itself for generations, and of rendering human life humanly better rather than worse.

If ever I complained to my sister of those female angels and wondered how learned Jesuits could countenance such a lapse, she would say that angels were sexless, so that if artists might represent them as young men or boys or infants, why not, on occasion, as women? Theologically this was correct; angels are sexless, since they have no bodies, and according to St. Thomas, are each the only member of its species; so that in them any complications connected with reproduction are excluded *a priori*.* But theology—especially in regard to angels!—is something secondary: vision, inspiration, tradition, and literature come first. A Christian painter is not called upon to invent some form in which pure spirits might appear, nor is he likely to have seen them himself. What concerns him is not what they may be in heaven, but what they look like when visiting the earth. Now imagination has its specific hereditary idioms, just as the senses have; and if the artist be a Christian working for a Christian people he will be spontaneously borne along by the same tradition that has inspired the doctrines and visions of his Church; otherwise he would falsify the poetic character and tone of the themes that he illustrates. This will not deprive him of originality; he can be stylistic, hieratic, or picturesque,

* I refer to Catholic theology. In the *Jewish Book of the Jubilees*, assigned to about 100 B.C., we are informed that the angels in heaven are circumcised.

according to his taste or training: but he will cease to be a religious artist if he contradicts the revelation he has inherited.

Now in what form have angels appeared? The angels that came to Abraham's tent and the one that wrestled with Jacob were certainly men; and in the Old Testament it often seems that angels were strangers or travellers that gave some warning or left a mysterious impression and only afterwards were recognized to have been "angels of the Lord," or vehicles for a divine oracle. The Angel that appeared to Mary is understood to have been the archangel Gabriel, certainly no less masculine, if less military, than his companion Michael; so much so that his figure, like that of St. Joseph, was avoided in early Christian art, until the idiom of faith had become native to the popular imagination, and it could be left free without danger of becoming equivocal. Then those innumerable charming Annunciations could be designed, where Gabriel is a royal page, as deferential as he is smiling and beautifully attired, gracefully bending the knee, gracefully delivering his embarrassing but important message, and ready gracefully to retire, perfectly pleased with himself and with his performance.* Or if direct and strangely crude evidence on the sex of angels were required it might be found in Genesis, where the angels sent to warn Lot cause a most embarrassing commotion in Sodom. Graver ambassadors are the two "young men" in white raiment seen sitting by the empty tomb on Easter morning, who speak mystically of not looking for the living among the dead. It is as if the soldiers on guard had turned, in the Evangelist's fancy, into young priests. They come to bring tidings of martyrdom and of a transfigured life. Sex is not absent here, as it is not absent in the monk or the mystic; it is expressly mentioned; yet it appears only in the firmness with which it is suppressed.

---

* *Cf.* Saint Bernard in Dante:

> *Baldezza e leggiadria,*
> *Quanta èsser può in angelo ed in alma,*
> *Tutta è in lui: e sì volém che sia.*
> Par. XXXII, 109–111.

Such was the mechanism of logic or poetry in mere ideas that occupied my mind when a boy: not expressed, of course, as I now express it, but intensely felt by me to determine the only right or beautiful order possible for the universe. Existence could not be right or beautiful under other conditions. But was existence beautiful or right? Quite the opposite; according to my youthful heart, existence was profoundly ugly and wrong. The beautiful remained imaginary. My daily life had nothing to do with it. Reality meant a dull routine of getting up in the morning, walking to school, sitting there for five hours, walking home, eating not very palatable food, and going to bed again. I was bored. I hadn't enough to do or enough to learn. At school there was nothing but lessons; and lessons in a large class, with indulgent teachers and slack standards of accuracy, meant perpetual idleness. I could have learned twice as much in half the time, had a better pace been set for me and more matter. In the absence of matter, I dreamt on a hungry stomach. But those ideal universes in my head did not produce any firm convictions or actual duties. They had nothing to do with the wretched poverty-stricken real world in which I was condemned to live. That the real was rotten and only the imaginary at all interesting seemed to me axiomatic. That was too sweeping; yet allowing for the rash generalizations of youth, it is still what I think. My philosophy has never changed. It is by no means an artificial academic hypothesis; it doesn't appeal at all to the professors; it is a system of presuppositions and categories discovered already alive and at work within me willy-nilly, like existence itself, and virtually present not only in the boy but in the embryo.

I say "within me," because there I have finally deciphered it by analysis; but it was not peculiar to me. It was common then in certain circles and was called pessimism. Pessimism is an accidental moralistic name for it; because the philosophy in question is a system of cosmology, a view of nature and history; moral preferences or judgments are not central in it. Whether a particular man is pessimistic because he dislikes the truth, or likes the truth and feels optimistic, makes but a slight difference in that total truth;

and such a feeling, turned into a sentence pronounced on the universe, seems, either way, rather impertinent. We speak of the fair, says a Spanish proverb, as we fare in it: and our personal fortunes may justly color our philosophy only if they are typical and repeat the fortunes of all living beings. I am not ashamed of my childish pessimism; it was honest; and it showed my courage in not letting my preferences cloud my perceptions nor my perceptions abash my preferences. The clash between them was painful, but not unnatural, and was destined to grow less painful with time, and this without any loss either of realism or of honor.

In spite, then, of my religious and other daydreams, I was at bottom a young realist; I knew I was dreaming, and so was awake. A sure proof of this was that I was never *anxious* about what those dreams would have involved if they had been true. I never had the least touch of superstition. To follow the logic of dogma and keep the feasts, if not the fasts, of the Church, was a part of the game; and the whole allegorical pseudo-historical pageant passed through my mind unchallenged, because I felt intimately the dramatic logic that had inspired it. But no logic can upset the facts. Thus it never occurred to me to shudder at the doctrine of eternal damnation, as the innocent Unitarians did or to be overawed by it, as were the innocent Calvinists. Hell is set down in the bond, like Shylock's pound of flesh: the play requires it. Of course damnation must be eternal, because every loss and every pain is irremediable. The consolation or peace said to wipe evil away, cannot wipe it out: you may forget it, but if you say you have annulled it, you are lying. Nothing that has ever occurred can be annulled. That is what eternal damnation means, or might be said to mean by a thinking being. But if you suppose that in an Inferno like Dante's you may soon be jumping about naked in a fiery furnace, you are dreaming. You are confusing poetry with fact. Never had I the least fear of a material hell or desire for a material heaven. The images were so violent, so childish, as to be comic.

The force of images is equivocal, reversible, hard to recover in memory. Two of my earliest effusions in verse were entitled: *To the Moon* and *To the Host*. The images were similar, and the sentiment in both cases was similar. The Host, I said, was "clear in faith's divine moonlight." It was "my only friend," much as the moon, to Endymion, might be the only goddess. And I sighed that my faith was "too like despair." The last word, what I really aspired to, was "peace." For this purpose the machinery of the sacraments was not needed, I had no wish to go to confession and communion, else I should have done so. My faith was indeed so like despair that it wasn't faith at all; it was fondness, liking, what in Spanish is called *afición*; I indulged in it, but only north-northwest, and keeping my freedom. I heartily agreed with the Church about the world, yet I was ready to agree with the world about the Church; and I breathed more easily in the atmosphere of religion than in that of business, precisely because religion, like poetry, was more ideal, more freely imaginary, and in a material sense falser.

Those verses were written when I was fifteen or sixteen, and before my prize poem. Seven years later, when I had studied philosophy and travelled, the same position is described, more cynically in the Byronic manner. The lines are entitled *At the Church Door*; I will quote one stanza from memory.

> Ah, if salvation were a trick of reason
> How easily would all the world be saved!
> But roses bloom not in the winter season
> Nor hope of heaven in a heart enslaved.
> To break the bond with earth were easy treason
> If it were God alone the bosom craved;
> But we have chosen thrift and chosen rest
> And with our wings' plucked feathers built our nest.*

* A friend of mine who was a bird-fancier (I mean who liked shooting) observed that here I had hit on a true simile without knowing it; some birds did pluck their feathers in nest-building, but from their breasts. I believe I corrected my manuscript accordingly, spoiling the sense: because what I meant was that we sacrificed our capacity for flight, under pressure of blind commitments or in mere apathy.

Here the drama had become frankly subjective: the turn it would take depended on the weather. Ideal flights, reason, heaven and union with God did not compose another world or carry us there; they were methods, directions, or goals of thought, habits that the human spirit developed under favorable conditions, when it was free. But for the most part, and especially then (in the 1880's), the mind was wretchedly servile, vulgarized, and absorbed in instrumentalities. And the worst of it was that we had lost courage and foresworn our vocation. We were not like a good dog that, if compelled to cross a river, hurries to the other bank, and shakes the water vigorously from his skin as soon as he gets there; we wallowed in our muddy bath like pigs in a sty, pretended that we positively enjoyed it, and paid our philosophers in obsequiousness if not in money for telling us that at least we were doing our duty.

From the boy dreaming awake in the church of the Immaculate Conception, to the travelling student seeing the world in Germany, England, and Spain there had been no great change in sentiment. I was still "at the church door." Yet in belief, in the clarification of my opinions, I had taken an important step. I no longer wavered between alternate views of the world, to be put on or taken off like alternate plays at the theatre. I now saw that there was only one possible play, the actual history of nature and of mankind, although there might well be ghosts among the characters and soliloquies among the speeches. Religions, *all* religions, and idealistic philosophies, *all* idealistic philosophies, were the soliloquies and the ghosts. They might be eloquent and profound. Like Hamlet's soliloquy they might be excellently reflective criticisms of the play as a whole. Nevertheless they were only parts of it, and their value as criticisms lay entirely in their fidelity to the facts, and to the sentiments which those facts aroused in the critic.

Two other important steps remained to be taken before my philosophy was wholly clarified and complete: I shall speak of them when it comes to my successive books. Yet it may be well to mention those two points here, in order that the skein of my meditations at the Immaculate Conception may be seen unravelled. One step was to overcome moral and ideal provinciality, and to see that every form of life had its own perfection, which it was stupid and cruel to condemn for differing from some other form, by chance one's own. The other step, rising above the moral dissolution that might invade a man who cultivated an indiscriminate sympathy with every form of life, made it clear that sympathy and justice themselves are only relative virtues, good only in their place, for those lives or forms of life that thereby reach their perfection: so that integrity or self-definition is and remains first and fundamental in morals: and the right of alien natures to pursue their proper aims can never abolish our right to pursue ours.

Why, before taking these final steps, had I stood so long "at the church door," with regret at never having really lived inside? I might prefer ideally an imaginary Atlantis to any earthly island: but how puerile and helpless to languish after it and not at once to make the best of the real world! I think there was a congenital transcendentalism in me, long before I heard of transcendental philosophy or understood it. I had a spontaneous feeling that life is a dream. The scene might entirely disappear at any moment, or be entirely transformed. There could be no *a priori*, strictly even no empirical, presumption against anything whatsoever. The volume and solidity of one apparition, of one imposed world, could never insure its perpetuity, much less prevent the reality of perpetuity of a thousand other worlds.

Now this, I am still convinced, is an invincible intuition: yet this invincible intuition, in its absoluteness and purity, leaves the mind empty and rescinds all faith. If it were the principle of life (which it is not) it would condemn us to suspended animation and the sense of infinite potentiality unrealized: the crystal vision, umbilical contemplations, and my childish verses *To the Moon* and *To the Host*. The light of spirit is indeed pure and unprejudiced, open, like the young eye, to whatsoever there may be. But this light is kindled by something else and it must fall on something else, if it is to reveal anything. It is kindled in an animal psyche, in a living perishable heart; and it falls on the world in which that heart and that psyche have been formed, and is deeply dyed in their particular passions. If, then, we are to see or to believe in anything, it must be at the bidding of natural accidents, by what I call faith: and the alternatives open to pure spirit are not open to rational belief. Rational belief must have other guides than sheer imagination exploring infinite possibilities. Those guides can be, logically, nothing but accidents; but they have a compulsory presence and evoke an inescapable adhesion, confidence, and trust; which trust is fortified by experiment and found trustworthy.

My instinctive transcendentalism or solipsism was, as I think, quite right analytically; but I was confused in playing with it as a criterion or judge of beliefs. Beliefs have an earthly origin and can be sanctioned only by earthly events.

CHAPTER XII

FIRST FRIENDS

IT WAS also at the age of sixteen that I began to notice the characters and quality of the other boys, and to find my ideal affinities. I say ideal affinities, because I had always had instinctive or canine friends: boys or girls—for there were several girls—with whom I played or prattled, or danced at the dancing school. There, at about the age of ten, I had a sort of *amourette*: absolutely groundless and silent, but absolutely determined. I remember the child perfectly. She had a dark complexion and curly black hair, and stood very straight, but gracefully. She was the first example to me of that admirable virtue cultivated by French actresses; eloquent stillness. I don't think she ever said a word, and I very few: but we always took each other out to dance, and were partners for the cotillion. Her name was Alice White, and I have never seen or heard of her since then. It was the friendship of two genteel kittens, who played gravely with the same ball, and eschewed the rest of the litter.

A less enigmatic companionship of my boyhood was with Charlie Davis. He was a soft blond youth, a little older and taller than I, but mentally younger: our great pleasure was to laugh about everything, like silly girls. But in our daily walks from school we must have gabbled on many subjects, because after some years —he left school young to go into an office—he became a Catholic, and asked me to be his sponsor at his christening. I was; and I remember later his desire to enter a religious order, to which his previous incidental entanglements with the fair sex proved a fatal obstacle. Must all novices be virgins? Probably only in that (Paulist) order, and in America. Our friendship died out: but he con-

178

tinued all his life to write occasionally to my sister Susana, partly on religious subjects and partly in a tone of amiable banter and comic pessimism. Let us hope, if I didn't save my own soul, that I saved the soul of Charlie Davis.

He was by no means my first friend. The first was Gorham Hubbard, at Miss Welchman's Kindergarten; the next was Bob Upham, at the Brimmer School: and in him I first tasted two of the sweets of friendship, which had regaled me since in many a "nice fellow"; guidance or good judgment in practical matters— which it is always a pleasure for me to follow if I can trust the guide—and the quality of simple gentleman, a clean upstanding independence and a sureness in everything personal and moral. My favorite young gentlemen haven't always turned out well; they have often gone to the dogs; but that was on account of a virtue which lent them a chivalrous and aristocratic charm, namely, indifference to public opinion, and courage in running risks.

I had also had several fancy-friends—little more than dream images of a foolish sentimental sort. The reality of their persons mattered little; they were simply knobs on which to hang my own reveries. But now, in my second class year, the manly note sounds for the first time. A common intelligence, a common readiness— *spes animi credula mutui*—allies two young men in the presence of a common world.

My first real friend was Bentley Warren. We two with Dick Smith (who afterwards took his mother's name Weston) formed what we called the Triumvirate. Warren was the link between the other two of us, who hadn't very much in common, except perhaps a better breeding than most of the boys at the Latin School. This school, being public (i.e. free), was naturally frequented by the ambitious poor—Irish boys wishing to be priests, lawyers, or doctors, Jews wishing to be professors, and native Americans, like Warren and Smith, whose families were in reduced circumstances. It was my mother's straitened means that caused her to send me there, instead of to some private school; and I should perhaps have seemed an entirely different person, and had an entirely different

life, if this genteel poverty and this education in a public day
school, among children of humble parents, had not fortified me in
the spirit of detachment and isolation. Not that the most luxurious
of American surroundings—such as I afterwards had some contact
with—would ever have made an American of me. America in those
days made an exile and a foreigner of every native who had a temperament at all like mine.

Warren's father, who had recently died, had been a Democratic congressman, elected in an off year of public dissatisfaction
in a suburb of Boston, usually Republican; but two years of life
in Washington, together with inherited dissentient opinions, had
given his son a freer intelligence and a more varied experience
than little Bostonians were apt to have. I often went to Mrs. Warren's to tea on holidays; and Warren sometimes came to lunch at
our house. His Democratic views—if he had them—were not
rabid; his most intimate friends were Harry and Jim Garfield, sons
of the future President of the United States; and he left school
at the end of our second class year in order to enter Williams College with the Garfields, a year before the rest of us were expected
to be ready for the university. Dick Smith, too, on account of the
tiff his father had with the Headmaster, left school early during
our last year; so that as far as friendship was concerned—so new to
me but so important—the end of my school life might have been
desolate.

Not that my relations with Warren were broken off: we wrote
each other long letters; and four years later, in 1885, I went to
Williamstown for the festivities at his graduation. I think it was
my first journey undertaken merely for pleasure, and at my own
expense. Ward Thoron had invited me to his grandfather's at
Lenox, and I combined the two visits. I have been to Williams and
to Lenox again: to read a lecture in the one (on Shelley) and to
"Ja" Burden's wedding in the other. There had been intervals of
twenty or twenty-five years: Harry Garfield was president of the
College; we spoke of Bentley Warren and of the old days, but with
how different a sentiment! For me those things had passed into

the empyrean, into an eternal calm where their littleness or their greatness was nothing and their quality, their essence, everything; for him they were merely early unimportant phases of the business which occupied him now, and not to be regarded on their own account. When I mentioned Bentley Warren, Garfield said: "Oh, yes. He is one of the Trustees of our College." From this I gathered two things: that Warren had been "successful" and was now rich; and that for Garfield this fact was what counted in Warren rather than their early friendship. I expressed surprise that in their Faculty Room they had no portrait of his father—an old member of the College and a President of the United States: and he said it was not for him to suggest that. Why not? Because it might seem egotistical? But why didn't his Trustees or whoever governed behind him—for Presidents of Colleges are secondary powers—take a gentle hint or spontaneously attend to something so obviously proper? I suppose they were always thinking of the future. A portrait in the Faculty Room would hardly have been an advertisement; it would only have been an act of homage. Let the past paint its own pictures.

My school friends were gone; but just beyond school bounds a new friend appeared, Edward Bayley. I was Lieutenant Colonel of the Boston School Regiment, the Colonel that year being from the English High School which, back to back with the Latin School, was housed in the other half of the same new building. In some matter of vital importance to our forces it became necessary for me to consult my superior officer. We met by appointment, and found that the high questions of epaulettes or of buttons were soon disposed of; but that first interview made us fast friends. We happened to live in the same quarter of the town, the Back Bay, about a mile from our schools, and we at once established the custom of waiting, he for me or I for him, at the corner, so as to walk home together. Yet this did not last many weeks, because that winter my mother moved to Roxbury, having at last got rid of the dreadful burden of our Beacon Street house; so that I saw my new friend only occasionally, or by express appointment. But that made no difference. The bond was established, silently of course, but safely. Even the fact that he was not going to College, but directly into some place of business, so that as it actually came about, we never saw each other after that year, and hardly a letter passed between us, made no difference in our friendship, though it entirely separated our lives. Strange enchantment! Even today, the thought of that youthful comradeship, without incidents, without background, and without a sequel, warms the cockles of my heart like a glass of old port.

There is a sort of indifference to time, as there is a sort of silence, which goes with veritable sympathy. It springs from clear possession of that which is, from sureness about it. Those who are jealous, jealous of time, of rivals, of accidents, care for something vague that escapes them now, and that would always escape them; they are haunted souls, hunting for they know not what. Not so those who know what they love and rest in it, asking for nothing more. If circumstances had led Bayley and me to go through life together, we should have stuck to each other against any incidental danger or enemy; there would have been something to tell about our comradeship; but there would have been nothing new in our friendship. Clearness and depth in the heart, as in the intellect, transpose everything into the eternal.

Is that all? What did he do? What did he say? What did he stand for? I confess that after sixty years I have to invent a theory to account for this fact. I have to compare that sudden, isolated, brief attachment with other friendships of mine that had something of its quality, but were circumstantially more describable. We were eighteen years old, and there was nothing in us except ourselves. Now, in himself, apart from circumstances, Bayley was like Warwick Potter, only stronger. In Warwick the same type of character, weaker although at the time of our intimacy he was much older, was made describable by his social background and breeding. He had been brought up in the most select and superior way in which it was then possible to be brought up in America. Not through mere wealth or fashion, because his widowed mother

I asked a Boston friend who turned up at Cortina about these very first friends of mine, Warren and Bayley. Did he know them? Were they still living? What had become of them? And I was not surprised to hear the warmest eulogy of both, although my informant was a Lyman of the Lymans and a Lowell of the Lowells, while Warren and Bayley were not descendants of the Boston Brahmins. And I said to myself, "Oh, my prophetic soul!" My earliest friendships were not illusions.

CHAPTER XIII

THE HARVARD YARD

I F FORTUNE had been unkind to me in respect to my times
—except that for the intellectual epicure the 1890's were
enjoyable—in respect to places fortune has been most
friendly, setting me down not in any one center, where
things supposed to be important or exciting were happening, but
in various quiet places from which cross-vistas opened into the
world. Of these places the most familiar to me, after Avila, was
the Harvard Yard. I lived there for eleven years, first as an undergraduate, later as an instructor and proctor. No place, no rooms,
no mode of living could have been more suitable for a poor student and a free student, such as I was and as I wished to be. My
first room, on the ground floor in the northeast corner of Hollis,
was one of the cheapest to be had in Cambridge: the rent was
forty-four dollars a year. I had put it first for that reason on my list
of rooms, and I got my first choice. It was so cheap because it had
no bedroom, no water, and no heating; also the ground floor seems
to have been thought less desirable, perhaps because the cellar
below might increase the cold or the dampness. I don't think I was
ever cold there in a way to disturb me or affect my health. I kept
the hard-coal fire banked and burning all night, except from Saturday to Monday, when I slept at my mother's at Roxbury. An
undergraduate's room in any case is not a good place for study, unless it be at night, under pressure of some special task. At other
times, there are constant interruptions, or temptations to interrupt
oneself: recitations, lectures, meals, walks, meetings, and sports. I
soon found the Library the best place to work in. It was not
crowded; a particular alcove where there were philosophical books

at hand, and foreign periodicals, soon became my regular place for reading. I could take my own books and notebooks there if necessary; but for the most part I browsed; and although my memory is not specific, and I hardly know what I read, except that I never missed *La Revue des Deux Mondes,* I don't think my time was wasted. A great deal stuck to me, without my knowing its source, and my mind became accustomed to large horizons and to cultivated judgments.

As to my lodging, I had to make up my sofa bed at night before getting into it; in the morning I left the bedding to be aired, and the "goody," whose services were included in the rent, put it away when she came to dust or to sweep. I also had to fetch my coal and water from the cellar, or the water in summer from the College pump that stood directly in front of my door. This was economy on my part, as I might have paid the janitor to do it for me; perhaps also to black my boots, which I always did myself, as I had done it at home. But my life was a miracle of economy. I had an allowance from my mother of $750 a year to cover all expenses. Tuition absorbed, $150; rent, $44; board at Memorial Hall, with a reduction for absence during the week-end, about $200; which left less than one dollar a day for clothes, books, fares, subscriptions, amusements, and pocket money. Sometimes, but very rarely, I received a money-prize or a money-present; I had no protection or encouragement from rich relations or persons of influence. The Sturgises were no longer affluent, and as yet they hardly knew of my existence. Later, when their natural generosity could (and did) express itself, it did so in other ways, because I was already independent and needed no help. Yet on my less than one dollar a day I managed to dress decently, to belong to minor societies like the Institute, the Pudding, and the O.K., where the fees were moderate, to buy all necessary books, and even, in my Junior year, to stay at rich people's houses, and to travel. Robert had given me his old evening clothes, which fitted me well enough: otherwise the rich people's houses could not have been visited.

Doing my "chores" was something I rather liked, as I still brush and pack my own clothes for pleasure, and shave myself, and walk everywhere rather than drive, circumstances permitting. A little manual work or physical exercise changes the stops agreeably, lengthens the focus and range of vision, reverts to the realm of matter which is the true matrix of mind, and generally brings judgment and feeling back into harmony with nature. I have never had a man servant and later when I lived in hotels I seldom called on the servants for any personal service not in their common routine. This trait is a heritage from the humble condition of my father's family and my mother's reduced circumstances during my boyhood. I had not an aristocratic breeding; not only was I not served, but I was taught no aristocratic accomplishments, not even riding or driving or shooting or dancing. What is a gentleman? A gentleman is a man with a valet: originally he also had a sword, but in my time that was obsolete except for officers in full uniform; a bank account could take its place. But having many servants, though it makes a man a master, does not make him a gentleman. He is not one because his wife may keep servant girls in the house; he is one only if he has a body servant of his own. This defines the Spanish gentleman as well as the English gentleman, yet differently. The relation in Spain is or was more confidential, more general, more moral: the man served his master in all his affairs. In England, it is more a matter of laying out all his master's things. However, I confess that the mere fop is not a complete gentleman, however dependent he may be on his valet. To be a complete gentleman he should also have a horse, and should ride it gallantly. Don Quixote, too, had a horse, as well as a servant.

Life in the Yard for me, during my second period of residence there, 1890–1896, had a different quality. I hadn't a horse or a valet, but could count on enough pocket-money, a varied circle of friends, clubs, and ladies' society in Boston and Cambridge, and the foreglow and afterglow of holidays spent in Europe. The first year, when I had only one foot in the stirrup and was not yet in the saddle as a Harvard teacher, I lived in Thayer; graceless quarters and the insecure stammering beginnings of a lecturer. The only thing I remember is the acquaintance I then made with my next-door neighbor, Fletcher, who was afterwards a professor of Comparative Literature and made a translation of the *Divina Commedia*. He was also a football player; and I remember one day when I was violently sick at my stomach—my digestion in those days being imperfect—he thought to help me by holding my head (a common illusion among helpful people) and his grasp was like a ring of iron. He was a very good fellow, with a richer nature than most philologists, and firm morals. We had long talks and discovered common tastes in literature and the arts; but he didn't remain at Harvard, and I lost sight of him. Even if he had been at hand, we should hardly have seen each other often: there were things in us fundamentally inaccessible to one another. Besides, though I became a professor myself, I never had a real friend who was a professor. Is it jealousy, as among women, and a secret unwillingness to be wholly pleased? Or is it the consciousness that a professor or a woman has to be partly a sham; whence a mixture of contempt and pity for such a poor victim of necessity? In Fletcher, and in the nobler professors, the shamming is not an effect of the profession, but rather, as in inspired clergymen, the profession is an effect of an innate passion for shamming. Nobody feels that passion more than I have felt it in poetry and in religion; but I never felt it in academic society or academic philosophy, and I gave up being a professor as soon as I could.

The next year I again had my pick of rooms in the Yard, securing No. 7 Stoughton, in the southeast corner of the first floor, where I stayed for six winters. Here there was a bedroom, and my coal and water were brought up for me by the janitor; on the other hand I often made my own breakfast—tea, boiled eggs, and biscuits—and always my tea in the afternoon, for I had now lived in England and learned the comforts of a bachelor in lodgings. Only —what would not have happened in England—I washed my own dishes and ordered my tea, eggs, milk and sugar from the grocers: domestic cares that pleased me, and that preserved my nice china— a present from Howard Cushing—during all those years. There was a round bathtub under my cot, and my sister's crucifix on the wall above it: only cold water, but the contents of the kettle boiling on the hearth served to take off the chill. I had also acquired a taste for fresh air, and my window was always a little open.

One day a new goody left the bathtub full of slops, explaining that she hadn't known what to do with it; it was the only bathtub in her entry. I had myself taken only recently to a daily sponge bath. When I was an undergraduate few ever took a bath in Cambridge; those who lodged in private houses might share one bathroom between them, and those who went to the Gymnasium might have a shower bath after exercise; but your pure "grind" never bathed, and I only when I went home for the week-end. In Little's Block I believe there was a bathroom on each floor; but Beck was the only luxurious dormitory where each room had its private bathroom. Habits, however, were rapidly changing. Violent exercise and fiercely contested sports were in the ascendant among the athletes; this involved baths, but not luxury. Yet luxury was in the ascendant too; and the polite ideal of one man one bathroom, and hot water always hot, was beginning to disguise luxury under the decent names of privacy and health.

My father used to say that the English had introduced baths into Christendom from India; but I suspect that it was luxury and the *femmes galantes* of the eighteenth century that did it. What could be more un-English than a languid female in a turban, not unattended, and not without a semi-transparent clinging garment, like that of a statue, getting in or out of a marble bath like an ancient sarcophagus, itself draped and lined with linen sheets? These were the refinements of luxury and mature coquetry. And the Christian background appears in the gown worn in the bath, according to the monastic precept of never being wholly naked. No such scruple exists in England, or among athletes. The tone there is masculine and hardy, with a preference for cold water and the open air. Robert Bridges, the most complete of Englishmen, at the age of eighty, used to take his cold bath every morning in the lounge-hall of his house, before a roaring wood fire. Here was Sparta rather than India transported to the chilly North.

In Spain, in those days, there were no baths in houses. My sister procured an immense zinc tub, in the middle of which, when it was full, a special stove had to be introduced to heat the water, which a special donkey laden with four earthen jars had to carry from the fountain; the thing didn't work, and I doubt that she took more than one or two baths. For me she got a manageable little hip bath which I found quite sufficient. Yet baths, medical baths, were not unknown in mediæval Avila. They were prescribed for certain ailments. You went to the establishment as to a pilgrimage; the water was that of a particular spring, mineral or miraculous, gushing forth at that spot; and you took always an odd number of baths, probably nineteen or twenty-one (never twenty!) according to some Pythagorean superstition of ancient medicine. When they were well the good people of Avila no more thought of bathing than of drinking tea; yet I never came across any decent person there who offended the nose. Complexions were seldom fresh or ruddy; but it is working people's clothes that smell; only the feet, head and hands gather dust and grime. The protected parts of the skin shed their excretions and become clean of themselves, if only the clothes are well washed and aired.

Hollis and Stoughton were twin red-brick buildings of the eighteenth century, solid, simple, symmetrical and not unpleasing. No effort had been made by the builders towards picturesqueness or novelty; they knew what decent lodgings for scholars were, and that there was true economy in building them well. The rectangular wooden window frames divided into many squares, flush with the walls, and painted white, served for a modest and even gay decoration. There was a classic cornice, and the windows immediately under it were square instead of oblong and suggested metopes, while the slope of the roof also was that of a temple, though without pediments at the ends. On the whole, it was the architecture of sturdy poverty, looking through thrift in the direction of wealth. It well matched the learning of early New England, traditionally staunch and narrow, yet also thrifty and tending to positivism; a learning destined as it widened to be undermined and to become, like the architecture, flimsy and rich. It had been founded on accurate Latin and a spellbound constant reading of the Bible: but in the Harvard of my day we had heard a little of everything, and nobody really knew his Latin or knew his Bible. You might say that the professor of Hebrew did know his Bible, and the professors of Latin their Latin. No doubt, in the sense that they could write technical articles on the little points of controversy at the moment among philologists; but neither Latin nor the Bible flowed through them and made their spiritual lives; they were not vehicles for anything great. They were grains in a quicksand, agents and patients in an anonymous moral migration that had not yet written its classics.

In both these old buildings I occupied corner rooms, ample, low, originally lighted by four windows, with window seats in the thickness of the wall, which a cushion could make comfortable for reading. Between the side windows the deep chimney stack projected far into the room, and no doubt at first showed its rough or glazed bricks, as the low ceiling probably showed its great beams. But an "improvement" had spoiled the dignity of these chambers. The rage for "closets" invaded America, why I am not antiquary enough to know. Was it that wardrobes and chests, with or without drawers, had become too heavy and cumbrous for an unsettled population? Or was it that a feminine demand for a seemly "bed-sitting room" had insisted on a place of hiding for one's belongings? Anyhow, in 19 Hollis both the side windows had been hidden by oblique partitions, going from the edges of the chimney stack to the front and back walls and enclosing the desired closets, not large enough for a bed, but capable of containing a washstand, trunks, and garments hanging on pegs. Luckily in 7 Stoughton this operation had mutilated only one angle, and left me one pleasant side window open to the South, and affording a glimpse of Holden Chapel and the vista then open over the grass towards Cambridge Common.

Yet it was the outlook to the east, from both rooms, that was most characteristic. The old elms in the Yard were then in all their glory, and in summer formed a grove of green giants, with arching and drooping branches, that swung like garlands in the breeze. This type of elm, though graceful and lofty, has a frail air, like tall young women in consumption. The foliage is nowhere thick, too many thin ribs and sinews are visible: and this transparency was unfortunate in the Harvard Yard, where the full charm depended on not seeing the background. In winter the place was ungainly and forlorn, and not only to the eye. The uneven undrained ground would be flooded with rain and half-melted dirty snow one day, and another day strewn with foul ashes over the icy pavements. This was a theme for unending grumbling and old jokes; but we were young and presumably possessed snow-boots called "arctics" or thick fisherman's boots warranted watertight. Anyhow we survived; and as bad going for pedestrians is made inevitable during winter and spring by the New England climate, the Yard was not much worse in this respect than the surrounding places.

Holworthy in my day was still nominally the "Seniors' Paradise," but not in reality: in reality those who could afford it lived in private houses, in Little's Block, or in Beck. Holworthy preserved, as it has sometimes recovered, only the charm of tradition. The two bedrooms to each study favored the pleasant custom of chumming; but as yet Holworthy had no baths, not even shower baths, and no central heating. Modern improvements seem to me in almost everything to be a blessing. Electricity, vacuum cleaning, and ladies' kitchens render life simpler and more decent; but central heating, in banishing fireplaces, except as an occasional luxury or affectation, has helped to destroy the charm of home. I don't mean merely the ancient and rustic sanctity of the hearth; I mean also the home-comforts of the modern bachelor. An obligatory fire was a useful and blessed thing. In northern climates it made the poetry of indoor life. Round it you sat, into it you looked, by it you read, in it you made a holocaust of impertinent letters and rejected poems. On the hob your kettle simmered, and the little leaping flames cheered your heart and ventilated your den. Your fire absolved you from half your dependence on restaurants, cafés, and servants; it also had the moralizing function of giving you a duty in life from which any distraction brought instant punishment, and taught you the feminine virtues of nurse, cook, and Vestal virgin. Sometimes, I confess, these cares became annoying; the fire kept you company, but like all company it sometimes interrupted better things. At its best, a wood fire is the most glorious; but unless the logs are of baronial dimensions, it dies down too quickly, the reader or the writer is never at peace; while a hard-coal fire (which also sometimes goes out) sleeps like a prisoner behind its iron bars, without the liveliness of varied flames. The ideal fire is soft coal, such as I had in England and also in America when I chose; like true beauty in woman, it combines brilliancy with lastingness. I congratulate myself that in the Harvard Yard I was never heated invisibly and willy-nilly by public prescription, but always by my own cheerful fire, that made solitude genial and brought many a genial friend who loved cheerfulness to sit by it with me, not rejecting in addition a drink and a little poetry; no tedious epic, but perhaps one of Shakespeare's sonnets or an ode of Keats, something fit to inspire conversation and not to replace it.

The quality of the Harvard Yard, both in its architecture and its manners, was then distinctly Bohemian: not of the Parisian description, since no *petite amie* or *grande amie* was in evidence, but of the red-brick lodging, tavern and stable-yard Bohemia of Dickens and Thackeray; yet being in a college, the arts and the intellect were not absent from it altogether. I had not been many days a Freshman when I had a glimpse of this. A note was slipped by hand through my door, inviting me to go that evening to a room in Holworthy, where two Seniors interested in things Spanish would be glad to see me and talk about them. I went. The two young men were commonplace and easy going. They didn't actually speak Spanish but had an idea that they loved gypsies and Moors, the *Alhambra* of Washington Irving and the *Carmen* of Mérimée. There was a mysterious curtain cutting off a corner of their room; and the talk soon drifted from Spain to painting Venuses from the model. Was that done here, I wondered, and was the model about to emerge from behind the curtain? That would surely have been contrary to College discipline; did these bold Seniors not care about that, or was I the greenest of Freshmen and were they trying to impose upon me? I saw little or nothing of them after that evening; probably I was less Spanish or less Bohemian than they expected. But by chance they gave me a useful hint. If I myself drew a little, why didn't I draw something for the *Lampoon*; and one of them suggested a subject: a mother with two or three daughters mistaking "Holyoke House" for a hotel and arriving with luggage and asking for rooms there. I made the drawing and sent it to the appropriate address; and soon I received a visit from the "President" of the *Lampoon* Board, who said they accepted my drawing but wished to keep it for the Class Day number—nine months hence—and meantime wouldn't I send them something else. Naturally I did so; and was thereupon elected a member of the *Lampoon* Board.

This was a decisive event in my Harvard life. Two other Freshmen, Felton and Sanborn, had also been elected; and they asked me to come and sit at their table in Memorial Hall. Felton's chum, Baldwin, was also there, and some other friends; so I immediately found myself in a little circle of more or less lively wits that congregated every day at meals, apart from any personal sympathies. In time, the inner circle narrowed down to four, the three I have mentioned and myself. We kept up our comradeship at table for four years; and Sanborn and I became personal friends on intellectual grounds.

In those days Freshmen at Harvard were still at school. Courses were prescribed, and we sat in alphabetical order, to be marked present or absent. Sanborn and I were likely to sit next to each other: not always, because those who had passed in French had to take German, and vice versa, and in some subjects the two hundred and fifty Freshmen were divided into more or less advanced classes. But I remember in Natural History 4, where Professor Shaler set forth "all the geology necessary to a gentleman," sitting next to Sanborn. We had separate chairs but one running desk in front of us, so that we could easily overlook one another's notebooks; and we amused ourselves in matching triolets, not always on that "concatenation of phenomena" which Shaler was impressing upon us.

Sanborn was a poet of lyric and modest flights but genuine feeling, not naturally in harmony with the over-intellectualized transcendentalism of Concord, Massachusetts, where his father was a conspicuous member of the Emersonian circle. There was more of Chaucer in him than of Emerson or Wordsworth: even Shakespeare—except in the songs—he found too heavy and rhetorical. These exclusions were involuntary; he was not in the least conceited about them, but on the contrary felt that he was a misfit, shy, ungainly in appearance, and at a disadvantage in the give and take of conversation or action. These maladjustments, a few years later, led to a tragic end. His father had found him a place in the office of *The Springfield Republican*. That town offered little to keep up his spirits. He fell into rather undesirable company, as at College he had sometimes succumbed to drink—not often, yet ungracefully. I think I understand the secret of these failings, gross as they seem for a man of such delicate sensibility. He was unhappy, he was poor, he was helpless. The sparkle of a glass, the glitter of a smile, the magic of a touch could suddenly transport him out of this world, with all its stubborn hindrances and dreary conventions, into the *Auberge Verte*, the green paradise, of his dreams. Yet this escape from reality was necessarily short-lived, and the awakening bitter and remorseful. The strain was too much for Sanborn. His discouragement became melancholia and began to breed hallucinations. He knew only too much about madness, as everybody did in old New England, and he feared it. He cut his throat in his bath with a razor, and we buried him in Concord, in sight of the optimistic Emerson's grave, after a parlor funeral, with the corpse visible, at which his father read a few not very pertinent passages from the Upanishads and the Psalms.

The other *Lampoon* men were more normal and better adapted to their social medium. Felton and Baldwin were not New Englanders, rather Southern, without crotchets and with unaffected old-fashioned literary tastes, leaning towards the sentimental and the nobly moral; leanings likely to grow more pronounced in later years, under the sacred influences of home and of political eloquence. They loved Thackeray; and Felton would read aloud *"Wait till you come to forty-year."* Their room, No. 1 Thayer, was the reality under the literary fiction of a *Lampoon* "sanctum." We gathered there to compose our parts of the fortnightly edition; chiefly drawings, although sometimes the column of puns entitled *By the Way* was concocted by us cooperatively, in the midst of a thousand interruptions. I never wrote for the *Lampoon*; even the text for my sketches was usually supplied for me by the others, who knew the idioms required. My English was too literary, too ladylike, too correct for such a purpose; and I never acquired, or liked, the American art of perpetual joking. What we printed was a severe selection from what we uttered: it had to be local, new or fresh, and at least apparently decent. Speech in this circle, if not always decent, never became lewd. There was an atmosphere of respect for holy things, of respect for distant or future ladyloves, and also of self-respect. We were not very intimate friends. The *Lampoon*, the Yard, the College had brought us together; and when we scattered the comradeship ceased. I scarcely knew what became of Felton or Baldwin. In recent years I unexpectedly received a letter from Baldwin, not reawakening old interests or old friendship, but full of conventional cordiality and platform sentiments. I should have preferred silence: because the young Baldwin had been an engaging person, who inspired trust and affection, and I recall the circle in which we moved with the warmest pleasure.

The man who gave the tone to the *Lampoon* at that time was Ernest Thayer, not one of our group. He seemed a man apart, and his wit was not so much jocular as Mercutio-like, curious and whimsical, as if he saw the broken edges of things that appear whole. There was some obscurity in his play with words, and a feeling (which I shared) that the absurd side of things is pathetic. Probably nothing in his later performance may bear out what I have just said of him; because American life was then becoming unfavorable to idiosyncrasies of any sort, and the current smoothed and rounded out all the odd pebbles.

In our last year or two, the *Lampoon* possessed a business manager whose name is known everywhere, and who is identified, perhaps more than any one else, with that inexorable standardizing current, namely William R. Hearst. He was little esteemed in the College. The fact that his father was a millionaire and a Senator from California gave him an independence that displeased the undergraduate mind, and his long cigars were bad form in the Yard. Yet his budding powers as a newspaper owner and manager made him invaluable to the *Lampoon* in its financial difficulties.

He not only knew how to secure advertisements, but he presented us with a material sanctum, carpeted, warmed by a stove, and supplied with wooden armchairs and long tables at which all the illustrated comic papers in the world were displayed as exchanges for our little local and puerile *"Lampy."* How easily a little cool impudence can deceive mankind! Yet the enterprise of our business manager in this affair, was of little use to us. Two or three times two or three of us may have gone into that new sanctum (for we were also supplied with keys) and looked at those startling comic papers, most of them unintelligible and grossly colored; especially the *Vie Parisienne* and the other French sheets, so different in prevalent theme from our decent and child-like fun. I myself actually read some of the longer stories in the *Vie Parisienne*: there was a certain overtone there of satire and subtle humor, sometimes even of pathos, as in Guy de Maupassant and Théophile Gautier; and the conventionalized illustrations showed a giraffe-like ideal of feminine beauty, very unlike the dumpy realities, as if a taste for elegance were struggling against mere sensuality. Yet the thing was horribly monotonous, and had been done better in *La Maison Tellier* and *Mademoiselle de Mau-*

pin. We turned a cold shoulder on Hearst's munificence, and continued to meet and to bring forth our labored witticisms, not without laughter, in Felton and Baldwin's room.

To the Harvard Yard in spirit, though not topographically, may be assigned my other contacts with college life during those first four years. Athletics did not figure among them. I never took any exercise except walking, and I seldom went, as yet, even to watch the games, which in the case of football was then done as in England, standing at the side lines, the crowd being kept back only by a chalk mark or a rope. This "Harvard indifference" was not due to intense study on my part or to misanthropy. I played the leading lady in the Institute Theatricals of 1884, and two years later, though I no longer looked at all deceptive in feminine clothes, I was one of the ballet in the Hasty Pudding play. These amusements, with rehearsals and a noisy trip to New York as a theatrical company, involved a good deal of intimacy for the moment, and I remember the names and faces of some of my companions, and some of the tunes we sang, chiefly from *Martha*; but for the most part scenes and persons are completely erased. I have a very short memory, except for such things as I absorb and recast in my own mind; so I am a good observer and critic, but a bad historian: let the reader of this book take warning.

One figure, however, still stands clear before me out of that medley: Crosby Whitman, our musician and director, in whom as in many a person, I felt a true potential friendship behind a slight acquaintance. Besides the love of music and of Miss Mary Anderson, he had a kind of cosmopolitan competence or normality that I seem to have noticed in the best people of the American West. They moved swimmingly in the midst of all the current conventions and noises, but they seemed to make light of them, as your good Bostonian never could. They were not "taken in" by the tastes, opinions, and pleasures that they played with as in a carnival. Crosby Whitman was a man of the world.

More intellectual, at least nominally, were the literary groups or societies of which, for me, the O.K. and the *Harvard Monthly*, when that was founded, were the most important. The members of the two were largely the same, and included *Lampoon* men as well; but the O.K., which later gave excellent dinners, had the advantage of running over into the class of merely intelligent or even athletic leaders of the College. In a commercial civilization, these were likely to be much *better beings* than the professional scholars or intellectuals, *better beings* even than the future lawyers, though these might have more historical and rhetorical attainments. I liked to feel a spark of sympathy pass from those sound simple active heirs of the dominant class to my secret philosophy: and sometimes the spark did pass, and in both directions. It was at the O.K. dinners in the 1890's, that I read my *Athletic Ode* and *Six Wise Fools*. Helped by the champagne, these trifles caught fire. The play of ordinary wit and sentiment, with a light touch and a masculine note, appeals to a side of the heart not reached in the standard poets; it moves from convention to sincerity, where the standard poets move from sincerity to convention.

The *Harvard Monthly* was founded by A. B. Houghton, afterwards American Ambassador at Berlin and London. His literary quality was in marked contrast with Sanborn's, as was also his character and fate. Houghton was as rich as Sanborn was poor; he was ambitious and bitter, nominally preoccupied with socialism and pessimism, not, I think, in a clear speculative spirit, but rather as scandals and dangers that the leaders of liberalism and plutocracy must somehow overcome. His conscience and critical faculty were not at peace about the way in which his father made money: it was chiefly in a glass factory: and the son would ask himself how many glass blowers died each year from blowing into those furnaces. In the good old times they would have died of famine, the plague, drink, war or the gallows—not perhaps gentler ways of keeping down the population below the means of subsistence. But that was not the question. The question was, Is material civilization worth while? Is the dull anonymous unhappiness that it steadily diffuses more tolerable than the sudden and horrible scourges that fall upon primitive peoples? Or should the question of happiness be ignored altogether, as German philosophy ignores it, and should the criterion be placed in more and more complex formal achievements? In the end Houghton would seem to have adopted the latter alternative, if we may judge by his brilliant career; but in his student days, at Harvard and in Germany, the problem of human suffering dominated his judgments. In verse he was scornful and revolutionary, with a good deal of verbal facility and technical ingenuity, after the manner of Swinburne. His versification was not slovenly, even when it was empty or trite. This was remarkable in America, and indicated a certain documentary precision and authority in his mind, that doubtless contributed to his subsequent official distinction.

I knew Houghton very well; we discussed all manner of subjects. In 1898 he unexpectedly made me a visit in Brattle Street. He glanced about my quarters disapprovingly, sucked his enormous cigar, and said magisterially that it was a sad mistake to try and swim against the stream. I have never been aware of swimming against any stream: I have merely stood on the bank or paddled about in the quiet backwaters. From there I may have observed that the torrent was carrying down more or less wreckage. My philosophy throws no challenge to those who rush down the very middle of the rapids and rejoice in their speed. However, the monition addressed to me by the wise Houghton revealed the dilemma in which he had found himself, and his own decision never to swim against the current. I wonder if he was ultimately satisfied with his career? Perhaps his success fell short of his hopes, and perhaps his conscience about the way the world is run was never quite at rest. Yet he was actively abetting the dominant procedure, no doubt wishing to improve it in detail, but in any case determined to keep it going full blast. Was it faith in a divine direction of things and in the course of history as the Last Judgment? Or was it the force of vested interests and formed habits drowning the still small voice of the spirit?

After this glance into the great world, taken from the Harvard Yard, I will add nothing more about that place. It has lost its character and its importance. When President Lowell was planning his "Houses" to be built by the river, he very kindly urged me to remain and take part in the experiment. I could have lived very like a don at Oxford or Cambridge. But it was too late. My heart might have been in the thing twenty years earlier, and perhaps then the transformation of Harvard into a university of colleges might have been socially more successful. But by 1912 the non-collegiate additions had become too numerous and too important for such a reorganization. The community too had outgrown the instinct for a secluded life. Colleges were fundamentally conventual and religious; on which foundation specific precious traditions, social and sporting, might develop together with an exact but familiar and humanistic learning. Now looser, wider, more miscellaneous interests had invaded every mind. But I am not writing a history of Harvard University. I know very little about it. I knew only the Harvard Yard.

CHAPTER XIV

FIRST RETURN TO SPAIN

THE chief event of my Freshman year occurred towards the end of it. I received—what was unprecedented—a note from home, asking me to be in my room on the following evening, because my mother and sisters were coming to lay before me an important proposal. I guessed at once what it would be, although no hint had been dropped on the subject. I was to go to Spain that summer to see my father.

My mother evidently felt profoundly the recent relief to her finances, and wished to be generous. Sending me to College, even on my modest allowance, had already consumed perhaps a fourth of her income; yet she still had money to spare, and desired to do more. She had done nothing for my father during these ten years; in a certain sense she had done nothing for *me*; for giving me food and lodging and a hundred dollars a year for clothes, books and pocket-money, was something she owed to herself. She would not have allowed a child of hers to beg or go in rags; and even in sending me to College she was carrying out a plan of her own, and trying to make me into what she wished me to be, rather than into what my father or I secretly desired. But now in letting me go to see him, she was doing us an unselfish kindness, relenting as it were and letting us, for a moment, have our own way. Neither my father nor I had made any such suggestion; but it was impossible that he shouldn't wish to see his son grown up; and everybody knew at home how I longed to travel, to see again with my own eyes old towns, cathedrals, castles, and palaces, and also the classic landscape of Europe: because in America, at least in the parts I knew, nature as well as society seemed to lack contrast and definition, as if everything were half formed and groping after its essence.

Late in June I started accordingly on my first journey alone, and sailed from New York for Antwerp. Robert had looked up the various routes possible, and it had been decided that I should go and return by the Belgian or Red Star Line. The ship was decent as standards stood in those days, but second-rate, perhaps of 5,000 tons; and as usual I was dreadfully seasick; so much so that the doctor and the stewardess took pity on me, some ladies became interested (I was nineteen years old) and a bed was rigged up for me on deck, where as they said I should enjoy the sunshine and the air. The fresh air was indeed a relief but the glare an added nuisance; and the coming and going of people, and their talk, only intensified the general instability of everything. I was too ill for the moment to be ashamed of myself; but when I once got back to my cabin, although I wasn't alone even there, the feeling of shame came over me. They say dying animals go into hiding; and I could understand that instinct. There are phases of distress when help is neither possible nor desired. It is simpler, easier, more honest to be seasick alone, and to die alone. The trouble then seems something fated, not to be questioned, like life itself; and nature is built to face it and to see it out. Much as I suffered at sea, I was always ready to go to sea again: such a trial leaves the will unaffected, as nightmares do: you start afresh as you were, perhaps more merrily and with a deeper courage. The thing will pass, the ghosts will vanish. There is no reason for changing your purpose.

When I appeared on deck again, looking and feeling perfectly well, shaved and in fresh linen, I was congratulated. One particular lady of uncertain age, who now explained that she was Mrs. X. of Cincinnati, Ohio, had to be thanked for the kindness she had shown, or at least intended, on the day of that disgusting exhibition which I was heartily sorry to have made of myself. A young man should be hardier, and I had been sicker than any girl. Mrs. X. had brought me a raw egg in brandy, and insisted I should swallow it, which I had done with dire results: brandy on such occasions is a brutal remedy that my throat, not to say my stomach, abhors. Now, it was eleven o'clock in smooth sunny weather, there was no question of brandy, but only of a cup of broth and a biscuit, which we had together. I must come, she said, to sit in *their* chairs, and take a vacant place that was at *their* table. *They*, she explained, were her son (she had been married very young) and her niece, not *daughter*, who was sixteen. I had to say of course that a young girl of sixteen couldn't be her daughter. Even the boy seemed surprising. Yes, she said, he was very tall for his age; but she didn't tell me how old he was, because nice people mustn't lie.

A girl of sixteen might have seemed the natural affinity for a boy of nineteen: but not at all. The niece was to be regarded as a mere child, and my special friend was to be Mrs. X. herself. She certainly was more entertaining, deeply interested in all the higher subjects, very refined, and very religious. She spoke of "plumes," and embroidered the words *Holy, Holy, Holy* in gold upon altar-cloths. They were going all the way up the Rhine, it was such a beautiful trip, so romantic and so full of historic associations. Didn't it tempt me? It tempted me; but frankly I had no extra money for trips, and must go straight to Avila to see my father. It was too bad, she said, that I had no extra money; but it was nice that I should be going straight to see my old father, after such a long absence. Her husband too was old, too old to enjoy travelling, but he was happy in thinking how many interesting experiences the family were having, and it was wiser and pleasanter for him to remain at home, he so loved his dog and his garden and his beautiful books, all the English standard authors bound uniformly and making such a splendid decoration for his sunlit library wall. I must come some day to Cincinnati and see their delightful home. I should love it. And by the first of September they expected to be in Paris: perhaps I might be there at the same time, on my way back from Spain. We must try to arrange it.

We parted at Antwerp on these terms, having exchanged addresses, and promised to keep each other informed of our move-

ments. I had just time to see the market place with the Cathedral
spire, like a group of inverted icicles rising above it; and inside,
besides the general splendor of a great living place of worship, I
admired the two magnificent, if theatrical, pictures by Rubens at
the head of the two aisles, especially the *Descent from the Cross*.
Yet this is too classic, too Michelangelesque for Flanders; I could
have wished to carry away some humbler and more intimate memories: but the gorgeousness of Rubens blotted out the rest.

In Paris I saw nothing, merely driving from one station to the
other; but at the Gare d'Orléans I found myself in the sort of difficulty that inexperience will fall into. I was provided with just the
amount of French money that I had calculated would be sufficient,
leaving a decent margin for emergencies; and at the ticket-office I
asked, as planned, for a second-class ticket to Avila. I could have a
ticket to Avila, the man said, but only first class for the express:
the ordinary trains, with second and third class, would take more
than two whole days for the journey. I counted my money. I could
take a first-class ticket and have fifteen francs left. Would that be
enough for meals and tips on the journey? I would risk it. It was
only thirty-six hours, two nights and one day; I could have a sand-
wich instead of a dinner. It wouldn't kill me.

During the next ten years I repeated this journey many times;
the expense was about the same if I went first class without stopping, or second class with two or three stops on the way: a method
that avoided long nights in the train, and enabled me, by varying
my voyage and landing at Cherbourg or England, or even Gibraltar, to see the principal sights in all France and Spain, without
making trips expressly for that purpose. My architectural passion
was thus richly satisfied: it was only Italy that remained to be ex-
plored and lived in when I became relatively independent.

My fifteen francs, however, were just enough to pay my way
on that first occasion; and I found at Irun that I had only a few
coppers in my pocket and couldn't telegraph to my father, as had
been agreed, that I was arriving at 5:30 the next morning. It was
broad daylight, being early in July, and I recognized the walls and

the Cathedral tower, touched by the rising sun, before we reached the station. But there was nobody to receive me, and no vehicle. Not even anybody to carry my valise. I left it with the guard, and started alone on foot, immensely happy, and remembering perfectly that station road and the place among the first houses to the left, opposite the church and convent of Santa Ana, where Don Juan the Englishman's house stood, which was now my father's. There it was, the middle one of three humble two-story buildings, not properly lined up, and painted in varying weather-worn yellows or grays, with red tiled roofs. I pounded the middle door with the knocker. No answer. Finally a neighbor, from a window over the bakery in the house to the left, put out her dishevelled head and said "Knock hard. They are all deaf in that house." I knocked harder; until the window over my door was opened also, and another head, evidently the housemaid's, peered out, and looked at me with an air of inquiry. "*Don Agustín* lives here, doesn't he? I am his son." She smiled, wished me a good arrival, and said they were expecting me but not that morning. *El Señor* was still in bed; *la Señora* (his sister Maria Ignacia) was in the garden. And presently the door was opened for me. At the end of the stone-paved passage running through the house, I could see the so-called garden, and my aged aunt standing there, stooping a little, with a watering pot in her hand. The maid tactfully ran ahead and announced me loudly, and after embracing my aunt, whom I had never seen before, I had some difficulty in making her hear and understand why I hadn't telegraphed. Then I was led up to my father's room, where the same embraces and the same explanations, under the same difficulties, were duly repeated. But it was all right now; and rather characteristic of a young son from half round the world to arrive home with just twopence in his pocket.

My father looked much as I remembered him. When middle-aged he had seemed to me simply old; now that he was really old, he seemed no older, only deafer; a disadvantage for me—besides the fact that my powers of expression in Spanish were limited, for I had read, and even now have read, hardly any Spanish books.

But deafness was almost an advantage for him in conversation. It gave him a free field, and I soon discovered how entertaining and witty his talk could be. His views were distinctly *views*, partial, definite, and humorous. They were not at all the fruit of scientific thinking. He was rather like an ancient sage, a satirist and proverb-maker; his wit lay in putting things in a nutshell—into which naturally they couldn't go in their entirety. When he talked about persons and events these miniatures were excellent; they caught the traits relevant to his purpose. It was only when given out as general truths that his summings up become sophistical and monotonous.

To be monotonous, sophistical, and utterly intolerant is the characteristic of the liberalism that he seemed to have adopted as final and absolute: I belong to the next turn of the tide. The fifty years between our ages thus made a perfect contrariety in our fundamental principles; but they made him all the more valuable for me, so to speak, as a classic, as a point of reference in thought; because the same principles, as they are found in English-speaking people, are not held so radically or intelligently but enveloped in various national, religious, commercial or sentimental interests that confuse the issue. In him the narrowing and desiccating force of this philosophy, helped no doubt by old age, became conspicuous; and I wondered how so penetrating a mind in regard to particular facts and persons, could be satisfied with such jejune second-hand theories. Anti-clericalism was the dominant crotchet: hatred of religion had acquired all the dogmatism and intolerance of religion, with none of its advantages. For it was noticeable in my father how comfortless (except for the assumption that things were improving and apparently were to go on improving forever)—I say how comfortless his philosophy was; whereas in the Anglo-Saxon world, it is all veiled and emotionalized by a sort of music, like the empty trite words by the swelling harmonies of an anthem.

This difference is capital. It makes the whole moral lesson and speculative interest of my many visits to my father, of which this was the first. And I think now I can distinguish wherein that difference lies. Liberalism, Protestantism, Judaism, positivism all have the same ultimate aim and standard. It is prosperity, or as Lutheran theologians put it, union with God at our level, not at God's level. The thing all these schools detest is the ideal of union with God at God's level, proper to asceticism, mysticism, Platonism, and pure intelligence, which insist on seeing things under the form of truth and of eternity. You must be content, they say, to see things under the form of time, of appearance, and of feeling. Very well: yet the question returns why my father's view, which doctrinally was the same as the Anglo-Saxon, was morally and emotionally so different. And to this question I reply, that prosperity may be the ideal of the poor, or it may be the ideal of the rich; and it may be accompanied by domestic, national, and religious joys, or by domestic, national, and religious bitterness. My father's was the bitter poor man's liberalism; the liberalism of the dominant Anglo-Saxon is that of the joyful rich man. This colors differently their common ideal of prosperity; but prosperity remains the ultimate ideal of both. For this reason Latins who are rich either in possessions or in sympathies can hardly be liberals. They love the beautiful.

This point touches the heart of my intellectual relations with my father, and also my judgment, very different from his, on English and American civilization. Both the side of it that he admired and the side of it that I admire and love, were foreshadowed in Bacon's *New Atlantis*. Bacon was the prophet of the rich man's Utopia; he had the liberal's worship of prosperity, and the pragmatic esteem for science and dominion over matter as means to that end: and when my father saw the partial realization of that prophecy in England and America, he was filled with respect and envy for it, and chagrin that his own country was so backward in those profitable inventions and methods. But Bacon's ideal had another side, the successful rich man's delight in nobility and splendor; he was a courtier, and still nursed the classic ideal of a hierarchy of the arts, with a magnificent pageant of virtues and dignities, like the celestial choirs come down to earth. His *New Atlantis* was not

to be merely prosperous, but solemnly ordered, glorious, and beautiful. Now just as in Bacon's mind this Roman or Byzantine ves-
ture clothed a pragmatic skeleton, so in England and even in the
United States, the cult of splendor and aristocratic ways of living
and feeling endured and in some circles entirely hid the commercial and industrial mechanism beneath it. There was an intense
poetic, sporting, and religious life. Of this my father knew nothing,
or shrugged his shoulders at it, as at vanities that may be forgiven
in a society that, in more serious matters, is thoroughly sound and
utilitarian. Now it was precisely this free, friendly, laughing side
of Anglo-Saxon civilization that I liked and cultivated. It could not
have existed, I know, without the material prosperity that supports
it; at least it could not have existed in these special forms. Yet
friendship, laughter, and freedom were not invented in the nineteenth century, and the modern forms of them are good only for
re-enacting those ancient glories.

It was not at long range only, like Lucretius, that my father
could observe the evils occasioned by religion. His only friend in
Avila, who at once courteously came to salute me, was a clerical,
and a sad wreck. Whether his ruin was due directly to clericalism
might be doubted; it was due rather to cards; but indirectly cards
might be due to indolence and boredom, these to lack of national
prosperity, and this in turn notoriously to clericalism. So that Don
Pelayo, for that was his name, was a victim of the system that he
so perversely advocated. Here was a perpetual thorn in my father's
side; and yet the prick was a stimulant. It enlivened him and kept
his exasperation always pleasantly fresh and green.

Don Pelayo expressed himself well, even grandly. His Castilian,
like my father's, was of the purest, only that he loved rhetoric, as
my father did not. His rounded periods were often Ciceronian.
His model among the living, however, was only Cánovas del Cas-
tillo, prime minister whenever the conservatives were in power,
whom he called *"el monstruo de la edad presente,"* the monster,
meaning the marvel, of the present age. Cánovas was neither a
monster nor a marvel, but a plausible intriguing politician who

made the best of a bad job. Perhaps he was less pernicious than his rival, the liberal Sagasta. He allowed Spain to draw her natural breath and to change spontaneously; he did not attempt to destroy her life and character, and to turn her into a capitalist plutocracy with an industrial proletariat, things equally contrary to her nature; because the Spanish people is a poetic people and Spanish greatness is a chivalrous greatness.

Sagasta, on the contrary, and the forces he represented, were corrupt to the core. I remember what my brother-in-law, a wiser head than Don Pelayo, said about Sagasta in 1898, after the battle of Santiago. The better Spanish cruisers had been sent to Cuba without their heavy guns. Where were those guns? In the pocket of the Minister of Marine. "How," I asked, "can Sagasta not be ashamed of himself, and how can he remain in office?" "He would have died of shame," my brother-in-law said dryly, "if he were capable of the feeling." * Such was Spanish Government under a foreign parliamentary regime.

Don Pelayo had studied at the University of Salamanca, but learning was not his strong point. Even the astronomy of Ptolemy was unknown to him. One evening we were walking in the Paseo de San Roque (a rough terrace by a convent wall, with an open view) and admiring the stars, particularly numerous and brilliant in the rarified atmosphere of Avila. "They say," Don Pelayo meditated, "that the earth is suspended in the void without any support. That is impossible. If it had no support it would fall to the ground." Unfortunately his practice was no wiser than his theory. In his youth he had divided a small patrimony with his two sisters, but had soon dissipated his share, and had gone to live with them at their expense. Finding nothing else to do, he continued to play cards in small taverns with only copper coins for stakes. As he was very near-sighted and his companions unscrupulous, he would find, even if he won, that he had only false pennies in his pocket. He would bring them up one by one in

---

* The original was more terse: "*Se hubiera muerto de vergüenza, si la tuviera.*"

the light to his better eye, and exclaim sadly: "But all these coins are ignoble." He felt himself Job-like; there was verbal majesty in his misery. My father used to say, that in spite of his grandiloquence, Don Pelayo would sell all his religious and political principles for one peseta. I think he might have sold them, because he needed the peseta; but he would have cheated the devil in doing so, because his ideal allegiance to them would have remained unchanged.

I was told that in winter, when my father took his walk soon after his midday dinner, Don Pelayo would sometimes arrive just before dinner was served. "No, thank you," he would say, "I have dined already; but if I may I will have the pleasure of sitting at table with you, while you eat." A place would be made for him; a heaping plate of chick peas and the other ingredients of the *puchero* would be placed before him, and he would resign himself to taste it. *"Empalmo,"* he would say: "I make a connection, I catch the branch train." It was true that the poor man had already dined—the day before yesterday.

My stay in Avila that year, 1883, was not long. I made a tour to Catalonia in order to visit relations, and by the way I saw a good many impressive things. I have already mentioned that my father and I made an excursion to the Escurial: later I went alone to Madrid and to the Prado, to Saragossa, to Tarragona, to Barcelona, and finally to Lyons and Paris. It was a varied feast for my hungry eyes. Most of those places have become familiar to me in later years, but of Saragossa, which I have hardly revisited, my memories belong to that early time, and are vivid. There was *La Seo*, the Cathedral, Gothic in style but preserving the square plan of the mosque that it replaced: seven lofty aisles, with rows of chapels in addition, and with the rich choir and sanctuary making an enclosed island in the middle. To me, who love shrines and individual devotions and freedom of movement in sacred places, this arrangement seemed ideal. A Jewish friend whom I once took to see the Pantheon in Rome pronounced it the first *religious* place he had found there; and I can understand that feeling. It belongs to what Spengler calls *Magian* religion and art: it reappears in the Mosque of Omar—a Christian Church—and in many other mosques. At Saragossa it is combined, as at St. Sophia, with the Christian theme of salvation, in all its complexities, historical, personal, and eschatological. There are a thousand mediations, unknown to the pure Moslem; but they do not destroy the sublimity or the inwardness of a total surrender of man to God. In Saragossa there is also *La Lonja*, a picturesque hall with twisted columns, the mediæval Merchants' Exchange. We are in the Mediterranean World; might be at Pisa or Palermo, or even at Damascus. Finally, there is *La Virgen dèl Pilar*; but here the architecture is vast, dreary, modern, and when I saw it, hideously painted. The only interest, the only beauty, is devotional and centered in the glittering shrine of the Pillar itself. *El Pilar* is the sanctuary of Spanish patriotism and chivalry: it is the point, as Delphi was to the Greeks, of their conscious contact with fate and with eternity. It is therefore truly sacred. That the legend should be childish or the statue ordinary makes no difference: what matters is the range of human need and aspiration that has been focussed here. I therefore went to the back of the shrine, where the jasper pillar is accessible to the public through an oval opening in the wall; and I kissed the hollowed place that had been worn down by the kisses of generations. Not that I expected any wish of mine to be furthered by such a ceremony: I was only offering up all my wishes, to be sacrificed or fulfilled as the issue might determine. In any case, I was quickening in myself the sense of their precarious fortunes and eternal claims. I kissed at once the beauty of the beautiful and the rod that smote me and drove me from its presence.

The goal of my journey, however, was Tarragona: for tnere a cousin and contemporary of my father's, Don Nicolás Zabalgoitia, was a canon in the Cathedral. Spanish custom calls a parent's cousin an uncle; courtesy therefore compels me to speak of the Canon as *tio Nicolás*; but he is not to be confused with my real uncle Nicolás Santayana, my father's brother, a major and my godfather, from whom I took my third Christian name. The Canon, however, was not my only relation in Tarragona. My father's eldest sister, my aunt Mariquita, lived with him and had kept house for him all their lives; and with them, at that time, lodged my father's youngest brother, Manuel, with his wife and their two children. More than half my entire Spanish connection lived under that roof: so that my father, who was always loyal to his family bonds, thought I ought to accept the invitation of my *tio Nicolás,* and make the acquaintance of that whole household.

Towards *tio Nicolás* my father had an old affection, as for a brother; yet like all my father's affections it was mixed with bitterness. In their youth Nicolás had been put in a monastery and had become a monk: yet scarcely had he taken his vows, when all the monasteries in Spain (except for a few devoted to supplying missionaries for the Colonies) were suppressed by the Government, and the monks dispersed. In time, a place was found for the waif as parish priest in some village, where he had to keep house and needed a housekeeper. Now my grandmother, as I have already indicated, was punctilious and vehement in her piety, poor, and burdened with a family of twelve children, for whom places had to be found in the world. Unfortunately the two eldest were daughters, not inclined apparently to become nuns; yet their mother doubtless thought that life in a clerical atmosphere would be better for their temporal and eternal welfare than would some modest commonplace marriage. Now that the young priest, their cousin, needed a housekeeper, would not the eldest sister, Mariquita, be suitable for that office? Surely a great confidence was manifested here in divine grace, to put a young man and a young woman, practically strangers to each other, under one narrow roof, where they were compelled by their cousinship to live on equal terms, not as master and servant, for day after day all summer, and night after night all winter. A triumph of chastity over propinquity would surely have been admirable in such circumstances, but the contrary was more probable. Could not my experienced grandmother or her confessor foresee it? A child, called a niece, before long was seen playing in that village parsonage; and although for some reason no more children appeared, the constraint and forced mendacity in such a household, added to its poverty, were not pleasant to consider.

My father's affectionate tone and loyal conduct towards his family never varied, whatever at any moment might be his feelings. He sometimes quarrelled with them, and spoke of them sharply to other persons; but the quarrels were soon made up, and he reverted to his fundamental tolerance and even deference towards all mankind. It was characteristic of him to combine a kind of enthusiasm and extreme courtesy of manner with a total absence of illusions about the person so favored. It was so, I suspect, that he had courted my mother, as it were against his will. Fate had allied him to her as it had to his blood relations. In itself the conduct of my *tio Nicolás* had nothing to surprise anybody. Everybody would say of him what Mephistopheles said of Gretchen: He was not the first. That was what his ecclesiastical superiors must have said of him. The thing was unfortunate but had to be overlooked: and it didn't interfere with his continuance in the priesthood or his ultimately becoming a canon.

Yet irregularities breed irregularities, and the worst, from my father's point of view, was yet to come. He had managed to secure for his youngest brother Manuel, a small post in the Philippine Islands. It opened a career for the young man and could ultimately secure him a pension. Spain was not then a capitalist country. Nobody had "money." There were some great landlords, and some modest ones, like my brother-in-law; there were lawyers and doctors; and the rest of the middle class, including the engineers, professors, military men, and ecclesiastics, held their positions under the government and expected pensions, not only for their widows and minor children, but for their unmarried daughters for life. A post under the government, especially in the Colonies which had a separate and less political administration, was a virtual settlement: it gave a relative sense of security. What, then, was

my father's chagrin, when his brother Manuel was leaving for
Manila with the prospect of a decent career, to find that his cousin
Nicolás and his sister Mariquita had married off their "niece" to
the young Manuel, who thus sailed on his first voyage already
burdened with a wife! It was an outrageous marriage. The girl was
not only a cousin but also a niece of her husband's; and he, who
as a young bachelor might have made his way in Manila in any
society, was condemned to wallow (*acochinado*, my father said) in
a tropical pigsty, poor, unknown, and without ambition. It was he,
retired on a miserable pension, with his wife Hermenegilda and his
two surviving children, Manuela and Juan, that I found living at
Tarragona, with my *tio Nicolás* and my Aunt Mariquita.

An unattractive family, unpleasantly complicated, crowded in a
modest ill-furnished flat: yet at once I had occasion to see the
human necessity of that loyalty to one's blood, apart from one's
inclinations, which my father practised, and to put it in practice in
my turn. For I brought no blessing to that family. On the contrary,
I involuntarily imposed upon them endless trouble and responsibility, which they faced bravely; and they placed me under a permanent obligation to acknowledge and to assist them.

It had been a hot journey to Tarragona: especially at the station
in Lérida, where I had to wait several hours between trains, the
heat had been oppressive. When I reached Tarragona, I easily
singled out my *tio Nicolás*, by his clerical robes; a stout, sound,
white-haired old gentleman, dignified and affable; and with him
my uncle Manuel, passive, modest, limp, and insignificant. At the
house, my two aunts and two cousins were duly embraced. I was
feeling a little dazed, not at all well. They had prepared an elaborate supper. I could eat nothing; excused myself on the ground
of fatigue and of the great heat. But finally my head began to
swim. I was unmistakably very ill, and had to be put to bed. They
told me afterwards that I had been delirious, talked sometimes in
English, sometimes in Spanish, but about imaginary things, and
that the doctor had spoken of a high gastric fever. But after a day
or two an eruption appeared. They said they were relieved. I was
better. It was "only smallpox," and a mild case.

It was nasty and for a time troublesome; but when the blisters dried up and the crusts fell off, I had rather a pleasant convalescence. They had told me not to scratch my face, as that would make the marks permanent; but I have no marks whatever on my body, where I was free to scratch, and a few, not very obvious, precisely on my nose. My father had come to Tarragona on hearing the news, and my mother had telegraphed asking for a bulletin by cable; and this could be brief and favorable, as by that time I was well, though the red spots remained visible for some months.

The Cathedral was directly opposite, and my father and I used to walk in the cloisters; we are both given to pacing a room, like a beast in a cage; but a continuous cloister has all the advantages of an enclosed smooth space with those of fresh air in addition. It was a nice cloister, with the dark gray castle-like Cathedral overshadowing it, and one immense slanting palm tree spreading its crown victoriously over all human obstructions in the direction of the sun. We were by the shores of the Mediterranean, and a short walk would take us to the ancient citadel, overhanging the nutshell port. It was my first glimpse of that sacred sea; but the foreground at that moment was more vividly in my mind than the distances, geographical and historical: only some years later, when I went by sea from Malaga to Gibraltar did the full sense of ploughing those Homeric waters come over me, of which I expressed something in the Ode written on that occasion. Here the accent fell on ancient Tarraco, with its Roman castle still standing, and its so Spanish mixture of Carthaginian and Celtic suggestions. This had been the capital of all northeastern Spain—how much more noble and Spanish than modern Barcelona!—and the archiepiscopal see still retained vestiges of its ancient preëminence. Its canons wore red silk cassocks, like cardinals, with purple stockings: and *tio Nicolás*, who had been a handsome man, looked very grand in his vestments.

He had a jovial temperament and carried his heavy burden, both of flesh and of responsibility, with a good grace. And he was no fool. When I heard him and my father talking together, though at least in my presence their conversation was discreet and general,

I couldn't help making comparisons and wondering which of them
had the sounder and riper mind. My father was far better informed and freer to express himself; yet *tio Nicolás* seemed to be
at home in a rich humanistic world of men, of affairs, of convention and of religion, on which my father had turned his back with
a strange hatred. I can sympathize with the preference for obscurity and solitude. I prefer them for myself also: but that does not
condemn the world in its own eyes, or in those of justice, or
remove the glory and inner interest of its adventures. I felt that
tio Nicolás liked all that was likable, without being deceived by
it; and this seemed a kindlier and wiser sentiment than constitutional derision of everything that one might have discarded in
one's own life. I could see why he had been made a canon. Without eminence for either learning or virtue, he had a certain native
elegance in speech and manners. His latinity, if not impeccable,
was familiar and pleasant, and he felt the full afflatus of theological poetry and wisdom, however qualified his faith might be.
Once when I complimented him on his robust health, he shook his
head with a smile, and said *"Senectus isa morbus;* do you understand that?" I certainly understood *senectus* and *morbus;* but what
was *isa?* Sounded like Greek for "equal," was it Latin? Yes, he
said; it meant "itself."—"Oh, *ipsa!* Old age is itself a disease."—Yes,
that was it; but they pronounced it *isa.* And we talked sometimes
of chants and church music. I knew only what I had heard at the
Church of the Immaculate Conception; but I used to sing parts
of the Mass and of Rossini's *Stabat Mater* about the house; something quite natural in that sort of family, where the housemaid
sings while she makes the beds. Spanish chants have no solemnity:
they are as precipitate and perfunctory as the recital of the Rosary;
which doesn't preclude a general devout posture of mind in the
process. It might even seem more religious only to indicate the
burden of a prayer rather than to mouth the words in order to
impress other people. Worship should be addressed to God, not to
an audience. Be that as it may, *tio Nicolás* was far from sancti-
monious; he liked sometimes to be a bit naughty. At three o'clock

he was obliged, in spite of the heat, to cross the street to the Cathedral, to be present at Vespers; for if a canon was absent, he was fined one peseta. Referring to this regulation, and smoothing his robe, he would recite as he went heavily down the stairs:

Cantemos del Señor las alabanzas,
para llenar nuestras panzas

"Let us sing the praises of the Lord, that we may fill our bellies." Pleasantry? Cynicism? I think a mixture of both. After all, the sentiment is not very different from the keynote of Hebrew piety; and the Psalter needs to be taken liturgically and very symbolically, if it is still to serve for spiritual expression. I don't wonder that the old canons should have found Vespers rather sleepy and useless, the music not having been raised, as in Anglican services, into an independent vehicle of sentiment, or stimulus for it.

What did *tio Nicolás* really think of his profession? I doubt that he knew himself, or much cared to ask. He was at home in the conventions, could not break away from them without ruining himself and his family, and had no inner desire to break away. It is not as if he had been a philosopher with a clear contrary system of beliefs. He was a man of the world without any contrary system. Your genuine and profound sceptic sees no reason to quarrel with any ruling orthodoxy. It is as plausible as any other capable of prevailing in the world. If you do not think so, it is simply because that orthodoxy is not familiar to you, or not congenial. In a different age, or with a different endowment, you would have rested peacefully in it like the rest of mankind. And from the point of view of happiness, decency, art, and imagination, you might have been better off. Such, I suspect, would have been the philosophy of *tio Nicolás*, if he had framed one for himself: but he was content to quote the approved answers to all puzzling questions, and to let the Church and the Fathers bear the responsibility. It was not our fault that we were born. Is it our fault that we believe what we believe? To be incurious and at peace in such matters might even be a mark of profound faith, if the intention were to conform to the divine order of things in courage and silence, without knowing what precisely this order may be.

The worst symptoms of infidelity that I saw in that family were in the women. Not unintelligibly. It was they who had suffered most from poverty, since there had always been enough to eat, but not enough to appear in the world as women like to appear. And it was they who had suffered most from the latent disgrace of their position, and the dread of gossip and insults. They owed society a grudge for making their life difficult. They had not sinned against nature, but the world had sinned against them by its cruel tyranny and injustice. They were therefore rebels, impotent rebels, against all the powers that be, celestial and earthly. My aunt Mariquita was smiling and silent; she smiled feebly, passively, equivocally at everything, even at death and illness, and hardly said anything. When *tio Nicolás* died and she came to live with us in Avila, she would lock herself up in her room, where she didn't allow even the servant to penetrate; and when she came out for meals, she would hardly eat, insisting on mixing vinegar with everything. These were crotchets of extreme old age; but what her secret thoughts must have been appeared in her "niece" Hermenegilda and in Manuela, Hermenegilda's daughter, who were loquacious, and betrayed their sentiments even when they didn't dare to express them frankly. They had a typical low-class esteem for small material advantages, with cynicism about all virtue and so-called higher interests. In the working classes, whose poverty does not come from decay, concern about little benefits and little losses is a sign of thrift: thrift that makes for a modest well-being and for mastery in some honest art. There is no mockery then about superior gifts or unselfish virtues; there is respect for them and ambition to cultivate them. There may be even great illusions about the superiority of superior people. From such illusions my female relations at Tarragona were scornfully free. They imagined that they knew perfectly the corrupt motives and morals of all the rich and famous. And yet they didn't love the poor or consent to be identified with them. Manuela, whose pension when she became an orphan was only forty pesetas or eight dollars a month, might have married a member of the *Guardia Civil* or Constabulary, who had courted her: but he was only a private or a non-commissioned officer, and she refused. She thereby became chiefly dependent on me, or on what I induced my sister Josefina to give her. I didn't dislike Manuela: her mind was common, and sometimes also her manners, but she was sincere and unprejudiced. You could talk with her as with a man, and though her judgments on people were ignorant and uncharitable, they were hypothetically penetrating: I mean, they showed what such people *might* be. Incidentally they revealed the quality of Manuela's education and character. She didn't belong to the Intelligentsia, because she had read nothing, but she belonged to the revolutionary party, to the Reds. Since we are all rascals, let us all be rascals at one level, with equal chances to worm our way to a false eminence.

These principles were not entirely theoretical. Before I left Tarragona, my father and I became aware that there was a plot afoot to marry me to Manuela. It was a repetition of the plot that had contrived the marriage of her father and mother. *Tio Nicolás* could not have been ignorant of this scheme, if not actually the author of it: something that rather lowered my esteem for him, and chilled a little my sense of the kind treatment I had received in his house. He may have thought: What is there wrong in mating these cousins? Why is young Manuela worse than any other girl that Jorge might marry? In the abstract there might seem to be nothing wrong; at their distance they could have no notion of my real circumstances in America, which made any marriage impossible. Perhaps they counted on keeping me in Spain: counted on my mother's help, without understanding her character.

Illness had prevented me from reaching Paris at the time when my steamer friend Mrs. X. of Cincinnati, Ohio, was to be there; but I had her address and wrote explaining what had happened, not disguising the disgusting and contagious nature of the illness but calling it smallpox in plain English. Having done the Rhine she was now going to do the Rhone; and as I was also passing that way, I suggested that we should meet in Lyons. Lyons turned out to be a lucky choice, and I spent a week there, not waiting for Mrs. X., but going every night to the theatre where Sarah Bernhardt happened to be performing. It was a great treat: *Phèdre, La Dame aux Camélias, Frou-frou, Adrienne Lecouvreur,* and *La Tosca.* The divine Sarah was still relatively young, serpent-like, with her "golden voice" fresh and not too monotonous; and while dramatically she seemed most adequate in *Frou-frou* and *La Dame aux Camélias,* poetically and verbally it was in *Phèdre,* and especially in the passage from *Phèdre* repeated in *Adrienne Lecouvreur* that she captivated me entirely: and I still repeat to myself at night, as if it were a prayer, that passage and others as nearly as I can after her fashion. It was liturgical: the text spoke as if it were an oracle, and the actress was a speaking statue, and her voice came, ideally, through a mask. In listening to *La Tosca,* on the contrary, in the scene where Mario is being tortured, I found the strain intolerable, and slipped out—being in the pit, near the door —for fear of fainting. This experience led me to understand that there is a limit to the acceptable terror and pity that tragedy may excite. They must be excited only speculatively, intellectually, religiously: if they are excited materially and deceptively, you are overcome and not exalted. The spectacle either drives you away, as it did me, or becomes a vice, an indulgence that adds to the evils of life rather than liberates from them. Sardou was not a tragedian; he was a contriver of sensational plays.

The rest of my journey is described briefly in one of my father's letters: it acknowledges one of mine from Antwerp, whence I was sailing on October 8th.

Avila, 9th of October, 1883.

. . . "I see with great pleasure that you have kept well, that the financial or cash question has been happily solved, and that you have nothing to complain of unless it be having missed your Conquest, who as appears from the letter that I enclose and that I opened to see if it shed any light on your whereabouts, has been playing with you at hide and seek. My cousin Nicolás had already maliciously guessed as much [lo ha maliciado], for being a priest he has a keen scent for everything that concerns women. He used to tell me he was sure that you would never find that lady, and attributed the fact to the smallpox. I think that you will not have been overmuch troubled at such a trifle, and that you will not go to look for her in Cincinnati, Ohio, but that you will wait tranquilly for her to send you that teacup, bought expressly for you, and the only one that was not broken, seeing that she has sworn not to let anyone use it but you."

The teacup never was sent and I never went to Cincinnati, Ohio, or had further correspondence with Mrs. X. Some ten years later, however, I received a visit from a beautifully dressed young clergyman who said he was the Reginald X. of Cincinnati, Ohio. Only an English military tailor who had been converted could have made a clerical coat look so like the smartest of officers' tunics. I remembered Mrs. X. saying how much she hoped that her son would become a "priest"; and putting two and two together I could imagine which way the wind blew in that young man's religious vocation. We talked of seasickness, of the sea, of the British Navy, of the Church. I spoke sorrowfully of the state of religion at Harvard, and hoped it was better in Cincinnati. Even the Episcopal Theological School in Cambridge was not traditional and Catholic enough for my taste; nevertheless on week days when their chapel was almost empty, I sometimes dropped in there for Vespers, if I got back early from my walk and it wasn't yet time for afternoon tea. He smiled and understood my banter perfectly; scoffers were half converted when they laughed at themselves; but when I asked about his mother, as I did repeatedly, his replies were curt and he changed the subject.

CHAPTER XV

COLLEGE FRIENDS

MY DEEPEST friendships were all individual. The bond was not due to belonging to the same circle or class or even nation. Chance having allowed us to discover each other, character, quality, and sympathy did the rest. Of such friendships I have mentioned only the two that I formed at school; they had little or no sequel, except in my inner mind. Now I come to others that, by chance, I formed at college: not like those friends I have described as figures in the Yard, where college life had brought us together. These chosen friends were picked out from that flowing mass precisely because they belonged elsewhere; the Yard where we happened to be did not unite us, nor does the memory of them take me back to the Yard.

First in time and very important, was my friendship with Charles Loeser. I came upon him by accident in another man's room, and he immediately took me into his own, which was next door, to show me his books and pictures. Pictures and books! That strikes the keynote to our companionship. At once I found that he spoke French well, and German presumably better, since if hurt he would swear in German. He had been at a good international school in Switzerland. He at once told me that he was a Jew, a rare and blessed frankness that cleared away a thousand pitfalls and insincerities. What a privilege there is in that distinction and in that misfortune! If the Jews were not worldly it would raise them above the world; but most of them squirm and fawn and wish to pass for ordinary Christians or ordinary atheists. Not so Loeser: he had no ambition to manage things for other people, or to worm himself into fashionable society. His father was the proprietor of a vast "dry-goods store" in Brooklyn, and rich—how rich I never knew, but rich enough and generous enough for his son always to have plenty of money and not to think of a profitable profession. Another blessed simplification, rarely avowed in America. There was a commercial presumption that a man is useless unless he makes money, and no vocation, only bad health, could excuse the son of a millionaire for not at least pretending to have an office or a studio. Loeser seemed unaware of this social duty. He showed me the nice books and pictures that he had already collected—the beginnings of that passion for possessing and even stroking *objets-d'art* that made the most unclouded joy of his life. Here was fresh subject matter and fresh information for my starved aestheticism—starved sensuously and not supported by much reading: for this was in my Freshman year, before my first return to Europe.

Loeser had a tremendous advance on me in these matters, which he maintained through life: he seemed to have seen everything, and to speak every language. Berenson had the same advantage, with a public reputation that Loeser, who wrote nothing, never acquired; but somehow I felt more secure under the sign of Loeser. He had perhaps more illusions, but also a more German simplicity and devotion to his subject. I felt that he loved the Italian renaissance and was not, as it were, merely displaying it. This was then in the future; for the moment it was only a question of reading a few books that he lent me, discussing them, and sometimes going together to the theatre—which was at his invitation. In those days there were foreign companies often playing for a week or two in Boston, French operetta, Salvini, Ristori, and grand opera. I saw everything, and in the first years it couldn't have been at my own expense. It might seem that all my life I have been "sponging" on my rich friends, or even that I have sought rich friends for that purpose. This was not the case: there were plenty of rich people about that I fled from. But with people with whom I was otherwise in sympathy, friendship was naturally more easily kept up and cemented if they had a house where they could ask me to stay, or could invite me to be their guest, partly or wholly, for trips or entertainments that I couldn't afford if left to my own resources. Loeser was my first Maecenas of this kind, and one of the most satisfactory. His invitations were specific, for particular occasions. Only once, when we were looking at some modern pictures, I stopped before one that I liked and said that it was painted as I should have wished to paint. "Why don't you do it," Loeser cried impulsively. "Why don't you stay in Paris and paint? I will help you." But I knew that this was an *ignis fatuus* in the case of both of us: I couldn't give up philosophy and an assured livelihood, and he couldn't commit himself to a responsibility that would have at once become a burden and a source of angry feelings. Ordinarily his favors were discreet, and made for his own pleasure. He never gave me money or presents, nor did any of my other friends. It was simply a question of making possible little plans that were beyond my unaided means. Thus when we travelled together in Italy, I contributed twenty gold francs a day to our expenses, and he, who knew the ropes and the language, made all the arrangements and paid all the bills. He might have been a sort of magic dragoman in my service, spiriting up the scenes and spiriting away the deficits.

At Harvard, Loeser was rather friendless. The fact that he was a Jew and that his father kept a "dry-goods store" cut him off, in democratic America, from the ruling society. To me, who was also an outsider, this seemed at first very strange, for Loeser was much more cultivated than the leaders of undergraduate fashion or athletics, and I saw nothing amiss in his person or manners. He was not good-looking, although he had a neat figure, of middle height, and nice hands: but his eyes were dead, his complexion muddy, and his features pinched, though not especially Jewish. On the other hand he was extremely well-spoken, and there was nothing about him in bad taste. To me he was always an agreeable companion, and if our friendship never became intimate, this was due rather to a certain defensive reserve in him than to any withdrawal on my part. Yet in the end, taking imaginatively the point of view of the native leading Americans, I came to see why Loeser could never gain their confidence. His heart was not with them, and his associations and standards were not theirs. He didn't join in their sports (as rich Jews have learned to do in England), he hadn't their religion, he had no roots in their native places or in their family circles. In America he floated on the surface, and really lived only in the international world of art, literature, and theory.

Yet there was something else at work: for, except for my connection with the Sturgises, all those things were true of me, with poverty added, yet I was never expressly excluded from anything in America. I was not isolated, except quite secretly in my own feelings, as any poetical or religious youth might have been anywhere. And I found afterwards, when Loeser lived in Florence, that while he knew the whole Anglo-American colony slightly, he seemed to have no friends. For a rich bachelor that was odd; and I suspect that he preferred to keep his gates shut, and prowled about, as if a little mad, in his own castle. There was usually a certain vagueness about his assertions and plans, as if he were afraid that people might interfere with him; and when he married, at fifty, a German Jewish pianist, the separation remained, except that his wife sometimes still performed, and with great power, in public or in private concerts. It surprised me, whenever I was at Strong's villa, that Loeser who had a good motor, never came to see me or asked me to go to his house, except once, to see his new tower. This made me doubt whether Loeser had ever had any affection for me, such as I had for him, and whether it was only *faute de mieux*, as a last resort in too much solitude, that in earlier years he had been so friendly. However, circumstances change, one changes as much as other people, and it would be unreasonable to act or feel in the same way when the circumstances are different. Loeser in any case had shown me Italy, initiated me into Italian ways, present and past, and made my life there in later years much richer than it would have been otherwise. Let him be thanked without any qualifications.

In the 1890's I saw him several times in London. He lived in the Burlington Hotel, behind the Arcade, amid a great lot of leather portmanteaux and hatboxes. He had become very English, much to my taste; his alien but expert knowledge of how an English gentleman should dress, eat, talk, and travel amused and instructed me vastly; but he didn't seem to have real friends among the English, other than Algar Thorold, son of the Bishop of Winchester, who (twice, I believe) had gone over to Rome. The first time he had essayed to be a Carthusian; but being disappointed and having a relapse, the second time he married and became an ordinary lay Catholic. He lived in Italy, in a truly Italian villa, where I was glad to hear him and his wife speak of Loeser with affection. It helped to relieve the latent uneasiness I felt about my friend. He had sometimes been so dark and inconsequential that I suspected a touch of madness in his nature. He would say and do things that might pass for jokes; but oddities when indulged may become illusions. He maintained that he had two original works of Michelangelo in his collection: one a rough ordinary *putto* from some fountain or altar, the other a truly beautiful panel in wax, a Madonna and Child (certainly after Michelangelo's earlier work) with a St. Joseph perhaps less convincing. I am no judge in the matter; but to have discovered two unknown and genuine Michelangelos, and got them cheap, is certainly a collector's dream, and incredible.

It was with Loeser that I first went to Rome and to Venice: my preference for these two cities, rather than for the Florence so dear to English-speaking people, may be partly due to a first impression gained under his auspices. His taste was selective. He dwelt on a few things, with much knowledge, and did not confuse or fatigue the mind. We reached Rome rather late at night. It had been raining, and the wet street and puddles reflected the lights fantastically. Loeser had a theory that architecture is best seen and admired at night. He proposed that we should walk to our hotel. He had chosen the *Russie*, where as he said only Russian Grand Dukes stayed, so that it was just the place for him and for me. We walked by the *Quattro Fontane* and the *Piazza di Spagna*—a long walk: but I doubt that the first loud accents that I heard on arriving at the Hotel were those of a Russian Grand Duchess. She said simply: "Oh my!"

Some ten years later, in 1905, Loeser had a spacious apartment in an old palazzo near the *Uffizi* in Florence. He said he couldn't offer me a room, but had secured a choice one (*choice* was a favorite word of his) for me, quite cheap, in a tower in the *Via dei Bardi,* with a loggia where I might have my breakfast, and wave to him across the river; for he too slept in a tower and had his bath in the open loggia at the very top of it. My room was indeed in a tower; there were 149 stone steps with hardly a door to pass on the way up: my choice room did have a bed in it, but the loggia was bitterly cold on those sunless mornings. This didn't matter, however, since there was no breakfast. My woebegone landlady had no idea of coffee, milk, or rolls, and her tea, in an open broken old dish, was half dust. However, I managed. I got up late, and went to breakfast in a good café, read the papers, sunned myself on the *Lungarno,* and by half past twelve was at Loeser's place, where I was expected daily for luncheon. But he said he had no dinner, only a bite of something by the fire in his library. One evening, however, I was invited to this frugal supper, and warned that Mrs. Y., of whom he had spoken to me, would be there also. Mrs. Y. was the wife of a British officer serving in India, and I had been given to understand that she and Loeser were on the best of terms. "But my servant, Antonio," he had added, "doesn't approve of her. I asked him if he was shocked." "Chè," said Antonio, "she is too thin!" I found Mrs. Y. most amiable, a slender blonde dressed like Botticelli's *Primavera,* hatless, with a workbasket beside her and evidently quite at home. Dinner was ample, served pleasantly at a low table in front of the fire. Apparently Mrs. Y. dined there every evening, and I began to understand that practically, if not nominally, she lived in that house. That explained why there had been no room to offer me, and why Loeser never "dined." Why hadn't he simply told me the facts? Did he think I should be shocked like Antonio? Or was he pro-

tecting the lady's reputation? But then why let out the secret in
the end? However, it was better to be inconsistently secretive than
to be mad.

In an earlier year, when I had been free in the spring, Loeser
proposed a walking tour across the Apennines. First we went to
Ravenna, which I hadn't seen, and thence to Pesaro where we
abandoned the railway and drove to Urbino. From there, sending
our things ahead by rail, we walked to San Sepolcro and La Vernia. It was travelling as in the Middle Ages, stopping at small inns
or at monasteries. At La Vernia we found the Franciscan community making a procession in their half-open cloister. The monks
were evidently peasants, some of them young yokels fresh from the
plough, no doubt ignorant and stupid; and Loeser's modern Jewish
standards betrayed themselves in his utter scorn of those mere
beasts, as he called them. I wondered if St. John the Baptist or
Elijah might not also have seemed mere beasts; but I didn't say so.
Being at once a beast and a spirit doesn't seem to me a contradiction. On the contrary, it is necessary to be a beast if one is ever
to be a spirit. The modern Jew recognizes verbal intelligence, but
not simple spirit. He doesn't admit anything deeper or freer than
literature, science, and commerce.

When we were at the top of the pass, after deliciously drinking,
like beasts on all fours, at a brook that ran down by the road, we
looked about at the surrounding hilltops. They were but little
above our own level, yet numerous, and suggested the top of the
world. "What are you thinking of?" Loeser asked. I said: "Geography." "I," he retorted, "was thinking of God." So that Loeser
would probably have reversed my judgment about not apprehending pure spirit, and would have said that the Latin or Catholic is
hopelessly materialistic even in his religion, whereas the Jew hears
the voice of an invisible God in the silence of nature. Very good:
but why not hear that voice also in the silence of beasts or of
monks? Perhaps the reason was that the mountains are the skeleton of that land which feeds and surrounds literature, science, and
commerce. To the Jew the earth seems a promised land, suggesting

the millennium, the triumph of God in the human world. Swine, epicureans, and monks, on the contrary, not being legally edible, seem not only useless for that purpose but positively unclean. This comes consistently enough of regarding God only as a power, the power that conditions our happiness. It is then no metaphor to say that God dwells in the mountains or in the whirlwind: their reality is his reality, and their work his work. In science, commerce, and literature you are tracing his ways. And the idea that all these vast and apparently dead forces secretly conspire to direct human history and to prepare the glory of Zion, becomes sublime. But if God were regarded rather as the *end* or the *good* in which happiness might be found, might he not seem to dwell far more directly and intimately in the monk and even in the beast than in commerce, literature, or science?

At the beginning of my Sophomore year, not in the Yard but in the Church of the Immaculate Conception, I made the acquaintance of Ward Thoron, destined to be my closest friend while we were undergraduates. He said in recent years that he was the original of Mario in my *Last Puritan*, and there is some truth in that assertion, especially in regard to his family relations; but I had other far more accomplished models for my young men, and gave him a different education, different motives, and a different career. Ward had not been educated at Eton, but at the Jesuit College in Fordham, New York. He had graduated there at seventeen; and on the strength of that degree he was mechanically and foolishly admitted to the Sophomore class at Harvard. We were in the same class, but he was three years younger than I, and younger than most Freshmen. This, together with his being a Catholic, gave me at once the feelings of an elder brother towards him, and a sort of mentor. Except that he was at home in scraps of Church Latin, he was utterly unprepared for the studies he was to take up; and not coming from any of the usual preparatory schools, he had no ready-made circle of acquaintances in the College, who might have adopted him and steered him more or less safely. Nevertheless, he had a social position much better than mine, and lived in a private house full of boys of good families, with plenty of money to spend. He was never lonely: and this was at once an advantage and a danger.

His grandparents, Mr. and Mrs. "Sam" Ward, of New York, were persons of high transcendental New England traditions, but at the same time rich and fashionable. Mrs. Ward was an impressive old lady, dressed in obsolete but regal garments and speaking in impassioned accents. "Ah," she would exclaim, "I could never close my eyes if I hadn't first opened wide my window and gazed at the stars!" In her youth she had been a colonist at Brook Farm with the social utopians; then she had passed from one Evangelical sect to another, until she finally landed in the Catholic Church. There she found inner peace, but socially she remained militant. She managed to convert her daughters and even her son, but her husband, alas! held on to his heathen idealism and Germanic intuitions: for he too was an ardent spirit, modified by luxurious living and much shrewd knowledge of the world. His grandson sent him an essay of mine on Free-Will, which had been printed in a College paper: on which the old gentleman made the penetrating observation that if I had anything to say I should be able to say it, that I knew the stock arguments on the subject, and that there were no others.

Not satisfied with converting her daughters, Mrs. Ward insisted on marrying them safely to Catholics, which at that time in her circle practically meant to foreigners. One of these, my friend's father, was a Frenchman who had occupied some post in the Levant; his wife had died; and their children had been adopted by their American grandparents. Ward saw his father but seldom; however, he could speak French easily, and took easily to his Catholic education and his American surroundings. He needed to sail before the wind. Rough seas and contrary blasts were not for him: I think he had no clear object in view that could have justified him in facing them. But given an open course he was clever enough to steer his festive voyage and enjoy himself thoroughly in doing so.

He once wrote an essay—it was only an exercise in composition, so that the views advanced didn't matter—on the *Art of Lying*, in which he gathered such arguments as occurred to him to prove the advantages of concealing or misrepresenting the truth; and then added that equal advantages could be found in telling it. He felt that he was playing a farce, and there seemed to be nothing else for him to do. Fordham had been a farce, Harvard was a farce also: yet if everything is a farce, the one in which you find yourself acting acquires, for the time being, all the values of reality.

This philosophy, hidden in a boy of seventeen under verbal sparkle and easy manners, but breaking down under pressure into genuine Catholic humility, had everything to please me. It was not even then my own philosophy. I was as convinced as I am now of the steady march of cosmic forces that we may, in a measure, enlist in our service, and thereby win the prize of life in the process of living, without laying any claims to dominate the universe, either physically or morally. But this is a comparatively mature, though very ancient, conclusion; and it is as well to become aware in the first place of the uncertainty and blindness of human opinion.

Ward and I didn't move in the same circles; I didn't know his friends nor he mine. Yet there were hours, especially the late afternoon hours, when we were much together, when the crowd were at their sports, in which neither of us took part. In the evening his casual boon companions would carry him off on their larks, perhaps too often for his tender years. He fell ill; and during a long convalescence, when he was confined to his sofa, I used to keep him company. During those long winter afternoons we read aloud alternately the whole of Tolstoi's *War and Peace* in French. It was no school task; we could talk instead, if there were anything to talk about; and we talked more or less about everything.

A feeling that we had moved into different climates came over me some years later when after his marriage he invited me to stay with him in Washington. He was living at his mother-in-law's, presiding at the other end of the table, while his wife sat with her sisters at the side, as if they were still children. He took me to see

Mr. Henry Adams, with whom he was on very friendly terms. "So you are trying to teach philosophy at Harvard," Mr. Adams said, somewhat in the gentle but sad tone we knew in Professor Norton. "I once tried to teach history there, but it can't be done. It isn't really possible to teach anything." This may be true, if we give very exacting meanings to our terms; but it was not encouraging. Still, both Mr. Adams' house and that of Ward's new family were luxurious. I got the impression that, if most things were illusions, having money and spending money were great realities. I also gathered that Ward no longer called himself a Catholic, but was more or less affiliated to his mother-in-law's church.

I have never seen Ward after that visit to Washington. He remained there while I was in America, or in summer resorts that I didn't frequent, and he has never, to my knowledge, been in Europe in the later years. But this material separation was not indifferent; it symbolized a separation in our interests and aims. I recognize the perfect right of anybody to surrender his personal inopportune advantages for the sake of others more social and opportune. That is the path of material evolution. But the evolution I admire and appreciate is not of that kind, which transforms the character and the ideal pursued. The evolution that interests me is that of a given seed, towards its perfect manifestation. From what I have heard about my friend in his maturity and old age, I gather that he played his part well and had his reward: but it was the sort of success by adaptability in essentials that leaves me cold: so that perhaps nothing was lost to him or to me by our separation; and our affectionate relation in youth retains its intrinsic value all the more distinctly by not being followed, as in the case of some of my other friendships, by later contacts that might obscure it.

Three other men in the Harvard class of 1886 belonged in the front rank of my friends: Herbert Lyman, Frank Bullard, and Boylston Beal. All these were pure and intense Bostonians of the old school, yet with differences that mark the range of Boston "culture" at that time. "Culture," with religious and philosophical preoccupations, belonged especially to Bullard. He was a nephew of Professor Norton, and I might almost say in fortunately delicate health; fortunately, because if he had been thoroughly sound, strong, and athletic, he would have had to go into "business" or into a profession no less businesslike and absorbing, because according to the ruling code this would have been his duty to society. That was what Herbert Lyman (also potentially rich) was obliged to do all his life. Business, together with music and a semi-administrative interest in King's Chapel, formed the entirely orthodox themes of his moral harmony. This harmony was beautifully achieved; yet it had cost him some renunciations and some moments of difficulty. He would have liked to devote himself entirely to music; but he had neither the great voice nor the exceptional musical genius that would have justified him in becoming a professional musician. Later his health faltered; but he pulled through, to the good age of seventy-seven. Only two years earlier, he was kind enough to make me a visit at Cortina, and seemed to me little changed from the memorable days that, fifty-five years before, we had spent together at Dresden. Of these, and of him, I will speak again. I mention him here lest he should seem to be forgotten in my catalogue of College friends.

Bullard and I hardly knew each other when undergraduates; but ten or fifteen years later he took to studying philosophy and came to hear some of my lectures. We then established an active exchange of moral and intellectual ideas. The influence of his uncle had led him to collect prints, especially Turner prints. They were very beautiful, and on the frequent occasions when I was a guest at his mother's house, we used to go up after luncheon to his study and look over his treasures. He had also some pre-Raphaelite prints that I couldn't praise so much; but the Turners and the photographed drawings by the old masters found us equally appreciative. It is not true, by the way, that the aerial effects in Turner's landscapes are exaggerated and melodramatic. Nature in England and elsewhere—for instance in Venice—is often like that, or even more emphatic; and the delicacy with which Turner preserves the special character and melody of the parts in the midst of that violent ensemble, shows a sincere love of nature and life and a devout imagination.

Frank Bullard and his collections did much more to educate my taste than my lectures did to clarify his intellect. He was interested and unprejudiced but, as he said, "bird-witted." His flights were short and flurried. He came to no large clear conclusions; what survived was only an open and ardent spirit. Christianity and Puritanism had here debouched into a sensitive humanity; yet the natural aims of life remained for him miscellaneous and conflicting. The day of fresh decisions and sharp exclusions had not yet dawned.

With Boylston Beal, too, my friendship grew after we had left College. We lived in the same boarding house one winter in Berlin, and we were constantly together at Cambridge in the early 1890's, he being at the Law School and I a young instructor, and both frequenting the same club. Later he married a cousin of my family, which established another bond. He travelled everywhere and knew the principal languages, and was as much at home in England and in European high life as it is possible for an American to be. During the war of 1914–1918 and afterwards he was Honorary Counsellor to the American Embassy in London, telling the ladies what to wear, the men what to say and how to address royalties and persons possessing complicated titles, by law or courtesy. It was happiness to him to live in beautiful places, among refined people, with simple, graceful, and honest minds; and so it would have been to me if my lot had been more often cast among them. I did taste such happiness in obscure modest places where perhaps it ran deeper, if less sparklingly, than in official or fashionable society; but Beal saw the thing in its spectacular as well as in its intimate forms. The spectacular and official side is easier to describe and to talk about, it gives one a glimpse of political history; yet I am sure that it was the quiet and domestic side that he loved and that colored his mature judgments and opinions.

A proof of this appeared in his attachment to traditional religion

—not to his home traditions, but to the Catholic and Anglican. In Rome, where he liked to spend, when he could, a part of the winter, he sometimes would take me to some sequestered little church that he had discovered, where there was a devotional atmosphere. He was not offended by modern images and pictures and flower pots; he didn't mind if the good nuns furnished their chapels like boudoirs; he felt the pious intention: they gave their best. This is even more Spanish than Italian: a domestication of the mind and heart in religion, and being tender in small things, rather than coldly despising them and confining religion to morality or to great tragic and cosmological vistas.

In politics also Beal reacted against the denials and abstractions of the reforming zealot, and was a pronounced Tory. I sympathized with all the affections that such a position implied; but I like to open the windows of the mind wider, and to recognize not only the inevitableness of moral mutations, but their fertility. One good thing is destroyed, but another good thing may be made possible. I love Tory England and honor conservative Spain, but not with any dogmatic or prescriptive passion. If any community can become and desires to become communistic or democratic or anarchical I wish it joy from the bottom of my heart. I have only two qualms in this case: whether such ideals are realizable, and whether those who pursue them fancy them to be exclusively and universally right: an illusion pregnant with injustice, oppression, and war.

CHAPTER XVI

COLLEGE STUDIES

WITH my return to Harvard, a fortnight late, from the journey to Spain, my College studies may be said to have begun. They did not begin well. I had failed in one subject—a half course in algebra—which I was obliged to pass later, as Freshman work was prescribed and no substitutions were permitted. I had done well enough in the rest of the prescribed mathematics, analytic geometry, which I had had some grounding in at school, and also in the physics, which interested me immensely: and even in the algebra there were points that struck my imagination, as for instance the possibility and advantages of duo-decimal notation: our decimal system being founded only on the stupid reason that we have ten fingers and ten toes. If my teachers had begun by telling me that mathematics was pure play with presuppositions, and wholly in the air, I might have become a good mathematician, because I am happy enough in the realm of essence. But they were over-worked drudges, and I was largely inattentive, and inclined lazily to attribute to incapacity in myself or to a literary temperament that dullness which perhaps was due simply to lack of initiation. With a good speculative master I might have been an eager pupil and cried at once: *Introibo ad altare Dei.*

I began badly also in not having a fixed plan of study. President Eliot's elective system was then in the ascendant. We liked it, I liked it; it seemed to open a universal field to free individuality. But to be free and cultivate individuality one must first exist, one's nature must be functioning. What was I, what were my powers and my vocation? Before I had discovered that, all freedom could be nothing but frivolity. I had chosen to go on with Latin and Greek, but disregarded the requirements for second-year honors in the classics, because those requirements involved Greek composition, which I couldn't attempt. I consciously continued my reading as an amateur, not as a scholar, I wasn't going to *teach* Greek or Latin. In this way I illustrated the complementary vices of the elective system: I was a smatterer, because things were arranged for the benefit of professionals.

So superficial was my study that I hardly remember what Latin authors I read or who was the professor. I read Lucretius, in a pocket edition without notes given me by a friend, somewhat pathetically, because he was leaving College. I couldn't properly understand the text, many a word was new to me, and I had to pass on, reading as I did at odd moments, or in the horse cars. But the general drift was obvious, and I learned the great passages by heart. Even the physical and biological theories seemed instructive, not as scientific finalities, if science could be final, but as serving to dispel the notion that anything is non-natural or miraculous. If the theory suggested were false, another no less naturalistic would be true: and this presumption recommended itself to me and has become one of my first principles: not that a particular philosophy called naturalism must be true *a priori,* but that nature sets the standard of naturalness. The most miraculous world, if it were real, would subdue the teachable mind to its own habit, and would prove that miracles were—as they are in the Gospels—the most ordinary and most intelligible of events. It made me laugh afterwards to read in pedantic commentators that Lucretius abandoned his atomism whenever he was poetical, and contradicted himself in invoking Venus, when Epicurus maintains that the gods do not trouble about human affairs. On the contrary, Lucretius might perfectly well have invoked Jupiter or Fate (as Leopardi constantly invokes Fate); for Fate, Jupiter, or Venus are names for the whole or some part of the life of nature. There is no incompatibility in these various appellations, if they are understood sympathetically as the ancients understood them. They were not gaping phenomenalists, but knew that our senses, no less than our poetry and myth, clothe in human images the manifold processes of matter. By these hidden processes they lived, before them they trembled, the promise and potency of them they sought to prophesy. Matter was the ancient plastic substance of all the gods.

I also took a half course in Latin composition which I audaciously neglected, "cutting" all the lectures except the first, but doing the prescribed exercises and taking the examinations. I passed with a mark of ninety per cent.

In Greek I did as badly as at school. Here again this was not the teacher's fault. He was the amiable Louis Dyer, who had studied at Balliol, married a Miss Macmillan, and later lived in Oxford, where I often saw him. He gave me his *Gods of Greece,* nicely bound, a book that had a great influence over me. Perhaps Matthew Arnold moved in the background and inspired us. But I was thirsting for inspiration, and Greek grammar and prosody didn't hold my attention. We were supposed to read the *Ajax,* but though in this case I went to all the lectures, I didn't study the text. The *Bacchæ,* however, was a revelation. Here, before Nietzsche had pointed it out, the Dionysiac inspiration was explicitly opposed to the Apollonian; and although my tradition and manner are rather Apollonian, I unhesitatingly accept the Dionysiac inspiration as also divine. It comes from the elemental god, from the chaotic but fertile bosom of nature; Apollo is the god of measure, of perfection of humanism. He is more civilized, but more superficial, more highly conditioned. His worship seems classic and established forever, and it does last longer and is more often revived than any one form of Dionysiac frenzy: yet the frenzy represents the primitive wild soul, not at home in the world, not settled in itself, and merging again with the elements, half in helplessness and half in self-transcendence and mystic triumph.

I have taken for a motto a phrase out of one of Euripides' choruses: Τὸ σοφὸν οὐ σοφία. It was this phrase, in that year, 1884, that led me to write my first sonnet, printed a year or two later, and reappearing as Sonnet III in my *Poems*; the first two having been composed afterwards on purpose to frame in the earlier ones and bring the argument to a head. I translated the dictum of Euripides in the rather thin and prosaic line: "It is not wisdom to be only wise"; and then, given that sentiment and that rhyme, I built the whole sonnet round them. Even when I wrote it, this sonnet was belated. I was twenty years old, and that sentiment was what I had felt at sixteen. But I still recognized, as I recognize now at nearly eighty, the legitimacy of that feeling.

The chief difference is that when, at sixteen or even at twenty, I said "faith," I meant the Catholic faith; and when now I oppose "faith" to reason I mean faith in the existence and order of nature, a faith in the assumptions made inevitably in daily life; yet I see far more clearly than I did in my youth that pure reason, a reason that is not based on irrational postulates and presuppositions, is perfectly impotent. It is not "smoky" or indistinct: on the contrary, it is mathematically precise, but abstract and in the air. What I had in mind then when I spoke of "knowledge" was the common sense and science of the day, which in fact were uncritically based on animal faith and empirical presumption, and which I, with a solipsistic breath, could at once reduce to a dream, not to say a nightmare. For that reason I called them "smoky," at once ugly, obscure, and unsubstantial. But it was immature of me to wish, lackadaisically and hopelessly, to substitute a religious myth for that sensuous obsession. And the rest of those twenty youthful sonnets pointed out well enough where a mature solution might be found: in obedience to matter for the sake of freedom of mind.

As to William James on Taine's *De l'Intelligence,* I am not conscious of any intellectual residuum, only of a few graphic memories touching his aspects and ways, which at that time were distinctly medical. He was impatient of the things he didn't like in philosophy; his latent pragmatism appeared only in its negative germ, as scorn of everything remote or pretentious; and his love of lame ducks and neglected possibilities, which later took the form of charity and breadth of mind, then seemed rather the doctor's quick eye for bad symptoms, as if he had diagnosed people in a jiffy and cried: "Ah, *you* are a paranoiac! Ah, *you* have the pox!" I remember his views better in another set of lectures on Herbert Spencer, or rather against him. James detested any system of the universe that professed to enclose everything: we must never set up boundaries that exclude romantic surprises. He retained the primitive feeling that death *might* open new worlds to us—not at all what religions predict but something at once novel and natural; also the primitive feeling that invisible spirits *might* be floating about among us, and might suddenly do something to hurt or to help us. Spencer was intolerable for shutting out such possibilities: he was also intolerable for his verbose generalities and sweeping "principles." There were no "principles," except in men's heads: there were only facts. James did not stop to consider whether this assertion was not itself a principle that might describe a fact.

Herbert Spencer, I think, taught me nothing. I agreed with his naturalism or materialism, because that is what we all start with: the minimum presupposition of perception and action. But I agreed with James about Spencer's theory of evolution: It was a tangle of words, of loose generalities that some things might sometimes suggest to us, and that, said properly, it might have been *witty* to say, but that had absolutely no value as "laws" or "causes" of events. Such "principles" might serve an "objective idealist," not a naturalist or a scientific man. James was characteristically masculine and empirical in his wrath at the "scandalous vagueness" of Spencer's ideas. For instance, what did it mean to say that things passed from the indefinite to the definite? Nothing can be indefinite. Make a blot of ink at random on a piece of paper. The spot is not indefinite: it has precisely the outline that it has.* But James, though trenchant was short-winded in argument. He didn't go on, for instance to consider on this occasion how, if there be

---

* Here was a hint of my "essences" given by an unintended shot, that hit the bull's-eye without seeing it. Forms are infinite in multitude and each perfectly concrete. James's radical empiricism was undoubtedly a guide to me in this matter. Also Berkeley's nominalism.

nothing indefinite, the notion of the indefinite comes into existence. Suppose that having made a random blot, shapeless as we
call it in spite of its perfectly definite shape, I at once folded the
paper in two. The blot would become two symmetrical blots, or a
larger blot bilaterally symmetrical. It might resemble an oak leaf.
It would then cease to have a nameless shape, but would become
Platonically or humanly specific. We should say it had a definite
shape, one that we could recognize and reproduce. Spencer, if we
interpret him critically and progressively, was therefore saying that
things change from forms that for our senses and language would
not be recognizable or namable into forms that we can distinguish
and name. This happens sometimes not because things grow more
definite, but because our senses and imagination have a limited
range and can arrest one form of things rather than another; so
that the world grows definite *for us* when we are able to perceive
more parts of it and their relations. Nature thereby has changed
but only intelligence has advanced; change is called evolution
when sense and language are thereby enabled better to distinguish
their objects. The notion that nature first acquired form as an
animal mind may gradually grow less stupid, belongs to the age of
fable. Spencer, unlike Lucretius and Spinoza, had no speculative
power. He meant to be a naturalist, but language and the hypos-
tasized idea of progress turned him into an idealistic metaphysi-
cian.

I will not attempt to describe here the many lessons that I
learned in the study of Spinoza, lessons that in several respects laid
the foundation of my philosophy. I will only say that I learned
them from Spinoza himself, from his *ipsissima verba*, studied in
the original in all the crucial passages; as a guide and stimulus I
had Sir Frederick Pollock's sympathetic book, with good render-
ings, and not much modern interpretation. It was a work, as he
told me himself forty-five years later, at the Spinoza commemora-
tion at the Hague, of his youth; and perhaps the science was emphasized at the expense of the religion. Yet that the object of this
religion was *Deus sive Natura*—the universe, whatever it may be,

of which we are a part—was never concealed or denaturalized. Royce himself seemed to suffer less from the plague of idealistic criticism in this case than usual; for instance, about the saying of Spinoza's that the mind of God resembled the mind of man as the Dog Star resembles the barking animal. Royce said only that this was too materialistic, without caring or daring to broach the question as to the diffusion or concentration of that cosmic "mind." The unified "universal thought" that Royce posited would not be a "cogitation" but only a truth, the total *system* of cogitations that may accompany the total movement of matter. If it were one actual intuition it would not *accompany* the movement of matter but either describe and command it from afar or merely imagine it. Royce had a powerful and learned mind, and it was always profitable, if not pleasant, to listen to him: not pleasant because his voice was harsh, his style heavy, repetitious and pedantic, and his monotonous preoccupation with his own system intolerable. To listen was profitable nevertheless because his comfortless dissatisfaction with every possible idea opened vistas and disturbed a too easy dogmatism: while the perversity and futility of his dialectic threw one back in the end on the great certainties and the great possibilities, such as made the minds of the great philosophers at once sublime and sane.

As I have said elsewhere, I regard Spinoza as the only modern philosopher in the line of orthodox physics, the line that begins with Thales and culminates, for Greek philosophy, in Democritus. Orthodox physics should inspire and support orthodox ethics; and perhaps the chief source of my enthusiasm for Spinoza has been the magnificent clearness of his orthodoxy on this point. Morality is something natural. It arises and varies, not only psychologically but prescriptively and justly, with the nature of the creature whose morality it is. Morality is something relative; not that its precepts in any case are optional or arbitrary; for each man they are defined by his innate character and possible forms of happiness and action. His momentary passions or judgments are partial expressions of his nature, but not adequate or infallible; and ignorance of the circumstances may mislead in practice, as ignorance of self may mislead in desire. But there is a fixed good relative to each species and each individual; so that in considering the moral ideal of any philosopher, two questions arise. First, does he, like Spinoza, understand the natural basis of morality, or is he confused and superstitious on the subject? Second, how humane and representative is his sense for the good, and how far, by his disposition or sympathetic intelligence, does he appreciate all the types of excellence towards which life may be directed?

James and Royce were then the "young" professors of philosophy, they represented the dangers and scandals of free thought, all the more disquieting in that their free thought enveloped religion. But Harvard possessed safe, sober old professors also and oldest of all, "Fanny" Bowen. He was so old that to be old, self-repeating, dogmatic, rheumatic, and querulous had become picturesque in him, and a part of his dramatic personage. He was a dear old thing, and an excellent teacher. Between his fits of coughing, and his invectives against all who were wrong and didn't agree with Sir William Hamilton, he would impress upon us many an axiom, many an argument belonging to the great traditions of philosophy: and when after spitting into the vast bandanna handkerchief that he carried for the purpose, he would drop it on the desk with a gesture of combined disgust and relief, he expressed vividly to the eye the spirit in which philosophic and religious sects have always refuted and denounced one another. History sat living before us in this teacher of history. Descartes, Leibniz and Spinoza would be quoted verbatim, and expounded (especially the first two) on their own presuppositions and in their own terms. It was not criticism but it was instruction. Spinoza was rather beyond Bowen's range; yet even here the words of the master would be repeated, and could be remembered in their terseness, while the professor's refutations would blow by like dead leaves. Unfortunately old Bowen did not always preach to his text. Sometimes he would wander into irrelevant invectives against John Stuart Mill, who in a footnote had once referred to

Bowen (who was then editor of a reputable review) as "an obscure American."

We had another right-thinking and edifying teacher, no less thoroughly well baked in all his opinions and mannerisms, but younger in years and following a later fashion in philosophy. Professor Palmer practised all the smooth oratorical arts of a liberal parson or headmaster; he conciliated opponents, plotted (always legally) with friends, and if things went against him, still smiled victoriously and seemed to be on the crest of the wave. He was the professor of ethics. His lectures were beautifully prepared, and exactly the same year after year. He had been professor of Greek also, and made anodyne translations from Homer and Sophocles in "rhymic" and sleepy prose. In his course on English moralists he brought out his selected authors in dialectical order; each successive view appeared fresh and plausible, but not sensational. They came in a subtle crescendo, everything good, and everything a little better than what went before, so that at the end you ought to have found yourself in the seventh heaven. Yet we, or at least I, didn't find ourselves there. I felt cheated. The method was Hegelian adapted to a Sunday School: all roses without thorns. All defects in doctrine (why not also in conduct?) were stepping-stones to higher things. We began with pungent, mannish, violent theories: Hobbes and Mandeville. We passed onward to something more feminine and refined, to Shaftesbury. From this we dialectically reacted, landing in the apparently solid, liberal, political reformer, John Stuart Mill: but no, that was not our divine destination. A breath of higher philosophy somehow blew over us. We levitated; and we knew not how or why, utilitarianism dissolved, lost in the distant valleys beneath us, and we realized the providential utility of utilitarianism in carrying us so far above it. "Purring pussy Palmer," my sporting friend "Swelly" Bangs used to call him: yet Palmer was a benign influence. The crude, half-educated, conscientious, ambitious young men who wished to study ethics gained subtler and more elastic notions of what was good than they had ever dreamt of: and their notions of what was bad became correspondingly discriminating and fair. Palmer was like a father confessor, never shocked at sin, never despairing of sinners. There must be a little of everything in the Lord's vineyard. Palmer was a fountain of sweet reasonableness. That his methods were sophistical and his conclusions lame didn't really matter. It was not a question of discovering or deciding anything final: the point was to become more cultivated and more intelligent. You could then define your aims and your principles for yourself. I found the authors read in Palmer's course, especially Hobbes, valuable in themselves; and Palmer's methods of exposition and criticism, sly and treacherous as they were, gave me a lesson in dialectic, and a warning against it. I began to understand that the cogency of dialectic is merely verbal or ideal, and its application to facts, even to the evolution of ideas, entirely hypothetical and distorting. If ideas created themselves (which they don't) or succeeded one another in the mind or in history by logical derivation (as again they don't), evolution might be dialectical: but as it is, dialectic merely throws a verbal net into the sea, to draw a pattern over the fishes without catching any of them. It is an optical illusion.

Dialectic didn't show its other, its honest, side to me until many years later, when I read Plato and knew Bertie Russell. Honest logicians never apply dialectic to history, and only in play to cosmology. Events are derived from one another materially and contingently. This is no less true when events are mental than when they are physical. It is *external* insights and interests that transform one system of philosophy into another, Socrates into Plato, Locke into Berkeley, Kant into Schopenhauer and Hegel. Each system remains logically and morally stable, like a portrait of its author. A philosophy that is radical and consistent cannot evolve. That which evolves is only the immature, the self-contradictory; and if circumstances do not permit it to ripen according to its inner potentialities, it withers and dissolves into dust, leaving no progeny. Each fact, each group of ideas, in fusion with other facts, passes into a new natural form, not evolved from the previous forms dialectically, but created by nature out of their matter and occasion, at each juncture with a fresh result.

I also studied Locke, Berkeley, and Hume under William

James. Here there was as much honest humanity in the teacher as in the texts, and I think I was not impervious to the wit and wisdom of any of them. Hume was the one I least appreciated: yet Palmer once said that I had Hume in my bones. In reality, whether through my immaturity only, or through James's bewilderment also, I seem to have gathered no clear lesson from those authors or from James himself. Verbally I understood them well enough; they were not superficially obscure; but critically, as to their presuppositions, their categories and their places in history, I understood nothing. Even when four years later I gave that very course, I didn't advance beyond a friendly literary interpretation of their meaning and of the psychological cosmos that they seemed to posit. I hardly questioned their ambiguous units, their "perceptions" or "ideas," but accepted them, as James then accepted them, as representing total scattered moments of "experience" or "life." This was historically just. This philosophy is purely literary and autobiographical. It sees "experience" as composed of the high lights that language and memory find in it retrospectively. It hypostasizes the description into the object. But such hypostasis is an indefensible trick of memory, a poetical or mythical substitution of images for events and of verbal for dynamic elements. It is as if I pretended, in writing this book, to have discovered the fundamental reality and total composition of myself, of my family, of Spain, America, Germany, England, and Italy. A monstrous trick of verbal legerdemain, a sophistical curiosity.

The only solid foundation for all my play with this subject was supplied by the sturdy but undeveloped materialism of Hobbes, powerfully supported by the psychology of Spinoza and insecurely by the early medical psychology of James: to which in Germany my passing enthusiasm for Schopenhauer may be added, because by that time I was able to discount the language of a system and perceive from what direction it drew its inspiration. The "Will" in Schopenhauer was a transparent mythological symbol for the flux of matter. There was absolute equivalence between such a system, in its purport and sense for reality, and the systems of Spinoza and Lucretius. This was the element of ancient sanity that kept me awake and conscious of the points of the compass in the subsequent wreck of psychologism. Such wrecks are not fatal. Psychologism lives, and must always live, in literature and history. In these pursuits we are living as we imagine others might have lived, and seeing things as they might have seen them. We are dramatically enlarging our experience. What was lost in that moral tempest was only the illusion that such play of imagination revealed any profound truth or dislodged Nature to put Experience in her place.

An event that had important consequences in the future course of my life occurred silently and almost unnoticed during my Senior year. A young man named Charles Augustus Strong—there was already something royal and German about that "Augustus" and that "Strong," though the youth was modesty and Puritanism personified—came from the university of his native Rochester, New York, to study philosophy for a year at Harvard. As I too was taking all the advanced courses in that subject, we found ourselves daily thrown together, gradually began to compare notes, and to discuss the professors and their opinions; and finally we founded a philosophical club, in order to discuss everything more thoroughly with the other embryonic philosophers in the place. Towards the end of the year we both became candidates for the Walker Fellowship, usually awarded to graduates who wished to study philosophy in Germany. This was a rivalry that I disliked and also feared; because, if I had the advantage of being a Harvard man and better known to the professors, and also of being more glib and more resourceful in examinations, he had the decisive advantage of inspiring professional confidence. When you learned that his father and his brother were Baptist clergymen, you recognized at once that he too was a Baptist clergyman by nature and habit, only that some untoward influence had crossed his path and deflected him from his vocation. He had lost his faith in revelation. Modernist compromises and ambiguities were abhorrent to his strict honesty and love of precision. You mustn't preach what you don't believe.

He turned therefore to the nearest thing to being a clergyman that he could be sincerely, which was to be a professor of philosophy. He was already, in aspect, in manner, in speech, in spirit, thoroughly professional. Moreover, for studying in Germany he was far better prepared than I in that he spoke German perfectly. He had been at school in Germany, in a Gymnasium at Güteslohe, and had received that strict training in all subjects which was not to be expected in free America. He was slow but accurate, and his zeal in the pursuit of truth was unflagging. He had the memory and solidity of the head boy of the class. Besides, when you observed him afresh, you saw that he was very good-looking, tall, firm, with curly black hair and noble features. It was only his shyness, reserve, and lack of responsive sympathy that obscured these advantages. Perhaps if he found his proper element and were happy they would shine out again.

How about me? Was I professional? Should I ever make a professor of philosophy? Everybody doubted it. I not only doubted it myself, but was repelled by the idea. What I wanted was to go on being a student, and especially to be a travelling student. I loved speculation for itself, as I loved poetry, not out of worldly respect or anxiety lest I should be mistaken, but for the splendor of it, like the splendor of the sea and the stars. And I knew I should love living obscurely and freely in old towns, in strange countries, hearing all sorts of outlandish marvellous opinions. I could have made a bargain with Mephistopheles, not for youth but for the appearance of youth, so that with its tastes but without its passions, I might have been a wandering student all my life, at Salamanca, at Bologna, in Oxford, in Paris, at Benares, in China, in Persia. Germany would be a beginning. If I never became a professor, so much the better. I should have seen the world, historical and intellectual: I should have been free in my best years.

Now my mother was going to assign me a permanent allowance of $500 a year, the sum that she received from "Uncle Russell" or that symbolically represented the $10,000 she had once received from "Uncle Robert," which she retained and meant to leave to me. The Walker Fellowship amounted to another $500. The two would make a neat sum, yet I knew that in Europe I could easily get on with less. From things that Strong had dropped in conversation, I had gathered that he was much in the same case. His father was well off and he too had an allowance. Perhaps he didn't need the whole Fellowship. I therefore did a sly thing. I asked him if he would be willing to agree that whoever of us got the Fellowship should divide it with the other. Then we should both be sure of going to Germany for the next year. He consented at once. I think he liked the idea of having me with him. Our discussions enlivened him. I should serve as a useful pace-maker in the pursuit of absolute truth.

Nevertheless my conscience was a bit uneasy. I felt in my bones that Strong would get the appointment, and I was simply robbing him of half his stipend. So I made a second proposal. Before agreeing to this plan, let us lay it before Professor Palmer, professional moralist and Head of the Department, practically the man who would decide between us. Let us ask him if he thought well of it. We went to see him together. I acted as spokesman, having the readier tongue. I said we supposed we were the only likely candidates for the Fellowship, that we both wanted it very much, and that we both had small allowances from our families, so that we could get on with less than the whole amount of the Fellowship. Would it be a fair thing for us to agree, whoever got it, to divide it between us?

Professor Palmer bit his lips, thought for a moment, and decided to be sympathetic. He saw no objection. The action would be equally unselfish in both of us. I knew it was not unselfish in me, yet Palmer's cant set me at rest. They must have been undecided about the choice in the Committee, otherwise Palmer would not have agreed to the division. Now they would give the Fellowship to Strong, knowing that I was to get half the money; so that really they would be voting half the money to me. Not quite satisfactory this, but excusable and rather ingenious.

I think this is the only occasion in my life when I have done something a little too clever in order to get money. Yet the result might have encouraged a person inclined to trickery, because I not only got what I wanted, but in consequence made a great haul, not exactly in money, but precisely in what I cared for more than for money, in travel, in residence in foreign parts, in a well-paved path open to all sorts of intellectual pleasures. Strong, for a family reason that I shall mention later, gave up the Fellowship at the end of one year. It was then awarded to me for two successive years. Later, Strong went to live in Europe, in Paris, in Fiesole. He had got used to having me to talk with. I was often his guest for long periods; and that division of his $500 let me into a series of favors that I was positively begged to receive. Strong had become rich, he was married and had a young daughter: yet his life was strangely solitary. He was no less bored than when he was younger. He would actually have paid me, as he paid one or two others, to live near him so as to have stated hours for philosophical discussions. He once expressly offered to guarantee me an income of $2,500 if I would give up my professorship and go and live with him in Paris. I didn't accept that offer; I waited before retiring until I had money enough of my own to make me independent; but I did make his apartment in Paris my headquarters for some years; which for me at that time was a great convenience and economy. I had a lodging at will, gratis, and I paid for food and service only when I was alone in the apartment or when we dined in restaurants, as we did every evening. At first on these occasions each paid for both on alternate days; later each always paid for what he ordered. Our tastes were becoming more different.

There was always a latent tension between us, because our reasons for living together were mixed and not the same in both of us. In both there was real sympathy up to a point and a real interest in the same philosophical problems and political and social matters; and our views if not identical were cooperative. They played round the same facts in the same speculative spirit. Yet we were not intimate friends. We were more like partners in the same business. And our motive for forming this partnership was in neither of us personal affection but in both only private interest.

Strong wanted a philosophical friend to talk with; at first mainly for the sake of company and stimulation, later rather in the hope of forcing his views and confirming himself in them by convincing someone else of their truth. I, on the other hand, wanted a material pied-à-terre, a place and a person or persons that should take the place of a home; and Strong offered these in a most acceptable form, especially when he lived in Paris. He was free from almost all the bonds from which I wished to be free; he was less entangling socially and financially than such attachments as I might have found in Spain or in England. Besides, I lived with him only at certain seasons, seldom longer than for a month or two at a time; and there was no pledge that our arrangement should be permanent. In fact, I constantly went off by myself, to Spain, to Oxford, to Rome, or even to other lodgings in Paris: because I found writing difficult, both materially and psychologically, when we lived together. His hours were inflexible, also his determination to revert daily to the same discussions; the limitations that had become tyrannical over him became tyrannical over others also. In this way, while the friendly partnership originally formed by us in dividing the Walker Fellowship accompanied us through life, the mixed motives that had prompted it accompanied us also. Strong was always being cheated, and a victim that complained of not being victimized enough; and I was always being punished by a sense of unnecessary dependence and constraint, when it was freedom and independence that I had sought.

These observations anticipate events that lay far in the future. For the moment I was plunged in work, more wholeheartedly perhaps than ever again, because I saw my future and my studies in an undivided prospect: my whole inner life would be in those studies, while those studies in turn would determine my career. And my bad beginning as a student at Harvard was redeemed by an honorable end. I received my bachelor's degree *summa cum laude*. In spite of mediocre standing in some subjects, my teachers thought that my speculative vocation and my understanding of the great philosophers entitled me to a first place. This was a repetition

with a difference, of my career at the Latin School. There I had, as
a person, carried the day against a middling record as a pupil: now
at Harvard I carried the day against the same handicap by force
of personal abilities in a special half-artistic direction.

I didn't wait, however, to receive my degree in person at Com-
mencement. Herbert Lyman took the parchment in charge and
brought it to me in Germany. On taking my last examination, I
had sailed without knowing what would be the result. I took a
German ship, not that I was bound directly to Germany, but that
it touched at Cherbourg whence second class this time, I could
travel leisurely to Avila and see a lot of cathedral towns: Caen, Le
Mans, Angers, Poitiers, Angoulême, Bordeaux, and Burgos. The
expense, stopping one night at each place, was not greater than
in going first class through Paris. I was to spend the summer
quietly in Avila, and in the autumn to join Herbert Lyman in
Dresden and Strong in Berlin.

The curtain drops here, to rise presently on those other scenes.

INDEX

INDEX